ATLA BIBLIOGRAPHY SERIES
edited by Dr. Kenneth E. Rowe

1. *A Guide to the Study of the Holiness Movement*, by Charles Edwin Jones. 1974.
2. *Thomas Merton: A Bibliography*, by Marquita E. Breit. 1974.
3. *The Sermon on the Mount: A History of Interpretation and Bibliography*, by Warren S. Kissinger. 1975.
4. *The Parables of Jesus: A History of Interpretation and Bibliography*, by Warren S. Kissinger. 1979.
5. *Homosexuality and the Judeo-Christian Tradition: An Annotated Bibliography*, by Tom Horner. 1981.
6. *A Guide to the Study of the Pentecostal Movement*, by Charles Edwin Jones. 1983.
7. *The Genesis of Modern Process Thought: A Historical Outline with Bibliography*, by George R. Lucas, Jr. 1983.
8. *A Presbyterian Bibliography*, by Harold B. Prince. 1983.
9. *Paul Tillich: A Comprehensive Bibliography ...*, by Richard C. Crossman. 1983.

PAUL TILLICH:
A Comprehensive Bibliography and Keyword Index of Primary and Secondary Writings in English

by
RICHARD C. CROSSMAN

ATLA Bibliography Series, No. 9

The American Theological
Library Association
The Scarecrow Press, Inc.
Metuchen, N.J., & London
1983

Library of Congress Cataloging in Publication Data

Crossman, Richard C.
    Paul Tillich : a comprehensive bibliography and
keyword index of primary and secondary writings in
English.

    (ATLA bibliography series ; no. 9)
    1. Tillich, Paul, 1886-1965--Bibliography.
2. Theology--Indexes. I. Title. II. Series.
Z8879.75.C76 1983   016.23'0092'4   83-15026
[BX4827.T53]
ISBN 0-8108-1650-4

CONTENTS

EDITOR'S NOTE

The American Theological Library Association Bibliography series is designed to stimulate and encourage the preparation of reliable bibliographies and guides to the literature of religious studies in all of its scope and variety. Compilers are free to define their field, make their own selections, and work out internal organization as the unique demands of the subject require. We are pleased to publish Richard C. Crossman's Tillich bibliography as Number 9 in our series.

Following undergraduate studies at Wittenberg University, Richard Crossman studied Theology at Hamma School of Theology, religion, and political science at the University of Chicago where he took the doctorate in 1976. An ordained minister in the Lutheran Church in America, Mr. Crossman is the author of several articles in learned journals and currently serves on the faculty of the Waterloo Lutheran Seminary, in Waterloo, Ontario, Canada.

Kenneth E. Rowe
Series Editor

Drew University Library
Madison, NJ 07940

INTRODUCTION

During his lifetime Paul Tillich established himself as one of the major theological figures of the twentieth century. He produced an extensive body of personal research and left a challenging legacy of thought. Through both of these accomplishments his influence has become widespread.

The extent of his personal research is manifest not only in the large volume of work he did (his research and writing was vigorously pursued over more than five decades), but also in the broad geographic range and interdisciplinary scope of his work. Tillich found other cultural contexts to be both stimulating and challenging. They embodied one type of boundary-situation out of which "New Being" might emerge. Consequently Tillich reached out to the cultures of Europe, North America, and Asia, living, teaching, and learning in all three of these geographical settings. Tillich's concerns also reached out across the boundaries of various academic disciplines. The focus of his writing extended from the interface between religion and the social sciences of psychology, sociology, and politics to philosophy, church missions, preaching, and Christian education. For Tillich reason and revelation were not compartmentalized entities but interdependent realities which touched all domains of the human enterprise.

Since his death, significant numbers of persons in a wide range of disciplines and countries have continued to find Tillich's thought helpful. Beyond the widespread impact of his insights on the writing of persons in the field of religion and philosophy, his thought has stimulated scholars in disciplines ranging from quantum mechanics in physics, to counseling in psychology, policy formation in political science, and pedagogical development in public education. Moreover, Tillich's insights have proven helpful not just for specialists and theoreticians; persons whose focus is more oriented to the "practice" side of their professions have found Tillich quite instructive. This holds true for persons throughout the world. Interest in Tillich's thought is found among the articles and books of persons from India to North America, from Japan to Australia, and from Europe to Africa. In short, it can be said that Tillich's prominence during his lifetime has not diminished after his death. If anything, his influence has become more widespread.

Given this widespread interest in Tillich's thought, it is not hard to recognize the difficulty which is posed for persons wishing to pursue Tillich-related research. Persons doing such research often are either hindered by not being aware of all the pertinent material available to them in their area of concern, or are forced to spend precious hours and days discovering where particular materials can be located.

These difficulties have been partially alleviated by the existence of a number of Tillich-related "selected" bibliographies. However, while some of these bibliographies have fairly thoroughly identified materials written by Tillich and some have also identified many of the materials written about Tillich on a selected subject or date basis, an important need still remains. Because of the large number of materials that are involved, a need exists for a comprehensive index of all Tillich-related material which is keyed to a set of comprehensive up-to-date bibliographies.

However, because this need involves such a large amount of material in English as well as in non-English languages, it was decided that two volumes would be required to complete the task. The first volume would collect and index the Tillich-related material in English. A proposed second book would do the same for the non-English Tillich-related materials.

It is the aim of this volume to address the first of these needs: the provision of a comprehensive set of up-to-date bibliographies of material written by and about Paul Tillich in English, excluding the unpublished documents of the Tillich archives, and of a comprehensive keyword index to the topics and persons included in these bibliographic materials.

Approach

The basic approach employed in preparing this volume has been that of indirect compilation. That is, a wide variety of available indexes, listings, reviews, catalogues and bibliographies was initially consulted and the resulting findings drawn together into a set of five complementary bibliographies. These findings were then supplemented by the process of direct compilation. This involved examining various primary resources to uncover previously unlisted material and to correct discovered inaccuracies in already catalogued citations.

Throughout this process of compilation the principle of inclusiveness was followed. Except in the area of book reviews, no discovered Tillich-related material was excluded from the compilation process. In the case of book reviews, space considerations prompted the focusing of citations primarily, though not exclusively, upon the book reviews done by Tillich and upon the longer, more analytical reviews done by others of Tillich's books.

It should be noted that where a cited book included a series of essays, such as a book of articles about Tillich or a book of sermons by Tillich, each of these essays was also given a separate bibliographical citation. In this way a more complete index of subjects was made possible.

After the compilation task was completed each entry of the five resulting bibliographies was surveyed for key search words to be placed in the indexes. These key words were selected on the basis of the topics and persons identified by the titles, annotations, and references of the entries. This body of terms was then divided into an index of persons and an index of topics. Finally, the two indexes and the five bibliographies were inserted into a computer, and a subsequent computer search related the indexed words to the bibliographical citations.

Sources

In preparing the bibliographies of this volume the following major sources were consulted.

1. Bibliography of English Writings, compiled by William B. Green. Poughkeepsie, New York, 1964.

2. Bibliography of English Writings from 1932 to September, 1956, compiled by Grace C. Leonard.   Harvard Divinity School, 1956.

3. Bibliothèque Nationale Listings.

4. The Book Review Digest, 1937-1981.

5. The British Humanities Index, 1937-1981.

6. British Museum Listings.

7. The Canadian Periodical Index, 1960-1981.

8. The Comprehensive Dissertation Index and Supplement, 1930-1981.

9. Dissertation Abstracts International, 1959-1981.

10. English Works By and About Paul Tillich, compiled by the Library Staff of the University of California at Santa Barbara, 1964.

11. The Index of Religious Periodical Literature, 1949-1976.

12. The International Index to Periodical Literature in the Social Sciences and Humanities, 1940-1981.

13. National Union Catalog of the Library of Congress, pre-1956-1981.

14. The Paul Tillich Archive Listings of Secondary Literature, 1938-1976.

15. The Philosopher's Index, 1940-1981.

16. The Readers' Guide to Periodical Literature, 1939-1981.

17. Religion and Culture: Essays in Honor of Paul Tillich, edited by Walter Liebrecht. New York: Harper & Row, 1959. Bibliography included.

18. Religion Index One: Periodicals, 1977-1981.

19. Religion Index Two: Festschriften, 1960-1969.

20. Religion Index Two: Multi-Author Works, 1970-1981.

21. Religious Studies Review, 1975-1981.

22. The Second North American Consultation on Paul Tillich Studies Summary of American Doctoral Dissertations on Paul Tillich, 1965-1972.

23. The Theology of Paul Tillich, edited by Charles W. Kegley and Robert W. Bretall. New York: The Macmillan Company, 1952. Bibliography included.

24. The Thought of Paul Tillich: A Selected Bibliographical Companion to the "Systematic Theology," Lawrence D. Bryan. Garrett Theological Seminary Library, 1973.

In addition to the above sources, the card catalogues and holdings of Wilfrid Laurier University and Harvard Divinity School were examined.   This activity proved particularly helpful in the direct compilation process noted earlier.

Before leaving this discussion of how the volume was prepared, the human side of the enterprise needs also to be acknowledged.   While it would be impossible to acknowledge my indebtedness and gratitude to all those whom I have consulted in the preparation of this document, special thanks should be given to the following persons.   First I shall always be grateful for the able assistance of my graduate student research assistants, Fred Grater, David Pfrimmer, and Blaine Barclay.   They made the tasks of searching, compiling, and recording a lot easier and saved me many hours of work.   I want also to make grateful mention of Carl Langford.   His helpful guidance made it possible for me to use the computer in preparing the indexes.   I am especially grateful to my family and colleagues for their personal encouragement and support. When a project extends over a long period of time, as this one did, the continued encouragement of those close to you can prove invaluable.   I also would like to thank the library staffs at Wilfrid Laurier University and Harvard Divinity School.   Their helpful assistance in answering my questions and locating pertinent resources made my library work in both locations unusually productive. Finally, I want to express my appreciation to the Waterloo Lutheran Seminary Board of Governors. The sabbatical leave which they provided enabled me to complete this important project in a much shorter time than would otherwise have been possible.

Features

As was mentioned earlier, the indexes in this volume are keyed to five complementary bibliographies. The topics of these bibliographies are as follows:

1. Writings by Paul Tillich in English

2. Dissertations and Theses About or Related to Paul Tillich in English

3. Reviews of Writings By or About Paul Tillich in English

4. Articles About or Related to Paul Tillich in English

5. Books or Portions of Books About or Related to Paul Tillich in English

Within each of these bibliographies the entries are placed in alphabetical order. In the first bibliography the entries are alphabetized by title. Titles beginning with the indefinite article (A) are listed at the beginning of this section. In bibliographies 2 through 5 the entries are alphabetized according to author. Regarding the matter of author's last names beginning with "Mc," such as McCann, the alphabetical pattern adopted here lists such last names after last names beginning with "Maz."

In each of the bibliographies the entries are numbered consecutively. In this way each entry is provided with an identifying number within its bibliography. These identifying numbers are then used to represent the entries in the indexes.

There are two keyword indexes in the volume: one of "persons" and the other of "subjects." Each is organized around an alphabetized list of search words. Following each search word is a list of entry numbers for those bibliographic items in which the word appears. These entry numbers are arranged in the sequence of the bibliographies (1 through 5) in which they occur. For example, after the search word "Holy" in the Index of Subjects the numbers 1: 164, 202 represent entries in the first bibliography. The following numbers, 2: 15, 174 represent entries in the second bibliography. If one locates the entries numbered 164 and 202 in the first bibliography one will find the search word "Holy" present in those citations. Similarly, the entries numbered 15 and 174 in the second bibliography will also contain material related to the subject

"Holy." The absence of entry numbers preceded by 3: or 4: or 5: indicates that the word does not appear in the third, fourth or fifth bibliographies.

Annotations have been included in a number of the bibliographical entries. Their purpose is to provide information regarding one or more of the following concerns: 1) the type of document that is cited, 2) the type of setting out of which the document cited emerged, 3) the alternative places where the document cited might also be located. It should be noted, however, that while alternative locations are often indicated, no systematic attempt has been made to identify all publishers or publications of the same title.

Following each of the entry numbers cited in the indexes one will find one or more of the letters, "T," "A," or "R." If a "T" appears this indicates that the search word occurs in the "title" of the work cited. If an "A" appears the search word will be found in the "annotation" of the citation. If an "R" is found the search word will appear in the title of a "reference" volume included in the citation.

The reader will notice that some citations include more information than others. This is due to the fact that the entries in this volume were initially drawn from a variety of sources, some of which were more complete than others. Nevertheless, every effort has been made subsequently to provide sufficient information in each entry for the efficient location of the document cited.

Future Editions

As was indicated earlier, every effort has been made to produce, outside the area of book reviews, as inclusive a set of bibliographies as was possible. In this regard I believe the present documentation represents a fairly thorough set of listings. Nevertheless, given the extensive and diverse nature of the Tillich-related materials already gathered, I suspect that further citations exist which need to be incorporated into this volume. It is as such citations are found that the volume's indexes can be made into even more effective research tools.

In light of this, I invite and urge all persons who might know of citations not included here to pass them along to me at Wilfrid Laurier University, Waterloo, Ontario, Canada. When sufficient additions have been collected it is my hope to produce a revised and up-dated edition of this volume.

Richard C. Crossman

1. WRITINGS BY PAUL TILLICH IN ENGLISH

1   "A Christian-Buddhist Conversation," Attitudes Toward Other
    Religions: Some Christian Interpretations, Owen C. Thomas,
    ed. New York: Harper and Row, 1969, pp. 175-189. Appears
    also in Jubilee, vol. 10, no. 11, March 1963, pp. 43-46.

2   "A Conscience Above Moralism," Conscience: Theological and
    Psychological Perspectives, C. Ellis Nelson, ed. New York:
    Newman Press, 1973, pp. 46-61.

3   A History of Christian Thought, Peter H. John, recorder and
    editor. New York: Union Theological Seminary, 1953. A
    stenographic transcription of Spring Term Union Theological
    Seminary lectures, 1953. This 1st stenographic edition contains
    the sermons, "Is There Any Word from the Lord?" "The Truth
    Will Make You Free," and "By What Authority?"

4   A History of Christian Thought, Peter H. John, recorder and
    editor. New York: Union Theological Seminary, 1956. A
    stenographic transcription of Spring Term Union Theological
    Seminary lectures, 1953. This 2nd stenographic edition con-
    tains the sermons, "Do Not Be Conformed," "Be Strong," "The
    Eternal Now," and "Heal the Sick ... Cast Out Demons."

5   A History of Christian Thought, Carl E. Braaten, ed. New
    York: Harper and Row, 1968.

6   A History of Christian Thought from Its Judaic and Hellenistic
    Origins to Existentialism, Carl E. Braaten, ed. New York:
    Simon and Schuster, 1972. This volume combines the book,
    A History of Christian Thought, edited by Carl E. Braaten
    (Harper and Row, 1968) with the book Perspectives on 19th
    and 20th Century Protestant Theology, edited by Carl E. Braaten
    (Harper and Row, 1967).

7   "A Letter from Tillich," Colby Library Quarterly, E. L.
    Strider, II, ed., vol. 6, no. 9 (March, 1964), p. 383.

8   "A Program for a Democratic Germany," Christianity and Crisis,

vol. 4, no. 8 (May 15, 1944), pp. 3-5. A declaration by the Council for a Democratic Germany, of which Tillich was Provisional Chairman.

9   "A Statement," Bulletin of the Council for a Democratic Germany, vol. 1, no. 1 (September 1, 1944), pp. 1, 4. Brief articles in other issues. Five issues published from September 1944 to May 1945.

10 "A Theology of Education," Theology of Culture, Robert C. Kimball, ed. New York: Oxford University Press, 1964, pp. 146-157. From a symposium held October 13-14, 1956, in celebration of the 100th Anniversary of St. Paul's School, Concord, New Hampshire.

11 "Across a Void of Mystery and Dread," The Universal God, Carl E. Voss, ed. New York: World Publishing Company, 1953, pp. 91-93.

12 "The Actuality of God," Contemporary Philosophic Problems: Selected Readings, Yervant H. Krikorian and Abraham Edel, eds. New York: The Macmillan Company, 1959, pp. 450-456. Reprinted from Paul Tillich's Systematic Theology: Volume I (University of Chicago Press, 1951), pp. 235-241. Also appears in Four Existentialist Theologians, edited by Will Herberg (Doubleday, 1958).

13 "Address," New York, 1964. An address on art given at the opening of the New Galleries and Sculpture Garden of the Museum of Modern Art on May 25, 1964. Mimeographed document, Harvard Divinity School Library.

14 "Address at Pacem in Terris Convocation," Peace Is Possible: A Reader for Laymen, Elizabeth Jay Hollins, ed. New York: Grossman Publishers, 1966, pp. 181-186.

15 Advanced Problems in Systematic Theology. New York: Union Theological Seminary, 1952. Lectures given at Union Theological Seminary, 1952. These lectures were privately recorded by Peter H. John and printed primarily for the personal use of Tillich's students.

16 "All Is Yours," The New Being, Paul Tillich. New York: Charles Scribner's Sons, 1955, pp. 110-114. A sermon.

17 "All Things to All Men," Union Review, vol. 6, New York, no. 3 (May, 1945), pp. 3-4. Revised as "The Theologian: Part 2" in The Shaking of the Foundations, Paul Tillich (Charles Scribner's Sons, 1948).

18 "Ambiguity of Perfection," Time, vol. 81 (May 17, 1963), p. 69. Excerpts from an address given at Time magazine's 40th Anniversary Dinner.

19   "An Afterword: Appreciation and Reply," Paul Tillich in Cath-
      olic Thought, Thomas F. O'Meara and Donald M. Weisser,
      eds. Dubuque, Iowa: Priory Press, 1964, pp. 369-380.

20   "An Ecumenical Dialogue. Ecumenical Perspectives: Protes-
      tant," Dublin Review, vol. 239 (Summer, 1965), pp. 162-182.
      Appears as "Ecumenical Perspectives: Protestant" in Ecumen-
      ical Exchange, no. 1, 1965, pp. 5-13.

21   "An Evaluation of Martin Buber: Protestant and Jewish Thought,"
      Theology of Culture, Robert C. Kimball, ed. New York: Ox-
      ford University Press, 1959, pp. 188-199.

22   "An Historical Diagnosis: Impressions of a European Trip,"
      Radical Religion, vol. 2, no. 1 (Winter, 1936), pp. 11-17.
      A description of impressions gained from a trip made between
      April and September of 1936.

23   "An Ontology of Anxiety," Dimensions of Faith: Contemporary
      Prophetic Protestant Theology, William B. Kimmel and Geof-
      frey Clive, eds. New York: Twayne Publishers, 1960, pp.
      456-486. Reprinted from chapter 2 of The Courage to Be,
      Paul Tillich (Yale University Press, 1952).

24   "Answer," The Minister's Own Mental Health, Wayne E. Oates,
      ed. Great Neck, New York: Channel Press, 1961, p. 307.
      A reply to William Rickel's essay, "Is Psychology a Religious
      Process?"

25   "Answer to Karl Barth," The Beginnings of Dialectic Theology,
      James McConkey Robinson, ed. Richmond, Virginia: John
      Knox Press, 1968, pp. 155-158.

26   "Anxiety, Religion, and Medicine," Pastoral Psychology, vol.
      3, no. 29 (December, 1952), pp. 11-17. An excerpt from
      The Courage to Be, Paul Tillich (Yale University Press, 1952).

27   "Anxiety-reducing Agencies in our Culture," Anxiety, Paul H.
      Hoch and Joseph Zubin, eds. New York: Grune and Stratton,
      1950, pp. 6, 17-26. An address delivered before the Amer-
      ican Psychopathological Association, New York, June 3, 1949.

28   Approaches to World Peace. New York: Harper and Brothers,
      1944. From a conference on science, philosophy, and religion
      in their relation to the democratic way of life.

29   "Art and Ultimate Reality," Cross Currents, vol. 10, no. 1
      (Winter, 1960), pp. 1-14. A lecture delivered at the Museum
      of Modern Art, New York City, February 17, 1959. Appears
      also in Art and the Craftsman: The Best of the Yale Maga-
      zine, 1936-1961, edited by Joseph Harned and Neil Goodwin
      {Southern Illinois University Press, 1961), pp. 185-200.

30   "Aspects of a Religious Analysis of Culture," Theology of
       Culture, Robert C. Kimball, ed.   New York: Oxford Univer-
       sity Press, 1959, pp. 40-51.

31   "The Attack of Dialectical Materialism on Christianity," Stu-
       dent World (Geneva), vol. 31, No. 2 (Second Quarter, 1938),
       pp. 115-125.   Reprinted in World's Youth (German), vol. 14,
       no. 2, Spring 1938, pp. 147-157.

32   "Authentic Religious Art," Arts Digest, vol. 28 (August, 1954),
       p. 13.   Appears also in Polemic, vol. 5, Spring 1960, and in
       Masterpieces of Religious Art, published by the Art Institute
       of Chicago, 1954, pp. 8-9.   Reprinted as "The Nature of Re-
       ligious Art" in Symbols and Society, edited by Lyman Bryson
       (Harper and Brothers, 1955), pp. 282-289.

33   "Authority and Revelation," Harvard Divinity School Bulletin,
       vol. 49, no. 8 (April 7, 1952), pp. 27-36.   The Dudlean Lec-
       ture for 1950-1951.   Appears also in The Livingstonian, a
       theological magazine of Rhodes University, Grahamston, South
       Africa, vol. 2, no. 1, October 1961.

34   "Author's Introduction," The Protestant Era, Paul Tillich.
       Chicago, University of Chicago Press, 1948, pp. ix-xxix.

35   "Autobiographical Reflections," The Theology of Paul Tillich,
       Charles W. Kegley and Robert W. Brettal, eds.   New York:
       Macmillan, 1952, pp. 3-21.

36   "Basic Features of Religious Socialism," James Luther Adams,
       tr.   1965.   Typescript document, Harvard Divinity School Li-
       brary.

37   "The Basic Ideas of Religious Socialism," Bulletin, The Inter-
       national House of Japan, no. 6 (October, 1960), pp. 11-15.

38   "Basic Principles of Religious Socialism," Political Expecta-
       tion, James L. Adams, ed.   New York: Harper & Row, 1971,
       pp. 58-88.

39   "Basis of Genuine Hope for Peace on Earth," Social Progress,
       vol. 55 (May-June, 1965), pp. 16-20.

40   "Be Strong," Christianity and Crisis, vol. 23, no. 14 (August
       5, 1963), pp. 144-7.   A sermon included in A History of
       Christian Thought, edited by Peter H. John, 2nd stenographic
       edition, Union Theological Seminary, 1956, and in The Eternal
       Now, Paul Tillich (Charles Scribner's Sons, 1963).

41   "Before One Can Be Creative, One Must Be Able to Listen
       Creatively," The London Free Press, December 10, 1960.
       An address at Huron College given upon receipt of an honor-
       ary degree.   The London Free Press is printed in London,
       Ontario.

42   "The Beginning of Wisdom," Pulpit Digest, vol. 36, no. 218
(June, 1956), pp. 27-31.

43   "Behold I Am Doing a New Thing," Union Seminary Quarterly
Review, vol. 2, no. 4 (May, 1947), pp. 3-9. A sermon included in The Shaking of the Foundations, Paul Tillich. Charles Schribner's Sons, 1948.

44   "Being and Love," Moral Principles of Action, Ruth Nanda
Anshen, ed. New York: Harper and Brothers, 1952, pp.
661-672. An essay included in Four Existentialist Theologians, edited by Will Herberg (Doubleday, 1958).

45   "Being and Love," Pastoral Psychology, vol. 5, no. 43 (March,
1954), pp. 43-46. An excerpt from Love, Power, and Justice,
Paul Tillich (Oxford University Press, 1954), pp. 24-34. It
also appears in Dimensions of Faith: Contemporary Prophetic
Protestant Theology, edited by William B. Kimmel and Geoffrey Clive (Twayne Publishers, 1960).

46   "Between Mountain and Plain," Time, vol. 60 (October 20,
1952), pp. 69-72. Includes a portrait of Tillich.

47   "Between Utopianism and Escape from History," Colgate Ro-
chester Divinity School Bulletin, vol. 31, no. 2 (1959), pp.
32-40. A lecture delivered March 30, 1959 as a part of the
Rauschenbusch Lectures.

48   "Beyond Religious Socialism: How My Mind Has Changed in
the Last Decade," Christian Century, vol. 66, no. 24 (June
15, 1949), pp. 732-733. Appears also in The Christian Century Reader, edited by Harold E. Fey and Margaret Frakes
(Association Press, 1962), pp. 123-127.

49   "Beyond the Dilemma of our Period," The Cambridge Review,
vol. 1, Cambridge, Massachusetts, no. 4 (November, 1955),
pp. 209-215.

50   "Beyond the Usual Alternatives," Christian Century, vol. 75,
no. 19 (May 7, 1958), pp. 553-555.

51   Biblical Religion and the Search for Ultimate Reality. Chicago: University of Chicago Press, 1955. A book based on
a lecture delivered for the James W. Richard Lectures in the
Christian Religion, University of Virginia, 1951-1952.

52   "Biblical Religion and the Search for Ultimate Reality," Con-
temporary Religious Thinkers from Idealist Metaphysicians to
Existentialist Theologians, John Macquarrie, ed. New York:
Harper and Brothers, 1968, pp. 279-285. An excerpt from
Biblical Religion and the Search for Ultimate Reality, Paul
Tillich (University of Chicago Press, 1955).

53   "Bibliography of English Material Related to a Study of

Christian Mystics Through Church History," Cambridge, Massachusetts: Harvard Divinity School, 1957. A typed manuscript, Harvard Divinity School Library.

54 Book Review: Bennett, John C., Christianity and Communism, Union Seminary Quarterly Review, vol. 4, no. 2 (January, 1949), pp. 41-42.

55 Book Review: Berdyaev, Nicolas, Slavery and Freedom, Theology Today, vol. 2, no. 1 (April, 1945), pp. 130-132.

56 Book Review: Blakeney, Raymond B., Meister Eckhart: A Modern Translation, Religion in Life, vol. 11, no. 4 (Autumn, 1942), pp. 625-626.

57 Book Review: Brunner, Emil, The Mediator: A Study of the Central Doctrines of the Christian Faith, The Christian Century, vol. 51, no. 49 (December 5, 1934), pp. 1554-1556.

58 Book Review: Brunner, Emil, Revelation and Reason, Westminster Bookman, vol. 6, no. 3 (January-February, 1947), pp. 5-7.

59 Book Review: Fromm, Erich, Psychoanalysis and Religion, Pastoral Psychology, vol. 2, no. 15 (June, 1951), pp. 62-66.

60 Book Review: Fromm, Erich, The Sane Society, Pastoral Psychology, vol. 6, no. 56 (September, 1955), pp. 13-16.

61 Book Review: Hessen, John, Platonismus und Prophetismus, Anglican Theological Review, vol. 23 (1941), pp. 82-83.

62 Book Review: Koestler, Arthur, The Yogi and the Commissar: and Other Essays, Journal of Religion, vol. 27, no. 2 (April, 1947), pp. 135-136.

63 Book Review: Marcuse, Herbert, Reason and Revolution: Hegel and the Rise of Social Theory, Studies in Philosophy and Social Science, vol. 9, no. 3 (1941-1942), pp. 476-478.

64 Book Review: Maritain, Jacques, The Rights of Man and Natural Law, Religion in Life, vol. 13, no. 3 (Summer, 1944), pp. 465-466.

65 Book Review: Niebuhr, Reinhold, The Nature and Destiny of Man: Volume I, Human Nature, Christianity and Society, vol. 6, no. 2 (Spring, 1941), pp. 34-37.

66 Book Review: Roberts, David E., Psychotherapy and a Christian View of Man, Pastoral Psychology, vol. 1, no. 8 (November, 1950), pp. 61-64.

67 Book Review: Santayana, George, The Idea of Christ in the

Gospels or God in Man: A Critical Essay, The Nation, vol.
163, no. 15 (October 12, 1946), pp. 412-413. This review is
entitled "Christianity without Paul."

68 Book Review: Stepun, Fedor, The Russian Soul and Revolution, Christendom, vol. 1, no. 2 (Winter, 1936), pp. 366-367.

69 Book Review: Thielicke, Helmut, Theologische Ethik, Volume
I: Dogmatische, Philosophische, und Kontroverstheologische
Grundlegung, Anglican Theological Reivew, vol. 35, no. 1
(January, 1953), pp. 64-65.

70 Book Review: Wieman, Henry Nelson and Horton, Walter
Marshall, The Growth of Religion, Journal for the Scientific
Study of Religion, vol. 1 (October, 1961), pp. 109-114. Orig-
inally published in Theologische Literaturzeitung, vol. 49,
1924, pp. 25-30. Appears also in Journal of Religion, vol.
20, no. 1, January 1940, pp. 69-72.

71 Book Review: Wiesengrund-Adorno, Theodor, Kierkegaard,
Konstruction de Aesthetischen, Journal of Philosophy, vol. 31,
no. 23 (November 8, 1934), p. 640.

72 "Born in the Grave," Classmate, vol. 71 (August, 1964), pp.
10ff. A sermon included in The Shaking of the Foundations,
Paul Tillich (Charles Scribner's Sons, 1948).

73 The Boundaries of Our Being. London: Collins, 1973. A
collection of Tillich's sermons that also includes an autobiographical sketch.

74 "By What Authority?" The New Being, Paul Tillich. New
York: Charles Scribner's Sons, 1955, pp. 79-92. Included in
A History of Christian Thought, edited by Peter H. John, 1st
stenographic edition, Union Theological Seminary, 1953.

75 "Can Religion Survive?" Albert Schweitzer's Realm, A. A.
Roback, ed. Cambridge, Massachusetts: Sci-Art Publishers,
1962, pp. 307-313. Based on a symposium.

76 "Can Uniting Love Never Unite Mankind?" The New Republic,
vol. 130 (March 29, 1954), p. 17. An excerpt from Love,
Power, and Justice, Paul Tillich (Oxford University Press,
1954).

77 "Challenge to Protestantism," The Protestant, vol. 4, no. 4
(February-March, 1942), pp. 1-4.

78 "Christ as the Center of History," Contemporary Thinking
about Jesus: An Anthology, T. S. Kepler, ed. Nashville:
Abingdon-Cokesbury, 1944, pp. 217-222. Excerpt from a
1938 address entitled "The Kingdom of God and History."

79   The Christ in Art. New York: National Council of the
     Churches of Christ in the U.S.A., Department of Worship and
     the Arts: Commission on Art, 1955. A list of 56 images of
     the Christ selected by Paul Tillich, Alfred H. Barr and others.

80   The Christian and the Marxist View of Man. Cambridge,
     Massachusetts: Harvard University Press, 1959. A mimeo-
     graphed pamphlet published in two editions for the Research
     Department of the Universal Christian Council for Life and
     Work.

81   "The Christian Churches and the Emerging Social Order in
     Europe," Religion in Life, vol. 14, no. 3 (Summer, 1945),
     pp. 329-339. Included in The Witness, vol. 14, Summer
     1945.

82   The Christian Conscience and Weapons of Mass Destruction.
     New York: The Department of International Justice and Good-
     will, Federal Council of the Churches of Christ in America,
     1950.

83   "The Christian Consummation: A Conversation," The Chap-
     lain, vol. 13, no. 2 (April, 1956), pp. 10-13, 18-19. A con-
     versation between Albert T. Mollegan, Nels F. S. Ferre, and
     Paul Tillich.

84   "Christian Criteria for Our Culture," Criterion, vol. 1, no. 1
     (October, 1952), pp. 1, 3-4.

85   "Christian Fortitude and Existential Despair," Dimensions of
     Faith: Contemporary Prophetic Protestant Theology, William
     Kimmel and Geoffrey Clive, eds. New York: Twayne Pub-
     lishers, 1960, pp. 456-486. A reprint from The Courage to
     Be, Paul Tillich (Yale University Press, 1952), chapter 2.

86   "Christianity and Emigration," Presbyterian Tribune, vol. 52,
     no. 3 (October 29, 1936), pp. 13, 16. An address on behalf
     of the American Committee for German Christian Refugees,
     October 6, 1936.

87   "Christianity and International Affairs," The Christian Answer,
     Henry P. Van Dusen, ed. New York: Charles Scribner's
     Sons, 1948. Reprinted as The World Situation, Paul Tillich
     (Fortress Press, 1965).

88   "Christianity and Marxism," Political Expectation, James
     Luther Adams, ed. New York: Harper & Row, 1971, pp.
     89-96.

89   "Christianity and Modern Society," Political Expectation,
     James Luther Adams, ed. New York: Harper & Row, 1971,
     pp. 1-9.

90 "Christianity and Other Faiths: Reply to John Macquarrie," <u>Union Seminary Quarterly Review</u>, vol. 20 (January, 1965), pp. 117-118.

91 <u>Christianity and the Encounter of the World Religions.</u> New York: Columbia University Press, 1963.

92 <u>Christianity and the Problem of Existence.</u> Washington, D.C.: Henderson Services, 1951. A collection of three lectures delivered in Andrew Rankin Chapel, Howard University, April 24, 1951. The lectures included are: "Naturalism Transcended," "The Existentialist Movement," and "Is There a Christian Answer?" Mimeographed document, Harvard Divinity School Library.

93 "The Church and Communism," <u>Religion in Life</u>, vol. 6, no. 3 (Summer, 1937), pp. 347-357.

94 "The Church and Contemporary Culture," <u>World Christian Education</u>, vol. 9, no. 2 (Second Quarter, 1956), pp. 41-43. An address given before the General Board of the National Council of the Churches of Christ in the U.S.A., June 8, 1955. Also published as a pamphlet by the National Council of the Churches of Christ in the U.S.A., Department of Worship and the Arts, New York, 1956.

95 "Church and Culture," <u>The Interpretation of History</u>, Paul Tillich. New York, Charles Scribner's Sons, 1936, pp. 219-241.

96 "The Class Struggle and Religious Socialism," James Luther Adams, tr. A translation of chapter 9 of Paul Tillich's <u>Religioese Verwirklichung</u>. Typewritten manuscript, Harvard Divinity School Library.

97 "Comment," <u>Presbyterian Outlook</u>, vol. 137, no. 50 (December 26, 1955), p. 6. A reply to criticisms made by Nels F. S. Ferre.

98 "Comment," <u>The Witness</u>, vol. 26, no. 45 (April 8, 1943), p. 4. Observations on the report of the Commission on a Just and Durable Peace.

99 "Comment," <u>Charlotte: A Diary in Pictures</u>, Charlotte Salomon. New York: Harcourt, Brace & World, 1963. Observations by Paul Tillich concerning this book and its author.

100 "Commentary," <u>The Metropolis in Modern Life</u>, Robert Moore Fisher, ed. Garden City, New York: Doubleday & Company, Inc., 1955, pp. 346-348. Paul Tillich's observations on part 7 of this book ("The Impact of the Metropolis on the Spiritual Life of Man").

101 "Comments on Beat Poetry," Wagner Literary Magazine, vol. 1 (Spring, 1959), p. 20. Wagner Literary Magazine is a publication of Wagner College, New York.

102 "Communicating the Christian Message: A Question to Christian Ministers and Teachers," Theology and Culture, Robert C. Kimball, ed. New York: Oxford University Press, 1959, pp. 201-213.

103 "Communicating the Christian Message Today," The Episcopal Overseas Mission Review, vol. 6, no. 1 (1960), pp. 23-26, 51-53.

104 "Communicating the Gospel," Pastoral Psychology, vol. 7, no. 65 (June, 1956), pp. 10-16. Appears also in The Evangel, May-June 1957, pp. 10-14, and in Union Seminary Quarterly Review, vol. 7, no. 4, June 1952, pp. 3-11.

105 "The Concept of God: Reply to W. T. Stace," Perspective, vol. 2, no. 3 (January, 1950), pp. 12-14.

106 "The Conception of Man in Existential Philosophy," Journal of Religion, vol. 19, no. 3 (July, 1939), pp. 201-215. Reprinted as "The Nature of Man" in The Examined Life: An Introduction to Philosophy, edited by Troy Wilson Organ (Houghton Mifflin, 1956).

107 "Conformity," Readings in Human Relations, Keith Davis and William G. Scott, eds. New York: McGraw-Hill, 1959, pp. 456-461. Appears also in Social Research, vol. 24, no. 3, Autumn 1957, pp. 354-360, and in Humanitas, vol. 1, Fall 1965, pp. 117-122.

108 "The Conquest of Intellectual Provincialism: Europe and America," Theology of Culture, Robert C. Kimball, ed. New York: Oxford University Press, 1959, pp. 159-176.

109 "The Conquest of the Concept of Religion in the Philosophy of Religion," What Is Religion? James Luther Adams, ed. New York: Harper & Row, 1969, pp. 122-154.

110 "The Conquest of Theological Provincialism," The Cultural Migration: The European Scholar in America, W. Rex Crawford, ed. Philadelphia: University of Pennsylvania Press, 1953, pp. 138-156. The Benjamin Franklin Lectures of the University of Pennsylvania, Spring 1952.

111 "Conscience in Western Thought and the Idea of a Transmoral Conscience," Crozer Quarterly, vol. 22, no. 4 (October, 1945), pp. 289-300. Reprinted as "The Transmoral Conscience" in The Protestant Era, Paul Tillich (University of Chicago Press, 1948).

112 The Construction of the History of Religion in Schelling's Positive Philosophy: Its Presuppositions and Principles, Victor Nuovo, tr. Lewisburg, Pennsylvania: Bucknell University Press, 1974. Paul Tillich's thesis, Breslau, 1910.

113 "Contemporary Protestant Architecture," Modern Church Architecture, Albert Christ-Janer and Mary Mix, eds. New York: McGraw-Hill, 1962, pp. 122ff. Appears also in Journal of the Liberal Ministry, vol. 3, no. 1, Winter 1963, pp. 16-21.

114 "Contribution," Christianity Today, vol. 3, no. 1 (October 13, 1958), p. 31. A contribution to the theme, "Theologians and the Moon."

115 "Conversation with Werner Rode," Wisdom: Conversations with the Elder Wise Men of Our Day, James Nelson, ed. New York: W. W. Norton and Company, 1958, pp. 163-171.

116 "Council for a Democratic Germany," Bulletin of the Council for a Democratic Germany, vol. 1, no. 1-5 (September, 1944 to May, 1945). Paul Tillich was Chairman of the Council during this period.

117 "Courage and a Dynamic Faith," Faith Is a Star, Roland Gammon, ed. New York: E. P. Dutton & Co., 1963, pp. 194-198.

118 "Courage and Individualization," Philosophy in the Twentieth Century: An Anthology, Volume 4, William Barrett and Henry David Aiken, eds. New York: Random House, 1962, pp. 652-667. An excerpt from The Courage to Be, Paul Tillich (Yale University Press, 1952).

119 "Courage and Transcendence," Philosophy in the Twentieth Century: An Anthology, Volume 4, William Barrett and Henry David Aiken, eds. New York: Random House, 1962, pp. 668-687. An excerpt from The Courage to Be, Paul Tillich (Yale University Press, 1952).

120 The Courage to Be. New Haven: Yale University Press, 1952. The Terry Lectures. Chapter 2 of this book is included in Dimensions of Faith: Contemporary Prophetic Protestant Theology, edited by William B. Kimmel and Geoffrey Clive (Twayne Publishers, 1960). Pages 174-190 of this book appear in Issues in Christian Thought, edited by John B. Harrington (McGraw-Hill, 1968).

121 "Creative Integrity in a Democratic Society," Polemic, vol. 5 (Spring, 1960).

122 "Creative Love in Education," World Christian Education, vol. 4, no. 2 (Second Quarter, 1949), pp. 27-34.

123 "The Creative Work of Love," <u>Dimensions of Faith: Contemporary Prophetic Protestant Theology,</u> William B. Kimmel and Geoffrey Clive, eds. New York: Twayne Publishers, 1960, pp. 486-501. An excerpt from <u>Love, Power and Justice,</u> Paul Tillich (Oxford University Press, 1954), chapter 2.

124 "The Crisis of Personality," <u>An Introduction to Social Science,</u> Nelson Noftalin and Calhoun Sibley, eds. Philadelphia: J. B. Lippincott, 1953, pp. 28-32.

125 "Critical and Positive Paradox: A Discussion with Karl Barth and Friedrich Gogarten," <u>The Beginnings of Dialectic Theology,</u> James M. Robinson, ed. Richmind, Virginia: John Knox Press, 1968, pp. 133-141.

126 "Critique and Justification of Utopia," <u>Utopias and Utopian Thought,</u> Frank Edward Manuel, ed. Boston: Houghton Mifflin, 1966, pp. 296-309.

127 " 'Critique' of articles by F. S. C. Northrop ('Philosophy and World Peace') and John A. Ryan ('Religious Foundations for an Enduring Peace')," <u>Approaches to World Peace,</u> L. Bryson, L. Finkelstein and R. M. MacIver, eds. New York: Harper, 1944, pp. 684-685, 816-817.

128 " 'Critique' of articles by Robert J. Havighurst ('Education for Intergroup Cooperation'), Rudolf Allers ('Some Remarks on the Problems of Group Tensions'), A. Campbell Garnett ('Group Tensions in the Modern World'), and Amos N. Wilder ('Theology and Cultural Incoherence')," <u>Approaches to National Unity,</u> L. Bryson, L. Finkelstein and R. M. MacIver, eds. New York: Harper, 1945, pp. 407-408, 522-523, 537, 923.

129 "The Dance," <u>Dance Magazine,</u> vol. 31, no. 6 (June 1957), p. 20. From a symposium on "The Dance: What It Means to Me."

130 "The Decline and the Validity of the Idea of Progress," <u>The Future of Religions,</u> Jerald C. Brauer, ed. New York: Harper & Row, 1966, pp. 64-79.

131 "The Demonic," <u>The Interpretation of History,</u> Paul Tillich. New York: Charles Scribner's Sons, 1936, pp. 17-122.

132 "Depth," <u>Christendom,</u> vol. 9, no. 3 (Summer, 1944), pp. 317-325. A sermon reprinted as "The Depth of Existence," in <u>The Shaking of the Foundations,</u> Paul Tillich (Charles Scribner's Sons, 1948).

133 "The Destruction of Death," <u>The Shaking of the Foundations,</u> Paul Tillich. New York: Charles Scribner's Sons, 1948, pp. 169-173. A sermon.

134 "Dimensions, Levels, and the Unity of Life," Kenyon Alumni Bulletin (Ohio), vol. 17 (October-December, 1959), pp. 4-8. A lecture given on December 5, 1958. Appears also in Buddhism and Culture, edited by Susumu Yamaguchi (The Nakano Press, 1960), pp. 181-190.

135 "Discussion," The Nature of Man in Theological and Psychological Perspective, Simon Doninger, ed. New York: Harper & Brothers, 1962, pp. 208-210. A discussion of Margaret Mead's essay, "The Immortality of Man," in this book. Appears also in Pastoral Psychology, vol. 8, no. 75, June 1957, pp. 17-24, and in In Search of God and Immortality: The Garvin Lectures, Julius Seelye Bixler and others (Beacon Press, 1961).

136 "The Disintegration of Society in Christian Countries," The Churches Witness to God's Design, World Council of Churches. New York: Harper and Brothers, 1948, pp. 53-64. This book is volume 2 of the Amsterdam Assembly Series.

137 "The Divine-Human Encounter and The Courage to Be," Man in Crisis: Perspectives on the Individual and His World, Joseph K. Davis, ed. Glenview, Illinois: Scott, Foresman and Company, 1970, pp. 45-54. A reprint of a portion of The Courage to Be, Paul Tillich (Yale University Press, 1952).

138 "The Divine Name," A Reader in Contemporary Theology, John Stephen Bowden, ed. Philadelphia: Westminster Press, 1967, pp. 46-53. A sermon that also appears in Christianity and Crisis, vol. 20, no. 7, May 2, 1960, pp. 55-58, and in The Eternal Now, Paul Tillich (Charles Scribner's Sons, 1963.

139 "Do Not Be Conformed," Pulpit Digest, vol. 38, no. 237 (January, 1958), pp. 19-24. A sermon included in A History of Christian Thought, edited by Peter H. John (2nd stenographic edition, Union Theological Seminary, 1956), and in The Eternal Now, Paul Tillich (Charles Scribner's Sons, 1963).

140 "Dr. Richard Kroner," Alumni Bulletin of the Union Theological Society, vol. 17, no. 1 (November, 1941), pp. 3-4.

141 "Doing the Truth," The Shaking of the Foundations, Paul Tillich. New York: Charles Scribner's Sons, 1948, pp. 114-118. A sermon.

142 Dynamics of Faith. New York: Harper and Brothers, 1956.

143 "The Effects of Space Exploration on Man's Condition and Stature," The Future of Religions, Jerald C. Brauer, ed. New York: Harper & Row, 1966, pp. 39-51.

144 "The End of the Protestant Era?" Student World (Geneva),

vol. 30, no. 1 (First Quarter, 1937), pp. 49-57. Included in The Protestant Era, Paul Tillich (University of Chicago Press, 1948), pp. 222-233.

145 "Environment and the Individual," Journal of the American Institute of Architects, vol. 28, no. 2 (June, 1957), pp. 90-92.

146 "The Escape from God," Best Sermons: 1949-1950, Paul G. Butler, ed. New York: Harper, 1949, pp. 138-146. A sermon included in The Shaking of the Foundations, Paul Tillich (Charles Scribner's Sons, 1948).

147 "Eschatology and History," The Interpretation of History, Paul Tillich. New York: Charles Scribner's Sons, 1936, pp. 266-284.

148 "Estrangement and Reconciliation in Modern Thought," Review of Religion, vol. 9, no. 1 (November, 1944), pp. 5-19.

149 The Eternal Now. New York: Charles Scribner's Sons, 1963. A book of sermons.

150 "The Eternal Now," The Eternal Now, Paul Tillich. New York: Charles Scribner's Sons, 1963, pp. 122-132. A sermon given at Union Theological Seminary on April 24, 1955. It also appears in A History of Christian Thought, edited by Peter H. John (2nd stenographic edition, Union Theological Seminary, 1956); in The Modern Vision of Death, edited by Nathan A. Scott, Jr. (John Knox Press, 1967); in Readings in Science and Spirit, edited by Camillus D. Talafous (Prentice-Hall, 1966); in The Meaning of Death, edited by Herman M. D. Feifel (McGraw-Hill, 1959); in Motive, vol. 24, January-February 1964, pp. 32-37; and in The Boundaries of Our Being, Paul Tillich (Collins, 1973).

151 "Ethics in a Changing World," Religion and the Modern World, Jacques Maritain, ed. Philadelphia: University of Pennsylvania Press, 1951, pp. 51-61. An address included in The Protestant Era, Paul Tillich (University of Chicago Press, 1948), and in Morality and Beyond, Paul Tillich (Harper and Row, 1963).

152 "The European Discussion of the Problem of Demythologization of the New Testament." New York: Union Theological Seminary, 1952. The Auburn Lecture delivered at Union Theological Seminary on November 10, 1952.

153 "The European War and the Christian Churches," Direction, vol. 2, no. 8 (December, 1939), pp. 10-11. Reprinted as "The War and the Christian Churches" in The Protestant Digest, vol. 3, no. 1, January 1940, pp. 15-20.

154 "Existence and Existentialism," Issues in Christian Thought, John B. Harrington, ed. New York: McGraw-Hill Book Company, 1968, pp. 365-369. Reprinted from Paul Tillich's Systematic Theology: Volume II (University of Chicago Press, 1957), pp. 24-26, 27-28, 44-47.

155 "Existential Analyses and Religious Symbols," Contemporary Problems in Religion, Harold A. Basilius, ed. Detroit: Wayne State University Press, 1956, pp. 35-55. The Leo M. Franklin Memorial Lectures, 1953-1954. Appears also in Four Existentialist Theologians, edited by Will Herberg (Doubleday and Company, 1958), pp. 277-291.

156 "Existential Philosophy," Journal of the History of Ideas, vol. 5, no. 1 (January, 1944), pp. 44-70. Appears also in Ideas in Cultural Perspective, edited by Philip P. Wiener and Aaron Noland (Rutgers University Press, 1962).

157 "Existential Philosophy: Its Historical Meaning," Theology of Culture, Robert E. Kimball, ed. New York: Oxford University Press, 1959, pp. 76-111.

158 "Existential Thinking in American Theology," Religion in Life, vol. 10, no. 3 (May, 1941), pp. 452-455. A critique of H. Richard Niebuhr's book, The Meaning of Revelation.

159 "Existentialism and Psychotherapy," Review of Existential Psychology and Psychiatry, vol. 1 (January, 1961), pp. 8-16. An address delivered to the Conference on Existential Psychotherapy in New York City on February 27, 1960. Appears also in Pittsburgh Perspectives, vol. 1, no. 2, June 1960, pp. 3-12.

160 "Existentialism and Religious Socialism," Christianity and Society, vol. 5, no. 1 (Winter, 1949), pp. 8-11.

161 "Existentialism, Psychotherapy and the Nature of Man," The Nature of Man in Theological and Psychological Perspective, Simon Doniger, ed. New York: Harper & Brothers, 1962, pp. 42-54. Appears also in Pastoral Psychology, vol. 11, no. 105, June 1960, pp. 10-18, and in Review of Existential Psychology and Psychiatry, Winter 1961.

162 "Existentialist Aspects of Modern Art," Christianity and the Existentialists, Carl Michalson, ed. New York: Charles Scribner's Sons, 1956, pp. 128-147.

163 "Existentialist Theology," Contemporary Protestant Thought, Charles J. Curtis, ed. New York: Bruce Publishing Company, 1970, pp. 150-165.

164 "The Experience of the Holy," The Shaking of the Foundations,

Paul Tillich. New York: Charles Scribner's Sons, 1948, pp. 87-93. A sermon.

165 "Faith and Symbols," <u>Classical Statements on Faith and Reason</u>, Eddie Le Roy Miller, ed. New York: Random House, 1970. pp. 200-218.

166 "Faith and the Integration of the Personality," <u>Pastoral Psychology</u>, vol. 8, no. 72 (March, 1957), pp. 11-14. An excerpt from <u>Dynamics of Faith</u>, Paul Tillich (Harper and Brothers, 1956), chapter 6, part 2.

167 "Faith and Uncertainty," <u>The New Being</u>, Paul Tillich. New York: Charles Scribner's Sons, 1955, pp. 75-78. A sermon.

168 "Faith in the Jewish-Christian Tradition," <u>Christendom</u>, vol. 7, no. 4 (Autumn, 1942), pp. 518-526.

169 "Flight to Atheism," <u>The Protestant</u>, vol. 4, no. 10 (February-March, 1943), pp. 43-48. A sermon reprinted as "The Escape from God," in <u>The Shaking of the Foundations</u>, Paul Tillich (Charles Scribner's Sons, 1948). Appears also in <u>Best Sermons: 1949-1950</u>, edited by George P. Butler (T. Y. Crowell Co., 1950).

170 "Foreword," <u>God Hidden and Revealed</u>, John Dillenberger, ed. Philadelphia: Muhlenberg Press, 1953, pp. vii-viii.

171 "Foreword," <u>The So-Called Historical Jesus and the Historic, Biblical Christ</u>, Martin Kaehler. Philadelphia: Fortress Press, 1964. This book was translated by Carl E. Braaten.

172 "Foreword," <u>Voice of Illness: A Study in Therapy and Prophecy</u>, Aarne Siirala. Philadelphia: Fortress Press, 1964, pp. v-vi.

173 "Foreword," <u>Voluntary Associations; A Study of Groups in Free Societies. Essays in Honor of James Luther Adams</u>, D. B. Robertson, ed. Richmond: John Knox Press, 1966, pp. 5-6.

174 "Forgetting and Being Forgotten," <u>Pulpit Digest</u>, vol. 42, no. 283 (December, 1961), pp. 37-42. A sermon included in <u>The Eternal Now</u>, Paul Tillich (Charles Scribner's Sons, 1963).

175 "The Formative Power of Protestantism," <u>The Protestant Era</u>, Paul Tillich. Chicago: University of Chicago Press, 1948, pp. 206-221.

176 "The Four Levels of the Relationship Between Religion and Art." New York: Union Theological Seminary, 1952. Appeared as notes in a catalogue entitled <u>Contemporary Religious Art</u> describing an exhibition of contemporary religious

art and architecture given at Union Theological Seminary, New York, 1952.

177   "Freedom and the Ultimate Concern," Religion in America: Original Essays on Religion in a Free Society, John Cogley, ed. New York: Meridian Books, 1958, pp. 272-286.

178   "Freedom in the Period of Transformation," Freedom: Its Meaning, Ruth Nanda Anshen, ed. New York: Harcourt Brace, 1940, pp. 123-144.

179   "Frontiers," Journal of Bible and Religion, F. H. Littell, tr., vol. 33 (January, 1965), pp. 17-23. An address given upon receipt of the German Book Trade Peace Prize, September 2, 1962. Included in The Future of Religions, edited by Jerald C. Brauer (Harper & Row, 1966).

180   The Future of Religions, Jerald C. Brauer, ed. New York: Harper and Row, 1966. A book of essays by and about Tillich, collected in tribute to Tillich's impact on America. Includes a series of photographs of Tillich in various settings.

181   "Genuine Hope for Peace," Concern, vol. 7 (March 16, 1965), pp. 5ff.

182   "Germany Is Still Alive: German-Americans Take a Stand for Democracy Against Nazis," Protestant Digest, vol. 1, no. 3 (February, 1939), pp. 45-46. A Madison Square Garden speech given November 21, 1938. Revised as "The Meaning of Anti-Semitism" in Radical Religion, vol. 4, no. 1, Winter 1938, pp. 34-36.

183   "The God above God," The Listener (London), vol. 66, no. 1688 (August, 1961).

184   "God as Man's Ultimate Concern," The New Christianity: An Anthology of the Rise of Modern Religious Thought, William Robert Miller, ed. New York: Delacorte, 1967, pp. 242-247.

185   "God as Reality and Symbol," Essays and Studies (Tokyo), vol. 9, no. 2 (March, 1961), pp. 101-109. The Takeshi Saito Lecture given at Tokyo Woman's Christian College, June 29, 1960.

186   "The God of History," Christianity and Crisis, vol. 4, no. 7 (May 1, 1944), pp. 5-6. A sermon appearing as "The Two Servants of Jahweh," in The Shaking of the Foundations, Paul Tillich (Charles Scribner's Sons, 1948). Appears also in Witness to a Generation: Significant Writings from Christianity and Crisis, edited by Wayne H. Cowan (Bobbs-Merrill, 1966), pp. 17-20.

187   "God's Pursuit of Man," The Pulpit, vol. 30, no. 4 (April,

1959), pp. 4-5, 21-22. A sermon given in Autumn 1957. Included in Alumni Bulletin of Bangor Theological Seminary, vol. 33, no. 2, April 1958, pp. 21-25, and in The Eternal Now, Paul Tillich (Charles Scribner's Sons, 1963).

188 "The Golden Rule," The New Being, Paul Tillich. New York: Charles Scribner's Sons, 1955, pp. 30-34. A sermon.

189 "The Good That I Will, I Do Not," Union Seminary Quarterly Review, vol. 14, no. 3 (March, 1959), pp. 17-23. A sermon that also appears in Counterpoint, no. 5, Spring 1959, pp. 9-16; in Pastoral Psychology, vol. 12, no. 113, April 1961, pp. 10-16; in Religion in Life, vol. 28, Fall 1959, pp. 539-545; in Rockefeller Chapel Sermons of Recent Years, edited by Donovan E. Smucker (University of Chicago Press, 1967), pp. 165-173; and in The Eternal Now, Paul Tillich (Charles Scribner's Sons, 1963).

190 "The Gospel and the State," Power and Civilization, David Cooperman and Eugene Victor Walter, eds. New York: Crowell, 1962, pp. 523-534. Appears also in Crozer Quarterly, vol. 15, no. 4, October 1938, pp. 251-261.

191 "Grandeur and Misery of Man," Christianity and Crisis, vol. 15, no. 19 (November 15, 1955), p. 149. A reprint of Tillich's introduction to The Grandeur and Misery of Man, by D. E. Roberts (Oxford University Press, 1955).

192 "Has Higher Education an Obligation to Work for Democracy?" Radical Religion, vol. 5, no. 1 (Winter, 1940), pp. 12-15.

193 "Has Man's Conquest of Space Increased or Diminished His Stature?" The Great Ideas Today 1963, Robert M. Hutchins and Mortimer J. Adler, eds. Chicago: Encyclopaedia Britannica, 1963, pp. 49-59.

194 "Has the Messiah Come?" The New Being, Paul Tillich. New York: Charles Scribner's Sons, 1955, pp. 92-97. A sermon.

195 "He Who Believes in Me," The New Being, Paul Tillich. New York: Charles Scribner's Sons, 1955, pp. 97-101. A sermon.

196 "He Who Is the Christ," The Shaking of the Foundations, Paul Tillich. New York: Charles Scribner's Sons, 1948, pp. 141-149. A sermon.

197 "Heal the Sick; Cast Out the Demons," Union Seminary Quarterly Review, vol. 11, no. 1 (November, 1955), pp. 3-8. A sermon included in A History of Christian Thought, edited by Peter H. John (2nd stenographic edition, Union Theological Seminary, 1956); in Religious Education, vol. 50, no. 6, November-December 1955, pp. 379-382; and in The Eternal Now, Paul Tillich (Charles Scribner's Sons, 1963).

198 "The Heart Doth Need a Language," The Universal God, Carl H. Voss, ed. New York: World Publishing Company, 1953, pp. 34-36.

199 "High Talk," Selected Papers of Conrad Wright. A manuscript of a lecture given at the University of Glasgow 500th Anniversary celebration. Harvard Divinity School Library.

200 "Historical and Non-Historical Interpretations of History: A Comparison," The Protestant Era, Paul Tillich. Chicago: University of Chicago Press, 1948, pp. 16-31.

201 "History as the Problem of Our Period," Review of Religion, vol. 3, no. 3 (March, 1939), pp. 255-264.

202 "Holy Waste," The New Being, Paul Tillich. New York: Charles Scribner's Sons, 1955, pp. 46-50. A sermon.

203 "Honesty and Consecration," Journal of the American Institute of Architecture, vol. 45 (March, 1966), pp. 41-45.

204 "Hope in Eternal Life," Christianity and Crisis, vol. 26, no. 5 (April 4, 1966), pp. 57-58. An Easter meditation based on excerpts from pp. 406-423 of Systematic Theology: Volume III, Paul Tillich (University of Chicago Press, 1963), and from the sermon, "The Right to Hope," as delivered by Paul Tillich at Rockefeller Memorial Chapel, University of Chicago, on October 22, 1965.

205 "How Much Truth Is There in Karl Marx?" Christian Century, vol. 65, no. 36 (September 8, 1948), pp. 906-908.

206 "How We Communicate the Christian Message," The New Christian Advocate, vol. 3, part 5 (May, 1959), pp. 12-17. An address delivered at the Evanston Ecumenical Institute, Evanston, Illinois, January 1959.

207 "Human Condition," Criterion, vol. 2 (Summer, 1963), pp. 22-24. Criterion is a publication of the University of Chicago.

208 "Human Fulfillment," Search for America, Huston Smith, ed. Englewood Cliffs, New Jersey: Prentice-Hall, 1959, pp. 164-174. The ideas in this essay are Paul Tillich's. The formulation of the ideas is Huston Smith's.

209 "Human Nature Can Change," American Journal of Psychoanalysis, vol. 12, no. 1 (1952), pp. 65-67. A symposium with Harold Kelman, F. A. Weiss, and Karen Horney. Appears also in The Nature of Man in Theological and Psychological Perspective, edited by Simon Doniger (Harper and Row, 1962), and in Pastoral Psychology, vol. 11, no. 107, October 1960, pp. 40-42.

210 "The Human Predicament," Earnest Enquirers After Truth:

A Gifford Anthology, Bernard E. Jones, ed. London: George Allen & Unwin Ltd., 1970, pp. 205-206. A reprint of Paul Tillich's Systematic Theology: Volume II (University of Chicago Press, 1957), p. 28.

211 "The Hydrogen-Cobalt Bomb," Pulpit Digest, vol. 34, no. 194 (June, 1954), pp. 32-34. A symposium in a special issue of Pulpit Digest.

212 "I Am an American," Protestant Digest, vol. 3, no. 4 (June-July, 1941), pp. 24-26.

213 "The Idea and the Ideal of Personality," The Protestant Era, Paul Tillich. Chicago: University of Chicago Press, 1948, pp. 115-135.

214 "The Idea of God as Affected by Modern Knowledge," Crane Review, vol. 1, no. 3 (Spring, 1959), pp. 83-90. Appears also in In Search of God and Immortality: The Garvin Lectures, Julius Seelye Bixler and others (Beacon Press, 1961), pp. 100-109.

215 "The Idea of the Personal God," Union Review, vol. 2, no. 1 (November, 1940), pp. 8-10. A reply to an address by Albert Einstein entitled, "Science and Religion."

216 "Ideology and Utopia," Gesellschaft, vol. 6 (1929), pp. 348-355. This article has been translated by James Luther Adams from Gesellschaft, vol. 6, 1929. Typescript.

217 "The Impact of Pastoral Psychology on Theological Thought," The Ministry and Mental Health, Hans Hoffman, ed. New York: Association Press, 1960, pp. 13-20. Appears also in Pastoral Psychology, vol. 11, no. 101, February 1960, pp. 17-23.

218 "The Importance of New Being for Christian Theology," Man and Transformation: Papers from the Eranos Yearbooks, Joseph Campbell, ed. New York: Pantheon Books, 1964.

219 "Impressions of Europe: 1956," Colgate-Rochester Divinity School Bulletin, May, 1957, pp. 22-29.

220 "In Everything Give Thanks," The Eternal Now, Paul Tillich. New York: Charles Scribner's Sons, 1963, pp. 173-185. A sermon.

221 "In Thinking, Be Mature," The Pulpit, vol. 34, no. 10 (November, 1963), pp. 4-6. A sermon given at Washington Cathedral on December 28, 1958, and at Chicago Sunday Evening Club on January 12, 1959. This sermon is also included in The Eternal Now, Paul Tillich (Charles Scribner's Sons, 1963), and in Washington Diocese, February 1959, pp. 16-19.

222 "Informal Report," Cambridge, Massachusetts: Harvard Divinity School, 1960. A report on Tillich's lecture trip to Japan in the Summer of 1960. Mimeographed document, Harvard Divinity School Library.

223 "Inner Aim," Time, vol. 77 (April 21, 1961), p. 57. A summary of an address.

224 The Interpretation of History. New York: Charles Scribner's Sons, 1936. A book of essays written by Tillich and translated by N. A. Rasetzki and Elsa L. Talmey.

225 "The Interpretation of History and the Idea of Christ," The Interpretation of History, Paul Tillich. New York: Charles Scribner's Sons, 1936, pp. 242-265.

226 "Introduction," The Grandeur and Misery of Man, David E. Roberts. New York: Oxford University Press, 1955, pp. v-viii. Appears also in Pastoral Psychology, vol. 6, no. 59, December 1955, pp. 12-13, and in Christianity and Crisis, vol. 15, no. 19, November 14, 1955, p. 149.

227 "Introductory Note," New Images of Man, New York Museum of Modern Art, ed. New York: Museum of Modern Art, 1959.

228 "Is a Science of Human Values Possible?" New Knowledge in Human Values, Abraham H. Maslow, ed. New York: Harper and Brothers, 1958, pp. 189-196.

229 "Is Psychotherapy a Religious Process?" Pastoral Psychology, vol. 7, no. 62 (March, 1956), pp. 39-40. Rejoinder to W. Rickel. Included in The Minister's Own Mental Health, edited by Wayne E. Oates (Channel Press), pp. 307f.

230 "Is There a Judeo-Christian Tradition?" Judaism, vol. 1, no. 2 (April, 1952), pp. 106-109.

231 "Is There Any Word from the Lord?" The New Being, Paul Tillich. New York: Charles Scribner's Sons, 1955, pp. 114-125. A sermon included in A History of Christian Thought, edited by Peter H. John (1st stenographic edition, Union Theological Seminary, 1953).

232 "Japan Is Split by Old and New," Chicago Maroon, vol. 60, no. 60 (February, 1961). Chicago Maroon is a publication of the University of Chicago.

233 "Jewish Influences on Contemporary Christian Theology," Cross Currents, vol. 2, no. 3 (May, 1952), pp. 35-42.

234 "The Jewish Question: A Christian and a German Problem," Jewish Social Studies, vol. 33 (October, 1971), pp. 253-271.

22 / Paul Tillich

235   "Justification by Doubt and the Protestant Principle," Toward
       a New Christianity; Readings in the Death of God Theology,
       Thomas J. J. Altizer, ed. New York: Harcourt, Brace and
       World, 1967, pp. 157-174.

236   "Kairos," The Protestant Era, Paul Tillich. Chicago: Uni-
       versity of Chicago Press, 1948, pp. 32-51. Appears also in
       A Handbook of Christian Theology, edited by Arthur A. Cohen
       and Marvin Halverson (Meridian Books, 1958), pp. 193-197.

237   "Kairos and Logos," The Interpretation of History, Paul Til-
       lich. New York: Charles Scribner's Sons, 1936, pp. 123-175.

238   "Karen Horney--September 16, 1885 to December 4, 1952,"
       Pastoral Psychology, vol. 4, no. 34 (May, 1953), pp. 11-13.
       A funeral address.

239   "Kierkegaard as an Existential Thinker," The Union Review,
       vol. 4, no. 1 (December, 1942), pp. 5-7.

240   "Kierkegaard in English," American-Scandinavian Review,
       vol. 3, no. 3 (October, 1942), pp. 254-257.

241   "The Kingdom of God and History," The Kingdom of God and
       History, H. B. Wood, ed. Chicago: Willett, Clark, 1938, pp.
       107-141. An address.

242   "Knowledge Through Love," The Shaking of the Foundations,
       Paul Tillich. New York: Charles Scribner's Sons, 1948,
       pp. 108-114. A sermon.

243   "The Language of Religion." Cambridge, Massachusetts:
       Harvard Divinity School, 1955. A lecture given November 13,
       1955 at Pennsylvania State University. Mimeographed docu-
       ment, Harvard Divinity School Library.

244   "Let Us Dare to Have Solitude," Union Seminary Quarterly
       Review, vol. 12, no. 2 (May, 1957), pp. 9-15. A sermon
       that appears as "Loneliness and Solitude" in University of
       Chicago Divinity School News, vol. 24, no. 2, May 1, 1957,
       pp. 1-7.

245   "Letter," Christianity and Crisis, vol. 16, no. 3 (March 5,
       1956), p. 24. A letter to Reinhold Niebuhr on Picasso's
       "Guernica" and its protestant significance.

246   "Letter," Partisan Review, vol. 24, no. 2 (Spring, 1962),
       pp. 311-312.

247   "Letter to Thomas Mann, May 23, 1943," The Intellectual
       Legacy of Paul Tillich, James R. Lyons, ed. Detroit:
       Wayne State University Press, 1969, pp. 101-107.

248 "Limit of Hope," Time, vol. 85 (February 26, 1965), p. 38.
A summary of an address on Pacem in Terris.

249 "Loneliness and Solitude," University of Chicago Divinity
School News, vol. 24, no. 2 (May 1, 1957), pp. 1-7. A
sermon that appears as "Let Us Dare to Have Solitude" in
Union Seminary Quarterly Review, vol. 12, no. 2, May 1957,
pp. 9-15. Appears also in Representative American Speeches:
1957-1958, edited by A. Craig Baird (H. W. Wilson Company,
1958), pp. 184-192; in Pulpit Digest, September 1958; in The
Reference Shelf, vol. 30, no. 4; and in The Eternal Now,
Paul Tillich (Charles Scribner's Sons, 1963).

250 "The Lost Dimension in Religion," Saturday Evening Post,
vol. 230, no. 50 (June 14, 1958), pp. 28-29, 76, 78-79. A
contribution to the magazine's series, "Adventures of the
Mind." Appears also in Issues in Christian Thought, edited
by John B. Harrington (McGraw-Hill, 1968), pp. 12-19, and
in Adventures of the Mind, edited by Richard Thruelsen and
John Kobler (Knopf, 1959), pp. 47-56.

251 "Love Is Stronger than Death," The New Being, Paul Tillich.
New York: Charles Scribner's Sons, 1955, pp. 170-175. A
sermon.

252 "Love, Power, and Justice," Christian Social Teachings: A
Reader in Christian Social Ethics from the Bible to the Pres-
ent, George W. Forell, ed. Garden City, New York: Anchor
Books, 1966, pp. 406-417.

253 "Love, Power, and Justice," The Listener, vol. 48, no. 1231
(October 2, 1952), pp. 544-545.

254 Love, Power, and Justice: Ontological Analyses and Ethical
Applications. London: Oxford University Press, 1954. A
book based on the Firth and the Sprunt Lectures. Chapter 2
of this book is included in Dimensions of Faith: Contemporary
Prophetic Protestant Theology, edited by William B. Kimmel
and Geoffrey Clive (Twayne Publishers, 1960), pp. 486-501.

255 "Love's Strange Work," The Protestant, vol. 4, no. 3
(December-January, 1942), pp. 70-75.

256 "Man and Earth," The Eternal Now, Paul Tillich. New York:
Charles Scribner's Sons, 1963, pp. 66-81. A sermon.

257 "Man and Society in Religious Socialism," Christianity and
Society, vol. 8, no. 4 (Fall, 1943), pp. 10-21.

258 "Man, the Earth, and the Universe," Christianity and Crisis,
vol. 22, no. 11 (June 25, 1962), pp. 108-112.

259 "Martin Buber, 1878-1965," Pastoral Psychology, vol. 16,
no. 156 (September, 1965), pp. 52-54.

260 "Martin Buber," A Reader in Contemporary Theology, John
Bowden and James Richmond, eds. Philadelphia: Westminster
Press, 1967, pp. 53-57.

261 "Martin Buber and Christian Thought: His Three-fold Contribution to Protestantism," Commentary, vol. 5, no. 6 (June,
1948), pp. 515-521.

262 "Marx and the Prophetic Tradition," Radical Religion, vol. 1,
no. 4 (Autumn, 1935), pp. 21-29.

263 "Marxism and Christian Socialism," Christianity and Society,
vol. 7, no. 2 (Spring, 1942), pp. 13-18. Appears also in
The Protestant Era, Paul Tillich (University of Chicago Press,
1948).

264 "Marxism and Christianity," The Protestant, vol. 6 (Spring,
1942), pp. 13-24. Appears also in Christianity in Society,
Spring 1942.

265 "The Marxist View of History: A Study in the History of the
Philosophy of History," Culture in History: Essays in Honor
of Paul Radin, Stanley Diamond, ed. New York: Columbia
University Press, 1960, pp. 631-641.

266 "The Meaning and Justification of Religious Symbols," Religious Experience and Truth, Sidney Hook, ed. New York:
New York University Press, 1961, pp. 301-321. From a
symposium sponsored by the New York University Institute of
Philosophy.

267 "The Meaning and Sources of Courage," Child Study, vol. 31,
no. 3 (Summer, 1954), pp. 7-11.

268 "The Meaning of Health," Perspectives, vol. 5, no. 1 (1961),
pp. 92ff. An address to the New York Society for Clinical
Psychiatry on January 14, 1960. Appears also in Perspectives in Biology and Medicine, vol. 5, no. 1, Autumn 1961,
and in The Graduate Journal (Austin, Texas), vol. 5, no. 2,
Winter 1963.

269 "The Meaning of Joy," The Spirit of Man: Great Stories and
Experiences of Spiritual Crisis, Inspiration, and Joy of Life
by Forty Famous Contemporaries, Whit Burnett, ed. Free-
port, New York: Books for Libraries Press, 1958, pp. 257-
264. A sermon included in The New Being, Paul Tillich
(Charles Scribner's Sons, 1955).

270 "The Meaning of Our Present Historical Existence," The
Hazen Conferences on Student Guidance and Counseling.
Haddam, Connecticut: Edward W. Hazen Foundation Inc.,
1938, pp. 19-29.

271 "The Meaning of Providence," The Shaking of the Foundations, Paul Tillich. New York: Charles Scribner's Sons, 1948, pp. 104-108. A sermon.

272 "The Meaning of the German Church Struggle for Christian Missions," Christian World Mission, William K. Anderson, ed. Nashville: Commission on Ministerial Training, The Methodist Church, 1946, pp. 130-136.

273 "The Meaning of the Triumph of Nazism," Christianity and Society, vol. 5, no. 4 (1940), pp. 45-46. A resume of an address.

274 "Meditation: The Mystery of Time," The Shaking of the Foundations, Paul Tillich. New York: Charles Scribner's Sons, 1948, pp. 34-38. A sermon.

275 "The Method of Theology," Varieties of Experience: An Introduction to Philosophy, Albert William Levi, ed. New York: The Ronald Press, 1957, pp. 514-518.

276 "Mind and Migration," Social Research, vol. 4, no. 3 (September, 1937), pp. 295-305. Reprinted as "Migrations Breed New Cultures," in The Protestant Digest, vol. 3, no. 2, February 1940, pp. 10-19.

277 "Misinterpretation of the Doctrine of Incarnation," Church Quarterly Review, vol. 147, no. 294 (January, 1949), pp. 113-132.

278 "Mission and World History," The Theology of the Christian Mission, Gerald H. Anderson, ed. New York: McGraw-Hill Book Company, 1961, pp. 281-289.

279 "Moralisms and Morality from the Point of View of the Ethicist," Ministry and Medicine in Human Relations, Iago Galdston, ed. New York: International Universities Press, 1955, pp. 125-140. From presentations given at the New York Academy of Medicine Conferences, May 11, 1950 and April 8 and 19, 1952.

280 "Moralisms and Morality: Theonomous Ethics," Theology of Culture, Robert C. Kimball, ed. New York: Oxford University Press, 1959, pp. 133-145.

281 Morality and Beyond. New York: Harper and Row, 1963. Chapters 4 and 5 are reprinted from The Protestant Era, Paul Tillich (University of Chicago Press, 1955).

282 My Search for Absolutes. New York: Simon and Schuster, 1967. From a lecture series delivered at the University of Chicago Law School in 1965. Includes drawings by Saul Steinberg.

283 My Travel Diary, 1936: Between Two Worlds, Jerald C.
Brauer, ed. New York: Harper and Row, 1970. A book
translated by Maria Pelikan.

284 Mysticism and Guilt Consciousness in Schelling's Philosophical
Development, Victor Nuovo, tr. Lewisburg, Pennsylvania:
Bucknell University Press, 1974. Paul Tillich's thesis, Halle,
1912.

285 "Nation of Time, Nation of Space," Land Reborn, vol. 8, no.
1 (April-May, 1957), pp. 4-5. A translation of a German
article entitled "The Jewish Question, A Christian and a German Problem."

286 "Natural and Revealed Religion," Contemporary Religious
Thought: An Anthology, T. S. Kepler, ed. New York:
Abingdon Press, 1941, pp. 64-68. Appears also in Christen-
dom, vol. 1, no. 1, Autumn 1935, pp. 159-170.

287 "Nature, Also, Mourns for a Lost Good," The Shaking of the
Foundations, Paul Tillich. New York: Charles Scribner's
Sons, 1948, pp. 76-87. A sermon.

288 "Nature and Sacrament," The Protestant Era, Paul Tillich.
Chicago: University of Chicago Press, 1948, pp. 94-112.

289 "The Nature and the Significance of Existentialist Thought,"
Journal of Philosophy, vol. 53, no. 23 (November 8, 1956),
pp. 739-748. A symposium with George Boas and George
Schrader, Jr., on "Existentialist Thought and Contemporary
Philosophy in the West."

290 "The Nature of a Liberating Conscience," Conscience: Theological and Psychological Perspectives, Carl Ellis Nelson, ed.
New York: Newman Press, 1973, pp. 62-71.

291 "The Nature of Authority," Pulpit Digest, vol. 34, no. 186
(October, 1953), pp. 25-27, 30-32, 34. A sermon reprinted
as "By What Authority," in The New Being, Paul Tillich
(Charles Scribner's Sons, 1955).

292 "The Nature of Man," Journal of Philosophy, vol. 43, no. 25
(December 5, 1946), pp. 675-677.

293 "The Nature of Man," The Examined Life: An Introduction to
Philosophy, Troy Wilson Organ, ed. Boston, Massachusetts:
Houghton Mifflin, 1956, pp. 339-346.

294 "The Nature of Religious Language," Theology of Culture,
Robert C. Kimball, ed. New York: Oxford University Press,
1959, pp. 53-67.

295 The New Being. New York: Charles Scribner's Son, 1955.
A book of Sermons.

296 "The New Being," Religion in Life, vol. 19, no. 4 (Autumn, 1950), pp. 511-517. A sermon included in Time, vol. 69, June 10, 1957, pp. 51-52; in The New Being, Paul Tillich (Charles Scribner's Sons, 1955); and in The Boundaries of Our Being, Paul Tillich (Collins, 1973).

297 "New Images of Man," Polemic, vol. 5 (Spring, 1960), pp. 11-13. Reprinted from New Images of Man, edited by Peter Selz (Doubleday, 1959).

298 "Nicholas Berdyaev," Religion in Life, vol. 7, no. 3 (Summer, 1938), pp. 407-415.

299 "Nietzsche and the Bourgeois Spirit," Journal of the History of Ideas, vol. 6, no. 3 (June, 1945), pp. 307-309.

300 "Now Concerning Spiritual Gifts," Union Review, vol. 6, no. 1 (December, 1944), pp. 15-17. A sermon appearing as "The Theologian: Part I," in The Shaking of the Foundations, Paul Tillich (Charles Scribner's Sons, 1948).

301 "The Nuclear Dilemma," Christianity and Crisis, vol. 21, no. 19 (November 13, 1961), pp. 203-204. Appears also in Witness to a Generation: Significant Writings from Christianity and Crisis, edited by Wayne H. Cowan (Bobbs-Merrill, 1966), pp. 253-260.

302 "On Catholicism and Protestantism," The Current, vol. 2, no. 4 (1961), pp. 148ff.

303 "On Healing," Pastoral Psychology, vol. 6, no. 55 (June, 1955), pp. 25-30. Excerpts of a sermon in The New Being, Paul Tillich (Charles Scribner's Sons, 1955).

304 "On Man and His Nature," Journal of Philosophy, vol. 43, no. 25 (December 5, 1946), pp. 675-677. An abstract of a paper read at the American Philosophical Association 43rd Annual Eastern Division meeting, Yale University, 1946.

305 "On Peace on Earth," Social Ethics: Issues in Ethics and Society, Gibson Winter, ed. New York: Harper and Row, 1968, pp. 225-232. Reprinted from To Live as Men: An Anatomy of Peace (Santa Barbara, California: Center for the Study of Democratic Institutions), 1965, pp. 12-23.

306 On the Boundary: An Autobiographical Sketch. New York: Charles Scribner's Sons, 1966. This autobiographical sketch also appears in The Interpretation of History, Paul Tillich (Charles Scribner's Sons, 1936), pp. 3-73.

307 "On The Boundary," The Boundaries of Our Being, Paul Tillich. London: Collins, 1973. A sermon.

308 "On the Boundary Line," Christian Century, vol. 77, no. 49

(December 7, 1760), pp. 1435-1437. Included in How My Mind Has Changed, edited by Harold E. Fey (Meridian Books, 1961), pp. 159-169.

309 "On the Idea of a Theology of Culture," What Is Religion? James Luther Adams, ed. New York: Harper & Row, 1969, pp. 155-181.

310 "On the Transitoriness of Life," The Shaking of the Foundations, Paul Tillich. New York: Charles Scribner's Sons, 1948, pp. 64-76. A sermon.

311 "On Wisdom," The Eternal Now, Paul Tillich. New York: Charles Scribner's Sons, 1963, pp. 163-173. A sermon given at Memorial Church, Harvard University, February 19, 1956.

312 "The Ontological Problems Implied in the Objective Side of Religion," Four Existential Theologians, Will Herberg, ed. New York: Doubleday & Co. Inc., 1958, pp. 323-331. Excerpt from Biblical Religion and the Search for Ultimate Reality, Paul Tillich (University of Chicago Press), 1955.

313 "Ontology and the Question of God," The New Christianity; An Anthology of the Rise of Modern Religious Thought, William Robert Miller, ed. New York: Delacorte, 1967, pp. 238-242.

314 "Our Disintegrating World," Anglican Theological Review, vol. 23, no. 2 (April, 1941), pp. 134-146. Appears also in Logical Review, vol. 23, April 1941, pp. 134-146.

315 "Our Protestant Principles," The Protestant, vol. 4, no. 7 (August-September, 1942), pp. 8-14.

316 "Our Ultimate Concern," The New Being, Paul Tillich. New York: Charles Scribner's Sons, 1955, pp. 152-161. A sermon.

317 "Pablo Picasso's Guernica," Together, December, 1959, p. 15.

318 "Pacem in Terris," Criterion, vol. 4 (Spring, 1965), Criterion is a publication of the University of Chicago.

319 "The Paradox of Prayer," Pulpit Digest, vol. 35, no. 206 (June, 1955), pp. 23-25. A sermon included in The New Being, Paul Tillich (Charles Scribner's Sons, 1955).

320 "The Paradox of the Beatitudes," The Shaking of the Foundations, Paul Tillich. New York: Charles Scribner's Sons, 1948, pp. 24-29. A sermon.

321 "Participation and Knowledge: Problems of an Ontology of Cognition," Sociologia; Aufsaetze, Max Horkheimer zum

sechzigsten Geburtstag gewidmet, Theodore W. Adorno and Walter Dirks, eds. Vol. 1 (Frankfurter Beitrage zur Soziologie). Frankfurt: Europaeische Verlagsanstalt (1955), pp. 201-209.

322 "Paul Tillich," Inquiry Magazine. New Haven, Connecticut: The Wesley Foundation at Yale, 1958. Excerpts from Paul Tillich's Yale University lectures given in March 1958. Inquiry Magazine is a special publication periodically produced by The Wesley Foundation.

323 "Paul Tillich," Wisdom, Nelson James, ed. New York: W. W. Norton and Company, 1958, pp. 163-171. Recorded conversations with Werner Rode, September 1955, on the NBC television series, "Wisdom."

324 "Paul Tillich and Carl Rogers: A Dialogue," Pastoral Psychology, vol. 19, no. 181 (February, 1968), pp. 55-64. A transcript of two successive television programs produced at San Diego State College, California, on March 7, 1965.

325 "Paul Tillich Converses with Psychotherapists," Journal of Religion and Health, vol. 11 (January, 1972), pp. 40-72.

326 "Paul Tillich in Conversation: Culture and Religion," Foundations (Baptist), vol. 14 (January-March, 1971 and April-June, 1971), pp. 6-17; pp. 102-115.

327 "Paul Tillich in Conversation: History and Theology," Foundations (Baptist), vol. 14 (July-September, 1971), pp. 209-223.

328 "Paul Tillich in Conversation on Psychology and Theology," Journal of Pastoral Care, vol. 26 (September, 1972), pp. 176-189.

329 "The Permanent Significance of the Catholic Church for Protestantism," Protestant Digest, vol. 3, no. 10 (February-March, 1941), pp. 23-31.

330 "Permanent Significance of the Catholic Church for Protestants," Dialog, vol. 1 (Summer, 1961), pp. 22-25.

331 "The Person in a Technical Society," Christian Faith and Social Action: A Symposium, John A. Hutchinson, ed. New York: Charles Scribner's Sons, 1953, pp. 137-153. Reprinted in Perspectives U.S.A., no. 8, Summer 1954, pp. 115-136, and in Social Ethics: Issues in Ethics and Society, edited by Gibson Winter (Harper and Row, 1968), pp. 120-138.

332 Perspectives on 19th and 20th Century Protestant Theology, Carl E. Braaten, ed. New York: Harper and Row, 1967.

333 "Philosophy and Fate," The Protestant Era, Paul Tillich. Chicago: University of Chicago Press, 1948, pp. 3-15.

334 "Philosophy and Theology," Religion in Life, vol. 10, no. 1 (Winter, 1941), pp. 21-30. Reprinted in Theology, vol. 44, no. 261, March 1942, pp. 133-143. Included in The Protestant Era, Paul Tillich (University of Chicago Press, 1948).

335 "The Philosophy of Religion," What Is Religion? James Luther Adams, ed. New York: Harper & Row, 1969, pp. 27-121.

336 "Philosophy of Social Work," Pastoral Psychology, vol. 14, no. 139 (December, 1963), pp. 27-30. Appears also in Social Service Review, vol. 36, March 1962, pp. 13-16.

337 Political Expectation, James Luther Adams, ed. New York: Harper and Row, 1971. A book of essays by Paul Tillich.

338 "The Political Meaning of Utopia," Political Expectation, James Luther Adams, ed. New York: Harper & Row, 1971, pp. 125-180.

339 "The Power of Love," The New Being, Paul Tillich. New York: Charles Scribner's Sons, 1955, pp. 15-25. A sermon.

340 "The Power of Self-Destruction," God and the H-Bomb, Donald Keys, ed. New York: Bellmeadows Press and Bernard Geis Associates, 1961, pp. 35-36.

341 "Pray Without Ceasing." Cambridge, Massachusetts: Harvard Divinity School, 1956. A sermon delivered in the Fall of 1956. Mimeographed document, Harvard Divinity School Library.

342 "Preface," Sunrise to Eternity: A Study of Jacob Boehme's Life and Thought, John Joseph Stoudt. Philadelphia: University of Pennsylvania Press, 1957, pp. 7-8.

343 "Prefatory Note," New Images of Man, Peter Selz. New York: Museum of Modern Art, 1959, pp. 9-10.

344 "Present Theological Situation in the Light of the Continental European Development," Theology Today, vol. 6, no. 3 (October, 1949), pp. 299-310.

345 "Principalities and Powers," The New Being, Paul Tillich. New York: Charles Scribner's Sons, 1955, pp. 50-63. A sermon.

346 "The Problem of Power," The Interpretation of History, Paul Tillich. New York: Charles Scribner's Sons, 1936, pp. 179-202.

347 "The Problem of Theological Method," Journal of Religion, vol. 27, no. 1 (January, 1947), pp. 16-26. A conversation between E. A. Burtt and Paul Tillich. Appears also in Four

Existentialist Theologians, edited by Will Herberg (Doubleday, 1958).

348 "The Prophetic Element in the Christian Message and the Authoritarian Personality," McCormick Quarterly, vol. 17, no. 1 (November, 1963), pp. 16-26. From an address delivered at McCormick Theological Seminary, Chicago, Illinois, on November 29, 1962.

349 The Protestant Era, James Luther Adams, tr. Chicago: University of Chicago Press, 1948. An abridged edition of this book, containing only chapters 1-15, was published by the University of Chicago Press in 1957.

350 "The Protestant Message," Newsweek, vol. 45 (May 2, 1955), pp. 89-90. Includes a portrait of Tillich.

351 "The Protestant Message and the Man of Today," The Protestant Era, Paul Tillich. Chicago: University of Chicago Press, 1948, pp. 192-205.

352 "The Protestant Principle and the Proletarian Situation," The Protestant Era, Paul Tillich. Chicago: University of Chicago Press, 1948, pp. 161-181.

353 "Protestant Principles," The Protestant, vol. 4, no. 5 (April-May, 1942), pp. 17-19. A statement by the Executive Council of The Protestant regarding the basic policy of the magazine. Paul Tillich was Chairman of the Council at this time.

354 "The Protestant Vision," Chicago Theological Seminary Register, vol. 40, no. 2 (March, 1950), pp. 8-12.

355 "Protestantism and Artistic Style," Theology of Culture, Robert C. Kimball, ed. New York: Oxford University Press, 1959, pp. 68-75.

356 "Protestantism and the Contemporary Style of the Visual Arts," Christian Scholar, vol. 40, no. 4 (December, 1957), pp. 307-311.

357 "Protestantism as a Critical and Creative Principle," Political Expectation, James Luther Adams, ed. New York: Harper & Row, 1971, pp. 10-39.

358 "Protestantism in the Present World-Situation," American Journal of Sociology, vol. 43, no. 2 (September, 1973), pp. 236-248. Reprinted as "The End of the Protestant Era?" in The Protestant Era, Paul Tillich (University of Chicago Press, 1948).

359 "Psychoanalysis, Existentialism and Theology," Faith and Freedom, vol. 9, no. 25 (Autumn, 1955), pp. 1-11. Reprinted

in the Christian Register, vol. 135, no. 3, March 1956, pp. 16-17, 34-63, and in Pastoral Psychology, vol. 9, no. 87, October 1958, pp. 9-17.

360 "Psychotherapy and a Christian Interpretation of Human Nature," Review of Religion, vol. 13, no. 3 (March, 1949), pp. 264-268.

361 "Purgation of Family Images," The Choice Is Always Ours, Dorothy Berkeley Philips, ed. New York: Harper and Brothers, 1960, pp. 45-46. An abridged version of the sermon "Who Are My Mother and My Brothers," in The New Being, Paul Tillich (Charles Scribner's Sons, 1955).

362 "Question and Answer," Earnest Enquirers After Truth: A Gifford Anthology, Bernard E. Jones, ed. London: George Allen & Unwin Ltd., 1970, pp. 120-121. A reprint of Paul Tillich's Systematic Theology: Volume II (University of Chicago Press, 1957), pp. 14-15.

363 "[Some] Questions on Brunner's Epistemology," The Theology of Emil Brunner, Charles W. Kegley and Robert W. Bretall, eds. New York: The Macmillan Company, 1962, pp. 99-107. An excerpt of this article appears in Christian Century, vol. 79, no. 43, October 24, 1962, pp. 1284-1287.

364 "Reading History as Christians," Christian Advocate, October, 1956, pp. 44-49.

365 "Realism and Faith," The Protestant Era, Paul Tillich. Chicago: University of Chicago Press, 1948, pp. 66-82.

366 "The Recovery of the Prophetic Tradition in the Reformation." Washington, D.C.: Organizing Committee, Christianity and Modern Man Publications (Henderson Services), 1950. A transcript of three lectures delivered at Washington Cathedral Library, November-December, 1950. The titles of these lectures are: "The Divinity of the Divine," "The Human Predicament," and "The New Community." Mimeographed document, Harvard Divinity School Library.

367 "Redemption in Cosmic and Social History," Journal of Religious Thought, vol. 3, no. 1 (Autumn-Winter, 1946), pp. 17-27.

368 "The Redemption of Nature," Christendom, vol. 10, no. 3 (Summer, 1945), pp. 299-306. A sermon reprinted as "Nature, Also, Mourns for a Lost Good," in The Shaking of the Foundations, Paul Tillich (Charles Scribner's Sons, 1948).

369 "Reinhold Niebuhr," Reinhold Niebuhr: A Prophetic Voice in Our Time, Harold R. Landon, ed. Greenwich, Connecticut: Seabury Press, 1962, pp. 29-41. Discussion, pp. 42-54.

Essays in tribute by Paul Tillich, John C. Bennett, and Hans J. Morgenthau.

370 "Reinhold Niebuhr's Doctrine of Knowledge," Reinhold Niebuhr: His Religious, Social, and Political Thought, Robert W. Bretall and Charles W. Kegley, eds. New York: Macmillan Company, 1956, pp. 35-43.

371 "A Reinterpretation of the Doctrine of the Incarnation," Church Quarterly Review, vol. 147, no. 294 (January, 1949), pp. 133-148.

372 "Rejoice Always." Cambridge, Massachusetts: Harvard Divinity School Library, 1956. A sermon given in the Fall of 1956. Mimeographed document, Harvard Divinity School Library.

373 "Rejoinder," Journal of Religion, vol. 46, no. 1, part 2 (January, 1966), pp. 184-196. Tillich's commentary on the articles written about his theology in this issue.

374 "Relation of Metaphysics and Theology," Review of Metaphysics, vol. 10, no. 1 (September, 1956), pp. 57-63.

375 "The Relation of Religion and Health," Healing: Human and Divine; Man's Search for Health and Wholeness through Science, Faith, and Prayer, Simon Doniger, ed. New York: Association Press, 1957, pp. 185-205. Appears also in Religion and Health, edited by Simon Doniger (Association Press, 1958); in Pastoral Psychology, vol. 5, no. 44, May 1954, pp. 41-52; and in The Review of Religion, vol. 10, no. 4, May 1946, pp. 348-384.

376 "The Relationship Today between Science and Religion," The Student Seeks an Answer, John A. Clark, ed. Waterville, Maine: Colby College Press, 1960, pp. 296-306. From the Ingraham Lectures in Philosophy and Religion.

377 "The Relevance of the Ministry in Our Time and Its Theological Foundation," Making the Ministry Relevant, Hans Hofmann, ed. New York: Charles Scribner's Sons, 1960, pp. 19-35.

378 "Religion and Education," Protestant Digest, vol. 3, no. 11 (April-May, 1941), pp. 58-61.

379 "Religion and Its Intellectual Critics," Christianity and Crisis, vol. 15, no. 3 (March 7, 1955), pp. 19-22. An abridged report of an address given at Union Theological Seminary, January 2, 1954. Appears also in Motive, May 1955, and in What the Christian Hopes for in Society: Cultural Perspectives from Christianity and Crisis, edited by Wayne H. Cowan (Association Press, 1957).

380 "Religion and Secular Culture," Journal of Religion, vol. 26, no. 2 (April, 1946), pp. 79-86. Included in The Protestant Era, Paul Tillich (University of Chicago Press, 1955).

381 "Religion and the Eternal Norms," Vox, vol. 2, no. 3 (Summer, 1959), pp. 4-12. Vox is a publication of Dartmouth College.

382 "Religion and the Free Society," Religion and Freedom, Donald McDonald, reporter and editor. New York: The Fund for the Republic, 1958, pp. 39-48. From a discussion between Abraham Heschel, Gustave Weigel, and Paul Tillich on "The Role of Religion in the Free Society."

383 "Religion and the Intellectuals: A Symposium," Partisan Review, vol. 17, no. 3 (March, 1950), pp. 254-256. Included in The Partisan Review Anthology, edited by William Phillips and Phillip Row (Holt Rinehart & Winston, 1962), pp. 424ff.

384 "Religion and the Visual Arts." Cambridge, Massachusetts: Harvard Divinity School Library, 1955. Part of a lecture given at Connecticut College, November 1955. Transcribed from Tillich's notes. Mimeographed document, Harvard Divinity School Library.

385 "Religion as a Dimension in Man's Spiritual Life," Theology of Culture, Robert C. Kimball, ed. New York: Oxford University Press, 1959, pp. 3-9. Included in Phenomenology of Religion, edited by Joseph D. Bettis (Harper & Row, 1969), pp. 173-178. First published in Man's Right to Knowledge (New York: H. Muschel, 1954).

386 "Religion as an Aspect of the Human Spirit," Man's Right to Knowledge, Herbert Muschel, ed. New York: Columbia University Press, 1955, pp. 78-83. A radio talk given on November 28, 1954. Reprinted in Perspectives U.S.A., no. 15, Spring 1956, pp. 43-48, and in The Gadfly (Great Books Foundation, Chicago), vol. 8, no. 1, July-August 1956, pp. 2-4.

387 "Religion in a Changing World," Religion and the Modern World, Jacques Maritain, ed. Philadelphia: University of Pennsylvania Press, 1941, pp. 51-61.

388 "Religion in the Intellectual Life of the University," Harvard Alumni Bulletin, January 17, 1957, pp. 298-299. An address to the Harvard University Board of Overseers, November 1957.

389 "Religion in Two Societies: America and Russia," Theology of Culture, Robert C. Kimball, ed. New York: Oxford University Press, 1965, pp. 177-187. From a lecture series held at the Metropolitan Museum of Art, New York, March 28-30, 1952.

390 The Religious Situation, H. Richard Niebuhr, tr. New York:
     H. Holt and Company, 1932. A translation of Paul Tillich's
     monograph, "Die Religioese Lage der Gegenwart,"

391 "The Religious Situation in Germany Today," Religion in Life,
     vol. 47, no. 3 (1978), pp. 361-370. A reprint from Religion
     in Life, vol. 3, no. 2, Spring 1934, pp. 163-173.

392 "Religious Socialism," Political Expectation, James Luther
     Adams, ed. New York: Harper & Row, 1971, pp. 40-57.

393 "The Religious Symbol," Journal of Liberal Religion, vol. 2,
     no. 1 (Summer, 1940), pp. 13-33. Reprinted in Symbolism in
     Religion and Literature, edited by Rollo May (George Braziller
     Publishers, 1960), pp. 75-98; in Daedalus, vol. 87, no. 3,
     Summer 1958, pp. 7-21; in Religious Experience and Truth,
     edited by Sidney Hook (New York University Press, 1961); and
     in Myth and Symbol, edited by Frederick W. Dillistone (The
     Talbott Press, 1966).

394 "Religious Symbols and Our Knowledge of God," Christian
     Scholar, vol. 38, no. 3 (September, 1955), pp. 189-197.

395 "Reply to Gustave Weigel: 'The Theological Significance of
     Paul Tillich,'" Gregorianum (Rome), vol. 37, no. 1 (1956),
     pp. 53-54. Reprinted in Cross Currents, vol. 6, no. 2,
     Spring 1956, pp. 141-155.

396 "Reply to Interpretation and Criticism," The Theology of Paul
     Tillich, Charles W. Kegley and Robert W. Bretall, eds. New
     York: The Macmillan Company, 1964, pp. 329-349. A re-
     sponse by Tillich to articles written about his theology in this
     book.

397 "Reply to Nels F. S. Ferre: 'Where Do We Go From Here
     in Theology?'" Religion in Life, vol. 25, no. 1 (Winter,
     1955), pp. 19-21.

398 "Reply to Reinhold Niebuhr," Christianity and Crisis, vol. 16,
     no. 3 (March 5, 1956), p. 24. In this reply Tillich addresses
     the subjects of art and architecture.

399 "Reply to William Rickel: 'Is Psychotherapy a Religious
     Process?'" Pastoral Psychology, vol. 7, no. 62 (March,
     1956), pp. 39-40.

400 "Response," Harvard Divinity Bulletin, vol. 30 (January,
     1966), pp. 23-28. Tillich's response to the address delivered
     at a program and dinner given in his honor, May 24, 1962.

401 "The Riddle of Inequality," Union Seminary Quarterly Review,
     vol. 13, no. 4 (May, 1958), pp. 3-9. A sermon reprinted in

Social Action, vol. 25, November 1958, pp. 20-25; in United Church Herald, vol. 6, no. 17, September 19, 1963, pp. 12-14; and in The Eternal Now, Paul Tillich (Charles Scribner's Sons, 1963).

402 "The Right Time," The New Being, Paul Tillich. New York: Charles Scribner's Sons, 1955, pp. 161-170. A sermon.

403 "The Right to Hope," Neue Zeitschrift für Systematische Theologie, vol. 7, no. 3 (1965), pp. 371-377. A sermon given at Memorial Church, Harvard University.

404 "Roman Catholicism and Protestantism," The Current, vol. 2, no. 4 (December, 1961), pp. 148-156.

405 "Russia's Church and the Soviet Order," Think, vol. 10, no. 1 (January, 1944), pp. 22-23. Reprinted in The Cathedral Age, vol. 19, no. 1, Easter 1944, pp. 14-15, 31-32.

406 "Salvation," Princeton Seminary Bulletin, vol. 57 (October, 1963), pp. 4-9. A sermon included in The Eternal Now, Paul Tillich (Charles Scribner's Sons, 1963).

407 "Science and the Contemporary World in the View of a Theologian," Public and Private Association in the International Educational and Cultural Relations of the United States, Department of State, U.S.A., Washington, D.C.: United States Department of State, February, 1961, pp. 67-70. An address given at the Massachusetts Institute of Technology, December 16, 1960, as a part of four conferences sponsored by the U.S. Department of State.

408 "Science and Theology: A Discussion with Einstein," Theology of Culture, Robert C. Kimball, ed. New York: Oxford University Press, 1959, pp. 127-132.

409 "Seeing and Hearing," The New Being, Paul Tillich. New York: Charles Scribner's Sons, 1955, pp. 125-135. A sermon.

410 "The Sermons of David E. Roberts," Pastoral Psychology, vol. 6, no. 59 (December, 1955), pp. 12-13. A reprint of Tillich's introduction to The Grandeur and Misery of Man, by David E. Roberts (Oxford University Press, 1955). Appears also as "The Grandeur and Misery of Man" in Christianity and Crisis, vol. 14, no. 19, November 14, 1955, p. 149.

411 "Shadow and Substance: A Theory of Power," Political Expectation, James Luther Adams, ed. New York: Harper & Row, 1971, pp. 115-124.

412 "The Shaking of the Foundations," The Shaking of the Foundations, Paul Tillich. New York: Charles Scribner's Sons, 1948, pp. 1-12. A sermon.

413 The Shaking of the Foundations. New York: Charles Scribner's Sons, 1948. A book of sermons by Tillich.

414 "The Significance of Kurt Goldstein for Philosophy of Religion," Journal of Individual Psychology, vol. 15, no. 1 (May, 1959), pp. 20-23.

415 The Significance of the Historical Jesus for the Christian Faith. Union Theological Seminary, 1938. Monday Forum Talk no. 5. From the lectures and discussion of Ernest F. Scott and Paul Tillich on February 28, 1938.

416 "The Significance of the History of Religions for the Systematic Theologian," The History of Religions: Essays on the Problems of Understanding by Joachim Wach and others, Joseph M. Kitagawa, ed. Chicago: University of Chicago Press, 1967, pp. 241-255. Included in The Future of Religions, edited by Jerald C. Brauer (Harper & Row, 1966).

417 "Signs of the Times," Christian Science Sentinel, vol. 66, no. 1 (January 4, 1964), pp. 43ff. Excerpts from the sermon "Salvation" which is included in The Eternal Now, Paul Tillich (Charles Scribner's Sons, 1963).

418 "Sin and Grace in the Theology of Reinhold Niebuhr," Reinhold Niebuhr: A Prophetic Voice in Our Time, H. R. Landon, ed. Greenwich, Connecticut: Seabury Press, 1962, pp. 27-54. Essays in tribute by Paul Tillich, John C. Bennett and Hans J. Morgenthau.

419 "The Social Functions of the Churches in Europe and America," Social Research, vol. 3, no. 1 (February, 1936), pp. 90-104.

420 The Socialist Decision, Franklin Sherman, tr. New York: Harper and Row, 1977.

421 "Spiritual Presence," Union Seminary Quarterly Review, vol. 17, no. 2 (January, 1962), pp. 121-128. A sermon delivered in the Spring of 1961 in James Memorial Chapel, Union Theological Seminary. Included in Pastoral Psychology, vol. 13, no. 127, October 1962, pp. 25-30; in Best Sermons: 1964, edited by George P. Butler (Van Nostrand, 1964); and in Sermons to Intellectuals from Three Continents, edited by Franklin H. Littell (Macmillan, 1963), pp. 149-160.

422 "Spiritual Problems of Post War Reconstruction," Christianity and Crisis, vol. 2, no. 14 (August 10, 1942), pp. 2-6. Included in The Protestant Era, Paul Tillich (University of Chicago Press, 1948).

423 "The State as Expectation and Demand," Political Expectation, James Luther Adams, ed. New York: Harper & Row, 1971, pp. 97-114.

424 "Storms of Our Times," Anglican Theological Review, vol. 25, no. 1 (January-April, 1943), pp. 15-32. An address with subsequent discussion among Frederick Grant, Angus Dun, Joseph Fletcher and George Thomas, pp. 43-44, 47-53. Also appears in The Protestant Era, Paul Tillich (University of Chicago Press, 1948), but without the discussion.

425 "The Struggle Between Time and Space," Theology of Culture, Robert C. Kimball, ed. New York: Oxford University Press, 1959, pp. 30-39.

426 "Symbol and Knowledge," Journal of Liberal Religion, vol. 2, no. 1 (Spring, 1941), pp. 202-206. Tillich's response to criticisms of his essay, "The Religious Symbol," made by W. W. Urban and E. E. Aubrey in Journal of Liberal Religion, Summer 1940, pp. 13-33.

427 "Symbols of Eternal Life," Harvard Divinity Bulletin, vol. 26, no. 3 (April, 1962), pp. 1-10. The Ingersoll Lecture on the Immortality of Man, 1962. Appears also in Pastoral Psychology, vol. 16, no. 153, April 1965, pp. 13-20.

428 "Symbols of Faith," Religion from Tolstoy to Camus, Walter Arnold Kaufmann, ed. New York: Harper and Brothers, 1961, pp. 383-390. Excerpts from Dynamics of Faith, Paul Tillich (Harper and Brothers, 1956).

429 "Symbols of Faith," Religious Language and the Problem of Religious Knowledge, Ronald E. Santoni, ed. Bloomington, Indiana: Indiana University Press, 1968, pp. 136-145.

430 "The System of the Sciences," James Luther Adams, tr. A typewritten manuscript, Harvard Divinity School Library.

431 Systematic Theology, vol. 1 (1951), vol. 2 (1957), vol. 3 (1963). Chicago: University of Chicago Press (1951-1963). Contents: Vol. I, Part 1, Reason and Revelation; Vol. I, Part 2, Being and God; Vol. II, Part 3, Existence and the Christ; Vol. III, Part 4, Life and the Spirit; Vol. III, Part 5, History and the Kingdom of God. In 1967 the University of Chicago Press combined all three volumes of Tillich's Systematic Theology under one cover.

432 "That They May Have Life," Christianity and Crisis, vol. 24, no. 15 (September 21, 1964), pp. 172-174. A sermon included in Union Seminary Quarterly Review, vol. 20, November 1964, pp. 3-8.

433 "Theism Transcended," The New Christianity: An Anthology of the Rise of Modern Religious Thought, William Robert Miller, ed. New York: Delacorte, 1967, pp. 232-237.

434 "The Theologian," The Shaking of the Foundations, Paul

Tillich. New York: Charles Scribner's Sons, 1948, pp. 118-130. A sermon.

435 "The Theological Significance of Existentialism and Psychoanalysis," Psyche and Spirit: Readings in Psychology and Religion, John J. Heaney, ed. New York: Paulist Press, 1973, pp. 261-274. Included in Theology of Culture, edited by Robert Kimball (Oxford University Press, 1959), pp. 112-125.

436 "Theology and Architecture," Architectural Forum, vol. 103, no. 6 (December, 1955), pp. 131-134. Portrait p. 105. Discussion, pp. 135-136. Reprinted as "Theology, Architecture, and Art" in Church Management, vol. 33, no. 1, October 1956, pp. 55-56. Discussion omitted.

437 "Theology and Counseling," Journal of Pastoral Care, vol. 10, no. 4 (Winter, 1956), pp. 193-200.

438 "Theology and Education," St. Paul's School Centennial Publication. Concord, New Hampshire: St. Paul's School, 1956. An address given in October 1956.

439 "Theology and Philosophy: A Question," Issues in Christian Thought, John B. Harrington, ed. New York: McGraw-Hill Book Company, 1968, pp. 215-225. Reprinted from Paul Tillich's Systematic Theology: Volume I (University of Chicago Press, 1951), pp. 18-28.

440 "Theology and Symbolism," Religious Symbolism, F. Ernest Johnson, ed. New York: Harper and Brothers (The Institute for Religious and Social Studies), 1955, pp. 107-116.

441 Theology of Culture, Robert C. Kimball, ed. New York: Oxford University Press, 1959. A book of collected essays by Paul Tillich.

442 "The Theology of Missions," Christianity and Crisis, vol. 15, no. 5 (October 4, 1955), pp. 35-38. Appears also in Occasional Bulletin of the Missionary Research Library, vol. 5, no. 10, October 10, 1954, and in Witness to a Generation: Significant Writings from Christianity and Crisis, edited by Wayne H. Cowan (Bobbs-Merrill, 1966), pp. 83-90.

443 "The Theology of Pastoral Care," Clinical Education for the Pastoral Ministry, Ernest E. Bruder and Marian L. Barb, eds. Washington, D.C.: Advisory Committee on Clinical Pastoral Education, 1958, pp. 1-6. Discussion, pp. 6-15. Drawn from the proceedings of the Fifth National Conference on Clinical Pastoral Education. Appears also in Christian Advocate, vol. 4, no. 13, June 23, 1960, pp. 4-6 (abridged), and in Pastoral Psychology, vol. 10, no. 97, October 1959, pp. 21-26.

444 "Tillich Challenges Protestantism," The Protestant, vol. 4, no. 4 (February-March, 1942), pp. 1-4. A speech made by Tillich at a dinner given in his honor on February 9, 1942 by friends of The Protestant magazine.

445 "Tillich Encounters Japan," Japanese Religions, vol. 2, no. 2 and 3 (May, 1961), pp. 48-55, 55-71. Edited from tape recordings by Robert W. Wood.

446 "Tillich Relates His Impressions of the Japanese Political Situation," Harvard Crimson, October 28, 1960.

447 "To the God Unknown," The Universal God, Carl H. Voss, ed. New York: World Publishing Company, 1953, pp. 61-63.

448 "To Whom Much Is Forgiven," Sermons from an Ecumenical Pulpit, Max F. Dascam, ed. Boston: Starr King Press, 1956, pp. 27-36. A sermon which appears in The Intercollegian, February 1956, as "The Source of Forgiveness and Love." Appears also in Best Sermons, 1955, edited by George P. Butler (McGraw-Hill, 1955), and in The New Being, Paul Tillich (Charles Scribner's Sons, 1955).

449 "The Totalitarian State and the Claims of the Church," Social Research, vol. 1, no. 4 (November, 1934), pp. 405-433.

450 "The Transmoral Conscience," The Protestant Era, Paul Tillich. Chicago: University of Chicago Press, 1948, pp. 136-149.

451 "Trends in Religious Thought that Affect Social Outlook," Outside Readings in Sociology, E. A. Schuler, ed. New York: T. Y. Crowell, 1952, pp. 420-430. Appears also in Religion and the World, edited by Frederick E. Johnson (Harper and Brothers, 1944), pp. 17-28.

452 "The Truth Will Make You Free," Pulpit Digest, vol. 33, no. 180 (April, 1953), pp. 17-23. A sermon included in A History of Christian Thought, edited by Peter H. John (1st stenographic edition, Union Theological Seminary, 1953), and in Campus Lutheran, November 1953.

453 "The Two Roots of Political Thinking," The Interpretation of History, Paul Tillich. New York: Charles Scribner's Sons, 1936, pp. 203-215.

454 "The Two Servants of Jahweh," The Shaking of the Foundations, Paul Tillich. New York: Charles Scribner's Sons, 1948, pp. 29-34. A sermon.

455 "Two Types of Philosophy of Religion," Theology of Culture, Robert C. Kimball, ed. New York: Oxford University Press, 1964, pp. 10-29. Included in Union Seminary Quarterly Review, vol. 1, no. 4, May 1946.

456 Ultimate Concern: Tillich in Dialogue, D. Mackenzie Brown, ed. New York: Harper and Row, 1965.

457 "Universal Salvation," The New Being, Paul Tillich. New York: Charles Scribner's Sons, 1955, pp. 175-179. A sermon.

458 "Vertical and Horizontal Thinking," The American Scholar, vol. 15, no. 1 (Winter, 1945), pp. 102-105. Reply, pp. 110-112. From a symposium with Ralph Demos and Sidney Hook on "The Future of Religion." Appears also in The American Scholar Reader, edited by Hiram C. Haydn and Betsy Saunders (Athenaeum, 1960), pp. 125-130.

459 "Victory in Defeat: The Meaning of History in the Light of Christian Prophetism," Interpretation, vol. 4, no. 1 (January, 1952), pp. 17-26.

460 "Visit to Germany," Christianity and Crisis, vol. 8, no. 19 (November 15, 1948), pp. 147-149.

461 "Waiting," The Shaking of the Foundations, Paul Tillich. New York: Charles Scribner's Sons, 1948, pp. 149-153. A sermon.

462 War Aims. New York: The Protestant Digest, 1941. A pamphlet published by The Protestant Digest of three previous Tillich articles on the aims of World War II. See, "What War Aims?" "Whose War Aims?" and "Why War Aims?"

463 "What War Aims?" The Protestant, vol. 4, no. 1 (August-September, 1941), pp. 13-18.

464 "Whose War Aims?" The Protestant, vol. 4, no. 2 (October-November, 1941), pp. 24-29.

465 "Why War Aims?" The Protestant, vol. 3, no. 12 (June-July, 1941), pp. 2-19.

466 "The Way as Openness to the New Creation," The Choice Is Always Ours, Dorothy Berkeley Phillips, ed. New York: Harper and Brothers, 1960, pp. 27-30. An abridged version of the sermon "The New Being," in The New Being, Paul Tillich (Charles Scribner's Sons, 1955).

467 "We Live in Two Orders," The Shaking of the Foundations, Paul Tillich. New York: Charles Scribner's Sons, 1948, pp. 12-24. A sermon.

468 "What Is Basic in Human Nature?" The American Journal of Psychoanalysis, vol. 22, no. 2 (1962), pp. 1-7. The Karen Horney Memorial Lecture. Reprinted in Pastoral Psychology, vol. 14, no. 131, February 1963, pp. 13-20.

469   "What Is Divine Revelation?" The Witness, vol. 26, no. 46
      (April 15, 1943), pp. 8-9.

470   What Is Religion? James Luther Adams, ed. New York:
      Harper and Row, 1969. Contains three essays by Tillich that
      were originally published between 1919 and 1925.

471   "What Is Truth?" Canadian Journal of Theology, vol. 1 (July,
      1955), pp. 117-124. A sermon included in The New Being,
      Paul Tillich (Charles Scribner's Sons, 1955).

472   "What Is Wrong With the 'Dialectic' Theology?" Journal of
      Religion, vol. 15, no. 2 (April, 1935), pp. 127-145.

473   "Where Do We Go from Here in Theology?" Religion in Life,
      vol. 25, no. 1 (Winter, 1955), pp. 19-21.

474   "Who Are My Mother and Brothers ... ?" The New Being,
      Paul Tillich. New York: Charles Scribner's Sons, 1955,
      pp. 105-110. A sermon.

475   "Who Are My Mother and My Brothers: Dangers of Psycho-
      therapy," The Choice Is Always Ours, Dorothy Berkley Phil-
      lips, ed. New York: Harper & Brothers, 1960, pp. 263-264.

476   "The Witness of the Spirit to the Spirit," The Shaking of the
      Foundations, Paul Tillich. New York: Charles Scribner's
      Sons, 1948, pp. 130-141. A sermon.

477   "The Word of God," Language: An Inquiry into its Meaning
      and Function, Ruth Nanda Anshen, ed. New York: Harper
      and Brothers, 1957, pp. 122-133.

478   "The Word of Religion to the People of This Time," The
      Protestant, vol. 4 (April, 1942), pp. 43-48. Reprinted as
      "The Word of Religion" in The Protestant Era, Paul Tillich
      (University of Chicago Press, 1948).

479   "The World Situation," The Christian Answer, Henry Pitt Van
      Dusen, ed. New York: Charles Scribner's Sons, 1945, pp.
      1-44. Included in this essay is a section entitled "Guideposts
      for the Christian Answer."

480   The World Situation. Philadelphia: Fortress Press, 1965.

481   "Yes and No," The New Being, Paul Tillich. New York:
      Charles Scribner's Sons, 1955, pp. 101-105. A sermon.

482   "The Yoke of Religion," The Shaking of the Foundations, Paul
      Tillich. New York: Charles Scribner's Sons, 1948, pp. 93-
      104. A sermon.

483   You Are Accepted. Chicago: National Student Council of the

YMCA and the YWCA, 1954. A booklet describing how the human situation of loneliness and insecurity is transformed in the Christian community.

484 "You Are Accepted," The Shaking of the Foundations, Paul Tillich. New York: Charles Scribner's Sons, 1948, pp. 153-163. A sermon that also appears in Sources of Protestant Theology, edited by William A. Scott (Bruce Publishing Company, 1971), pp. 333-339.

2. DISSERTATIONS AND THESES ABOUT OR RELATED TO PAUL TILLICH IN ENGLISH

1   Adams, James Luther, "Paul Tillich's Philosophy of Culture, Science, and Religion," University of Chicago, 1946. Ph. D. Dissertation.

2   Allen, Sydney Earl, Jr., "A Study of the Idea of Revelation with Special Reference to the Thought of Paul Tillich and Karl Barth," University of Nebraska, 1964. Ph. D. Dissertation.

3   Amelung, Eberhard A., "Religious Socialism as an Ideology: A Study of the 'Kairos-Circle' in Germany Between 1919 and 1933," Harvard University, 1962. Th. D. Dissertation.

4   "Arnink, Dale Edwin, "Symbolic Knowledge in Ernst Cassirer and Paul Tillich," School of Theology at Claremont, 1971. Ph. D. Dissertation.

5   Arnould, Eugene Robert, "The Theatre and Ultimate Reality: An Analysis of Paul Tillich's Writings on Theology and Art and their Application to the Theatre," Harvard Divinity School, 1972. M. Div. Senior Project.

6   Arther, Donald E., "The Philosophy of Life: Alfred North Whitehead and Paul Tillich," Eden Theological Seminary, 1977. Ph. D. Dissertation.

7   Ayers, Robert Hyman, "A Study of the Problem of Biblical Authority in Selected Contemporary American Theologians," Vanderbilt University, 1958. Ph. D. Dissertation.

8   Baker, Barry John, "The Mystical Theology of Paul Tillich," Trinity College, University of Toronto, 1971. M. Th. Thesis.

9   Barker, Alfred James, "The Concept of Sin in the Thought of Reinhold Niebuhr and Paul Tillich," Victoria University, 1959. Th. D. Dissertation.

10 Bartlett, Donald Elton, "The Concept of the End of History in

the Writings of Reinhold Niebuhr and Paul Tillich," Yale University, 1954. Ph.D. Dissertation.

11 Bash, John Adam, Jr., "The Nature of the Ontological and Theological Endeavors in the Thought of Paul Tillich," Yale University, 1965. Ph.D. Dissertation.

12 Bertaldt, Renzo, "Imago Christi: An Investigation of the Doctrine of Man According to the Later Writings of Paul Tillich (Systematic Theology II) and Karl Barth (Church Dogmatics III, 2)," McGill University, 1962. Ph.D. Dissertation.

13 Beyer, Carl Werth, "Being and the Question of God in the Philosophical Theology of Paul Tillich," American University, 1964. M.A. Thesis.

14 Bickley, Theodore Grant, "Person and Reality in the Thought of Paul Tillich and Edgar S. Brightman," Boston University, 1971. Ph.D. Dissertation.

15 Bird, Michael Shane, "Cinema and the Sacred: An Application of Paul Tillich's Theory of Art to the Film in the Aesthetic Apprehension of the Holy," University of Iowa, 1975. Ph.D. Dissertation.

16 Bond, Richard Ellison, Jr., "A Critical Analysis of the Concept of Justice in Paul Tillich, Heinrich Rommen, and Walter Rauschenbusch," Yale University, 1972. Ph.D. Dissertation.

17 Boozer, Jack S., "The Place of Reason in Paul Tillich's Concept of God," Boston University, 1952. Ph.D. Dissertation.

18 Bottoms, Robert Garvin, "The Practical Implications of Paul Tillich's Theology for a Doctrine of Church Renewal," Vanderbilt University Divinity School, 1972. D.Min. Dissertation.

19 Brigman, Johnnie Lee, "A Critique of the Existential Dimension of Revelation as Found in the Writings of Karl Barth and Paul Tillich," New Orleans Baptist Theological Seminary, 1962. Ph.D. Dissertation.

20 Bulman, Raymond Francis, "Theonomy and Humanism: An Examination of Paul Tillich's Interpretation of Secular Humanism," Columbia University, 1973. Ph.D. Dissertation.

21 Burden, Karl Niel, "Guilt, A Critical Examination of the Meaning of Guilt in the Writings of Erich Fromm, O. Hobart Mowrer, and Paul Tillich: A Critical Study of Three Theories of Guilt with a View to Assisting the Pastoral Counsellor in His Ministry of Healing," Victoria College, University of Toronto, 1971. Th.D. Dissertation.

22 Byer, Inez Vera Lord, "Tillich's Theory of God," University of Missouri, 1968. Ph.D. Dissertation.

46 / Paul Tillich

23 Cahoon, Guybert David, "Paul Tillich, Self-psychology, and
    Secular Education," Ohio State University, 1964. Ph.D. Dis-
    sertation.

24 Calvert, D. G. A., "An Examination of the Biblical and Dog-
    matic Character of Paul Tillich's Christology," Leeds Univer-
    sity, 1975. Ph.D. Dissertation.

25 Carey, John Jesse, "The Concept of History in the Thought of
    Paul Tillich," Duke University, 1965. Ph.D. Dissertation.

26 Catanzaro, James Lee, "The Problem of the Relation of Philos-
    ophy to Theology with Particular Attention to the Theologies of
    Karl Barth, Rudolf Bultmann, and Paul Tillich," School of The-
    ology at Claremont, 1964. Ph.D. Dissertation.

27 Cavanagh, Ronald Raymond, "Toward a Contemporary Construct
    of Providence: An Analysis of the Construct of Providence in
    the Systematic Theology of Paul Tillich and the Neoclassical
    Metaphysics of Charles Hartshorne," Graduate Theological Union,
    1968. Th.D. Dissertation.

28 Cawthon, Daniel Dee, "Towards a Theonomous Criticism of the
    Drama: Analogia Entis as the Basis of Paul Tillich's Meta-
    physics," Union Theological Seminary in the City of New York,
    1976. Ph.D. Dissertation.

29 Cho, Seogwhan, "The Theological Critique of the Marxist Idea
    of Man and the State in the Thought of Reinhold Niebuhr and
    Paul Tillich," Emory University, 1976. Ph.D. Dissertation.

30 Christian, Curtiss Wallace, "The Concept of Life After Death
    in the Theology of Jonathan Edwards, Friedrich Schleiermacher,
    and Paul Tillich," Vanderbilt University, 1965. Ph.D. Disser-
    tation.

31 Chuck, James, "Zen Buddhism and Paul Tillich: A Comparison
    of their Views of Man's Predicament and the Means of Its Res-
    olution," Pacific School of Religion, 1962. Th.D. Dissertation.

32 Chun, Paul Sang-Wan, "The Christian Concept of God and Zen
    'Nothingness' as Embodied in the Works of Tillich and Nishida,"
    Temple University, 1979. Ph.D. Dissertation.

33 Chun, Young Ho, "A Conceptual Analysis of Religion in Paul
    Tillich (1886-1965): With Particular Reference to His Positive
    Contribution towards a Theology of World Religions," Drew
    University, 1981. Ph.D. Dissertation.

34 Chung, Ha Eun, "Some Ethical Aspects of Existentialism in the
    Writings of Paul Tillich," Southeastern Baptist Theological
    Seminary, 1957. Th.M. Thesis.

35 Cieslak, William Marion, "Gabriel Marcel's Notion of 'Presence' and Paul Tillich's Concept of 'Religious Symbolism': Toward an Ecumenical Understanding of Eucharistic Memorial and the Manifold Presence of Christ," Graduate Theological Union, 1979. Ph. D. Dissertation.

36 Clark, Wayne Royce, "The Relation of Present Experience to Eschatological and Christological Uniqueness in Schleiermacher, Tillich, and Pannenberg," University of Iowa, 1973. Ph. D. Dissertation.

37 Connolly, John Richard, "The Compatibility of Faith and Doubt in Tillich's Theology and Its Significance for the Classical Catholic Notion of Faith," Marquette University, 1971. Ph. D. Dissertation.

38 Connolly, John R., Jr., "The Compatibility of Faith and Doubt in Tillich's Theology and its Significance for the Classical Catholic Notion of Faith," University of Manitoba, 1972. Ph. D. Dissertation.

39 Cooper, John Charles, "The Significance of the Pauline Spirit-Christology for the Doctrine of the Spiritual Presence in the Theology of Paul Tillich," University of Chicago, 1967. Ph. D. Dissertation.

40 Cowles, Ben Thomson, "The Ethical Implications of a Christian Estimate of Man with Special Reference to the Anthropologies of Carl Jung and Paul Tillich," University of Southern California, 1960. Ph. D. Dissertation.

41 Cox, Harvey Gallagher, "Religion and Technology: A Study of the Influence of Religion on Attitudes toward Technology, with Special Reference to the Writings of Paul Tillich and Gabriel Marcel," Harvard University, 1963. Ph. D. Dissertation.

42 Cox, Lafayette Hughes, "An Evaluation of Tillich's Intuitive-Ontological Approach to Philosophy of Religion in Contrast with Tennant's Empirical-Cosmological Approach," Yale University, 1963. Ph. D. Dissertation.

43 Craighead, Houston Archer, Jr., "Process and Being: The Concept of God in the Philosophies of Charles Hartshorne and Paul Tillich," University of Texas, 1970. Ph. D. Dissertation.

44 Crary, Stephen Trowbridge, "Idealistic Elements in Tillich's Thought," Yale University, 1955. Ph. D. Dissertation.

45 Crosby, Issac, "'Homo Religiosus': A Doctrine of Man in the Thought of Paul Tillich," Union Theological Seminary in Virginia, 1970. Th. D. Dissertation.

46 Crossman, Richard C., "Ethics and the International Order of

Political Development: A Study of Political Developmental Strategies in Latin America in the Light of Social Change Theory and the Theology of Paul Tillich," University of Chicago, 1976. Ph.D. Dissertation.

47 D'Arcy, Paul Wellington, "The Mode of God's Relation with the World in the Thought of Tillich, Altizer, and Cobb," School of Theology at Claremont, November 1975. Ph.D. Dissertation.

48 Davis, John Jefferson, "Paul Tillich and Religious Socialism: The Significance of the Early Socialist Writings for the Interpretation of His Later Thought," Duke University, 1975. Ph.D. Dissertation.

49 Deile, Carolyne Castleberry, "Paul Tillich's Philosophy of Communication," University of Illinois at Urbana-Champaign, 1971. Ph.D. Dissertation.

50 De Young, Quintin R., "A Study of Contemporary Christian Existential Theology (Kierkegaard and Tillich) and Modern Dynamic Psychology (Freud and Sullivan) Concerning Guilt Feelings," University of Southern California, 1959. Ph.D. Dissertation.

51 Doi, Masatoshi, "Paul Tillich's Eschatology and Its Social Implications," Hartford Seminary Foundation, 1955. Ph.D. Dissertation.

52 Dourley, John Patrick, "Paul Tillich and Bonaventure: An Evaluation of Paul Tillich's Claim to Stand in the Augustinian-Franciscan Tradition," Fordham University, 1971. Ph.D. Dissertation.

53 Duba, Arlo Dean, "The Principles of Theological Language in the Writings of Horace Bushnell and Paul Tillich and Their Implications for Christian Education Theory," Princeton Theological Seminary, 1960. Th.D. Dissertation.

54 Dwyer, John C., "Paul Tillich's Theology of the Cross," Tübingen University (Germany), 1973. Ph.D. Dissertation.

55 Dyal, Robert Allison, "The Function of Spiritual Presence in Paul Tillich's Theology of Culture," Boston University, 1968. Ph.D. Dissertation.

56 Dyke, Doris Jean, "The Significance of Paul Tillich's Protestant Principle for Public Education," Columbia University, 1967. Ed.D. Dissertation.

57 Earley, Glenn D., "Judaism in the Theology of Paul Tillich," Temple University, Ph.D. Dissertation in progress as of July 1981.

58 Edson, W. Doyle, "An Analysis of Identity from the Standpoint

of Erikson, Freud, Kroeber, and Tillich," School of Theology at Claremont, 1968. Ph.D. Dissertation.

59 Elmo, Francis Edward, "The Concept of Self-Actualization in the Theology of Paul Tillich and the Psychology of Abraham Maslow," Fordham University, 1974. Ph.D. Dissertation.

60 Fairweather, John Paul, "A Phenomenological Analysis of Love for Theological Ethics: Insights from Maurice Merleau-Ponty and Paul Tillich," Vanderbilt University, 1975. Ph.D. Dissertation.

61 Ferrell, Donald Ray, "The Relationship of Philosophy and Theology in the Thought of Paul Tillich," Graduate Theological Union, 1974. Ph.D. Dissertation.

62 Fisher, James Valentine, "Social and Intellectual Origins of Religious Socialism in Germany 1918-1923: A Study of Paul Tillich's Encounter with Socialism," Harvard University, 1978. Ph.D. Dissertation.

63 Foley, Grover, "Christ and Faith; Their Relationship in Contemporary Theology," University of Basel, 1971. Ph.D. Dissertation.

64 Ford, Lewis Stanley, "The Ontological Foundation of Paul Tillich's Theory of the Religious Symbol," Yale University, 1963. Ph.D. Dissertation.

65 Frein, Jeanne Marie Bordeau, "The Concepts of Courage, Anxiety, and Faith in the Writings of Paul Tillich and Their Implications for a Conceptual Model of Teacher and the Design of Teacher Preparation Programs," University of Massachusetts, 1974. Ph.D. Dissertation.

66 Fribley, Peter Craven, "The Pulpit Ministry to Alienation: A Dialectical Study of Alienation and the Preaching Ministries of Gerald Kennedy and George Arthur Buttrick, Using Sociological Criteria from Robert A. Nisbet and Theological Criteria from Paul Tillich and H. Richard Niebuhr, with Particular Emphasis upon 'Redemptive Alienation' as a Positive Heuristic for the Understanding of Sermonic Discourse," Princeton Theological Seminary, 1974. Ph.D. Dissertation.

67 Frick, Eugene George, "The Meaning of Religion in the Religionswissenschaft of Joachim Wach, the Theology of Paul Tillich, and the Theology of Karl Rahner: An Inquiry into the Possibility of a Christian Theology of the History of Religions," Marquette University, 1972. Ph.D. Dissertation.

68 Gardner, Romaine Luverne, "Theonomous Ethics: A Study in the Relationship between Ethics and Ontology in the Thought of Paul Tillich," Columbia University, 1966. Ph.D. Dissertation.

69 Garvin, Robert Merrill, "The Idea and the Ideal of Personality in the Thought of Paul Tillich and Erik Erikson," Columbia University, 1968. Ph.D. Dissertation.

70 Gibbs, Reagan Philip, "The Relevance of the Reformed Thought of Justification for a Contemporary Church as Illustrated in the Thinking of Paul Tillich," Vanderbilt University, 1972. Ph.D. Dissertation.

71 Gilkey, Roderick W., "The Development of Personality According to Erik Erikson and Paul Tillich," Harvard University, 1971. B.D. Senior Project.

72 Good, George Sterling, "The Christian Message in the Theology of Paul Tillich," University of Iowa, 1976. Ph.D. Dissertation.

73 Gordon, Donald M., "Myth and Symbol in Contemporary Existentialist Theology: An Examination of Myth and Symbol in the Writings of Rudolf Bultmann and Paul Tillich from the Point of View of Linguistic Analysis," Trinity College, University of Toronto, 1969. D.Min. Dissertation.

74 Graves, Barbara Lynne, "Understanding Rebirth and the Symbols Which Express It: A Study of Carl Jung and Paul Tillich," School of Theology at Claremont, 1976. D.Min. Dissertation.

75 Green, W. B., "The Concept of Culture in the Theology of Paul Tillich, with Incidental Reference to the Positions of Reinhold Niebuhr and Karl Barth," University of Edinburgh, 1956. Ph.D. Dissertation.

76 Gregory, Carlton Herbert, "The Problem of Descriptive Religious Statements with Special Reference to the Thought of Paul Tillich," Brown University, 1959. Ph.D. Dissertation.

77 Grosh, Gerald Russell, "The Notion of Anxiety in the Theology of Paul Tillich," Fordham University, 1973. Ph.D. Dissertation.

78 Groves, Richard Earl, "The Concept of Religion in the Writings of Dietrich Bonhoeffer and Paul Tillich," Baylor University, 1974. Ph.D. Dissertation.

79 Haas, Don, "Karl Barth and Paul Tillich on Revelation and the Spirit," School of Theology at Claremont, Ph.D. Dissertation in progress as of July 1980.

80 Hahnfeld, John Henry, "Paul Tillich and the Significance of Human Existence," Pennsylvania State University, 1971. Ph.D. Dissertation.

81 Hall, Richard Charles, "The Symbolic Relationship: Its Nature and Manifestation in the Works of Freud, Jung, Cassirer,

Urban, and Tillich," School of Theology at Claremont, 1970.
Ph.D. Dissertation.

82 Hammett, Jenny Lee Yates, "Existential Conceptions of Death:
Heidegger, Tillich, Rilke," Syracuse University, 1973. Ph.D.
Dissertation.

83 Hammond, Guyton Bowers, "The Idea of Self-Estrangement in
the Thought of Eric Fromm and Paul Tillich: A Comparative
Study with Emphasis on Implications for Theological Method,"
Vanderbilt University, 1962. Ph.D. Dissertation.

84 Hand, James Albert, "Teleological Aspects of Creation: A
Comparison of the Concepts of Being and Meaning in the Theologies of Jonathan Edwards and Paul Tillich," Vanderbilt University, 1969. Ph.D. Dissertation.

85 Harbuck, Donald Bradford, "A Critical Analysis of the Concept
of Religious Authority in the Writings of Paul Tillich," New
Orleans Baptist Theological Seminary, 1962. Ph.D. Dissertation.

86 Harris, Bond, "The Eschatological Destiny of the Individual in
the Thought of Paul Tillich," Drew University, 1970. Ph.D.
Dissertation.

87 Harrison, Jack Barham, "Paul Tillich and Psychotherapy,"
School of Theology at Claremont, 1967. Ph.D. Dissertation.

88 Hayward, John F., "The Theology and Philosophy of Mythical
Symbolism: A Study in the Function and Validity of Non-
Cognitive Symbols with Special Reference to the Writings of
Paul Tillich and Alfred North Whitehead," University of Chicago,
1949. Ph.D. Dissertation.

89 Hendrix, Harville, "The Fear of the Future: An Analysis of
the Essence of Anxiety in the Thought of Paul Tillich and Sig-
mund Freud," University of Chicago, 1971. Ph.D. Dissertation.

90 Henneman, Dennis Richard, "Chancel Drama and Ultimate Reality: An Application of Paul Tillich's Theory of Aesthetics to
the Functional Aspects of Chancel Drama Production," University of Nebraska at Lincoln, 1975. Ph.D. Dissertation.

91 Hill, Brennan R., "A Study of Tillich's Theology of Theonomy
as an Effective Synthesis of Pure Autonomy and Heteronomy,"
Marquette University, 1972. Ph.D. Dissertation.

92 Hiltner, Seward, "Psychotherapy and Christian Ethics: An
Evaluation of the Ethical Thought of A. E. Taylor and Paul
Tillich in the Light of Psychotherapeutic Contributions to Ethics
by J. C. Fluegel and Erich Fromm," University of Chicago,
1953. Ph.D. Dissertation.

93   Hirsh, Ruth, "Migration: A Problem for Theological Ethics. An Examination of the Significance for Theological Ethics of 'Migration' and of 'Exile' in their Relation to Cultural Contact, Criticism and Transformation, with Special Reference to the Rise of These and Similar Concepts by Certain Representative Theologians, Philosophers of History and Social Theorists," University of Chicago, 1956. M. A. Thesis.

94   Hoiteuga, Dewey James, Jr., "The Symbolic Theory of Religious Language," Harvard University, 1959. Ph. D. Dissertation.

95   Hopper, David Henry, "Presuppositions of the Method of Correlation: A Study of the Theological Method of Paul Tillich," Princeton Theological Seminary, 1959. Th. D. Dissertation.

96   Inbody, Tyron Lee, "Cultural Relativism and Theology: The Role of Philosophy in the Thought of Paul Tillich and Bernard Meland," University of Chicago, 1973. Ph. D. Dissertation.

97   Irwin, John E. G., "Psychoanalysis and Christian Thought: In Search of Man Through the 'Gestaltkreis,'" Drew University, 1975. Ph. D. Dissertation.

98   Jackson, George Andrew, Jr., "The Concept of Multidimensional Unity in Paul Tillich with Operational Implications for Interdisciplinary Methodology," School of Theology at Claremont, 1969. Ph. D. Dissertation.

99   Jackson, Harold Alan, "The Significance of Paul Tillich's Theology for a Philosophy of Religious Education," Stanford University, 1956. Ed. D. Dissertation.

100   Jackson, Jonathan, "The Relation of Religion and Higher Education in Paul Tillich and Theodore Brameld," Boston University, 1964. Th. D. Dissertation.

101   James, Robison Brown, "The Symbolic Knowledge of God in the Theology of Paul Tillich," Duke University, 1965. Ph. D. Dissertation.

102   Janes, Frances L., "A Theory of Learning and the Nature of Man: A Critical Evaluation of Nathanael Cantor in Light of Paul Tillich," University of Chicago, 1963. Ph. D. Dissertation.

103   Jelly, Frederick Michael, "The Notion of Theonomy in Paul Tillich's Systematic Theology: A Thomistic Evaluation for a Theology of Secularity," Dominican House of Studies, 1980. S. T. D. Dissertation.

104   Johnson, Barclay D., "How Americans Respond to Paul Tillich: A Case Study," Harvard University, 1960. B. A. Thesis.

105 Johnson, Ben Campbell, "A Comparison of the Cosmological Approach to a Theology of Evangelism in H. Orton Wiley and the Ontological Approach to a Theology of Evangelism in Paul Tillich," Emory University, 1980. Ph. D. Dissertation.

106 Johnson, Wayne Gustave, "Martin Luther's Law-Gospel Distinction and Paul Tillich's Method of Correlation: A Study of Parallels," University of Iowa, 1966. Ph. D. Dissertation.

107 Joshua, S. B., "A Critical Study of Some of the Basic Concepts in Paul Tillich's Theological System, with Comparitive Observations from Sankara's Advaita Vedanta," Birmingham University, 1975. Ph. D. Dissertation.

108 Kalita, Dwight Kenton, "They Call It Christianity; I Call It Consciousness: A Theological Correlation of Paul Tillich and R. W. Emerson," Bowling Green State University, 1972. Ph. D. Dissertation.

109 Kaufman, Gordon D., "The Problem of Relativism and the Possibility of Metaphysics: A Constructive Development of Certain Ideas in R. G. Collingwood, Wilhelm Dilthey, and Paul Tillich," Yale University, 1955. Ph. D. Dissertation.

110 Kelsey, David Hugh, "Tillich's Doctrine of Analogia Imaginis and the Authority of Scripture in Theological Argument," Yale University, 1963. Ph. D. Dissertation.

111 Kercher, R. Paul, "Tillich's Christology and the Classical Categories," Southeastern Baptist Theological Seminary, 1962. Th. M. Thesis.

112 Kim, Jong-Won, "Daisetz T. Suzuki and Paul J. Tillich: A Comparative Study of Their Thoughts on Ethics in Relation to Being," Graduate Theological Union, 1973. Th. D. Dissertation.

113 Kimball, Robert Charles, "Implications of the Thought of Freud and Tillich for Relating Psychotherapy and Theology, with Special Attention to the Methodology and Anthropology of Freud and Tillich," Harvard University, 1960. Ph. D. Dissertation.

114 Kincade, J., "A Critical Examination of the Views of Karl Barth and Paul Tillich on Philosophy and Ethics," University of Edinburgh, 1961. Ph. D. Dissertation.

115 King, Martin Luther, Jr., "A Comparison of the Conceptions of God in the Thinking of Paul Tillich and Henry Nelson Wieman," Boston University, 1955. Ph. D. Dissertation.

116 Kite, R., "Faith and History in the Theology of Paul Tillich," Birmingham University, 1972. M. A. Thesis.

117   Knudson, Robert Donald, "Symbol and Myth in Contemporary Theology, with Special Reference to the Thought of Paul Tillich, Reinhold Niebuhr, and Nicholas Berdyaev," Union Theological Seminary, 1952. Th. M. Thesis.

118   Kohak, Erazim Vaclav, "Evil and the Christian Symbol of Salvation," Yale University, 1958. Ph. D. Dissertation.

119   Kucheman, Clark Arthur, "Justice and the Economic Order: A Critical and Constructive Study of the Economic Thought of Paul J. Tillich," University of Chicago, 1966. Ph. D. Dissertation.

120   Lamb, Richard C., "The Prophetic Spirit in the Life and Writings of Paul Tillich," Eden Theological Seminary, 1974. Ph. D. Dissertation.

121   Lamore, George Edward, "Theories of Natural Evil in the Thought of Henry Nelson Wieman, Edwin Lewis, and Paul Tillich," Boston University, 1959. Th. D. Dissertation.

122   Lane, Dermot A., "The Saving Christ in Paul Tillich's Theology," University of Roma, 1970. Ph. D. Dissertation.

123   Langford, Thomas Anderson, "A Critical Analysis of Paul Tillich's Method of Correlation," Duke University, 1958. Ph. D. Dissertation.

124   Law, David Albert Clarke, "The Naturalistic Approach to Religion in the Philosophy of Erich Fromm, John Dewey, and Paul Tillich," University of Western Ontario, 1966. M. A. Thesis.

125   Lawson, Ernest T., "Tillich and Hartshorne: An Essay on the Sovereignty of God," University of Chicago, 1963. Ph. D. Dissertation.

126   Leidig, Daniel Gsell, "Existentialist Protestantism and Literary Criticism: A Study of the Relation of Tillichian Theology to the Work of Amos N. Wilder and Nathan A. Scott, Jr.," Florida State University, 1959. Ph. D. Dissertation.

127   Lewis, Granville Douglass, "Psychotherapeutic Concepts and Theological Categories: Some Problems in the Thought of Carl Rogers and Paul Tillich," Duke University, 1966. Ph. D. Dissertation.

128   Little, John Frederick, "The Role of Reason in the Apologetic Enterprises of Emil Brunner and Paul Tillich in Relation to the Myths of Genesis One to Three," Princeton University, 1961. Ph. D. Dissertation.

129   Liu, Shu Hsien, "A Critical Study of Paul Tillich's Methodo-

logical Presuppositions," Southern Illinois University, 1966.
Ph. D. Dissertation.

130 Lo, Samuel E., "Paul Tillich's Concept of Theonomy and Its
Implications for Pedagogical Principles of Christian Education," New York University, 1968. Ph. D. Dissertation.

131 Long, Wil, "A Secular Eucharist: Paul Tillich's View of the
Eucharist as a Focus for Secularization in Theology," Graduate Theological Union, 1969. Th. D. Dissertation.

132 Losee, John Price, Jr., "A Comparison of Methodological
Principles Basic to the Quantum Mechanics of Bohr and
Heisenberg, the Metaphysics of Emmet, and the Theology of
Tillich," Drew University, 1961. Ph. D. Dissertation.

133 Lounibos, John B., "The Idea of Power and Freedom in the
Theology of Paul Tillich," Fordham University, 1976. Ph. D.
Dissertation.

134 Loutzenhiser, Donald Ruel, "Faith and Ultimate Concern: St.
Paul and Paul Tillich," University of Southern California,
1960. Ph. D. Dissertation.

135 Luck, Donald George, "The Manifest and Latent Spiritual Community: The Essence of the Church in the Theology of Paul
Tillich," Union Theological Seminary, 1979. Ph. D. Dissertation.

136 Luebke, Neil Robert, "Paul Tillich's Philosophy and Theology
of History," The Johns Hopkins University, 1968. Ph. D. Dissertation.

137 Macleod, Alister Murray, "Paul Tillich's Conceptions of Ontology," Queen's University, 1966. Ph. D. Dissertation.

138 Maddock, James, "Developmental Psychology and Moral Anthropology: Some Implications in the Work of Paul Tillich
and Erik Erikson," University of Chicago, 1971. Ph. D. Dissertation.

139 Madsen, Truman Grant, "A Philosophical Examination of Tillich's Theory of Symbolic Meaning," Harvard University, 1960.
Ph. D. Dissertation.

140 Mahan, Wayne Wilbur, "Dislocations in the System and Method
of Paul Tillich's Systematic Theology," University of Texas at
Austin, 1967. Ph. D. Dissertation.

141 Mallow, Vernon Richard, "The Problem of the Demonic in the
Theology of Selected Contemporary Theologians (Karl Barth,
Edwin Lewis, and Paul Tillich)," The Southern Baptist Theo-
logical Seminary, 1966. Th. D. Dissertation.

142   Marieb, Joyce Marie, "The Myth of the Transcendent Fall: The Moral and the Tragic in Paul Tillich's Doctrine of Responsibility," Boston University, 1973. Ph.D. Dissertation.

143   Martin, Bernard, "The Philosophical Anthropology of Paul Tillich," University of Illinois at Urbana-Champaign, 1961. Ph.D. Dissertation.

144   Mattson, Alvin D., Jr., "Teilhard and Tillich: An Attempt to Demonstrate Their Use of a Common Method," The Hartford Seminary Foundation, 1971. Ph.D. Dissertation.

145   McCann, Michael W., "Occasional and Systematic: Two Styles of Theology," Harvard Divinity School, 1971. B.D. Senior Project.

146   McKelway, Alexander J., Jr., "The Systematic Theology of Paul Tillich: A Review and Analysis," University of Basel, 1963. Ph.D. Dissertation.

147   McLachlin, Alan M., "Tillich's Christology and the Problem of Docetism," Victoria University, 1967. Th.D. Dissertation.

148   McLean, George F., "Man's Knowledge of God According to Paul Tillich: A Thomistic Critique," The Catholic University of America, 1958. Ph.D. Dissertation.

149   Midgley, Louis Casper, "Politics and Ultimate Concern: The Normative Political Philosophy of Paul Tillich (Volumes 1 and 2)," Brown University, 1965. Ph.D. Dissertation.

150   Minter, David Curtis, "Christology in the Thought of Nels F. S. Ferre, W. Norman Pittenger, Paul Tillich," Boston University, 1968. Ph.D. Dissertation.

151   Minton, Frank D., "Providence and Evil: A Study Based on the Thought of Friedrich Schleiermacher and Paul Tillich," University of Chicago, 1969. Ph.D. Dissertation.

152   Mondin, John B., "Analogy Old and New: An Analysis and Criticism of Aquinas' Analogy of Intrinsic Attribution, Tillich's Symbolism, Barth's Analogy of Faith, and an Attempted Resolution of Some Historical, Philosophical, and Theological Problems Intrinsic to the Doctrine of Analogy," Harvard University, 1959. Ph.D. Dissertation.

153   Morrison, Roy Dennis, II, "Ontology and Naturalism in the Philosophies of John Herman Randall, Jr. and Paul Tillich," University of Chicago, 1972. Ph.D. Dissertation.

154   Mow, Joseph Baxter, "Redemption and the Demonic in Historical Process: A Study of the Theological Ethics of C. H. Dodd, Paul Tillich, and Henry N. Wieman," University of Chicago, 1964. Ph.D. Dissertation.

155 Mueller, Philip John, "The Centrality and Significance of the Concept of Ecstasy in the Theology of Paul Tillich," Fordham University, 1972. Ph.D. Dissertation.

156 Murakami, Paul Masayoshi, "From Historicism to Kairos: A Study of Paul Tillich's Method of Metalogic and Its Significance for His Interpretation of History," Hartford Seminary Foundation, 1972. Ph.D. Dissertation.

157 Muringathery, John P., "Theonomous Unity of Life: Paul Tillich's Doctrine of Spiritual Presence in the Context of His Apologetic Theology," Katholieke Universiteit te Leuven, 1975. Ph.D. Dissertation.

158 Murphey, Paul Warren, "The Concept of Death in the Theology of Nicholas Berdyaev, Paul Tillich, and Helmut Thielicke," Vanderbilt University, 1964. Ph.D. Dissertation.

159 Musil, Robert William, "Tillich's Theology of Education as a Correlate to His Protestant Principle," Boston University, 1969. Ph.D. Dissertation.

160 Myers, Dewitt Luther, Jr., "A Preliminary Study of Paul Tillich's Understanding of Faith," Southeastern Baptist Theological Seminary, 1959. Th.M. Thesis.

161 Nacpil, Emerito P., "Paul Tillich's Doctrine of the Fall: A Theological Interpretation of the Problem of Existence," Drew University, 1962. Ph.D. Dissertation.

162 Newman, P. W., "The Ontological in the Theology of Paul Tillich," St. Andrews University, 1964. Ph.D. Dissertation.

163 Nichols, Rodney Ralph, "Being and Symbol in Paul Tillich," University of Missouri at Columbia, 1974. Ph.D. Dissertation.

164 Niedenthal, Morris Jerome, "Preaching the Presence of God Based on a Critical Study of the Sermons of Paul Tillich, Karl Barth, and Herbert H. Farmer," Union Theological Seminary in the City of New York, 1969. Th.D. Dissertation.

165 Nikkel, David Henry, "Pantheism in Hartshorne and Tillich: A Creative Synthesis," Duke University, 1981. Ph.D. Dissertation.

166 Olmon, Luther E., "An Analysis and Evaluation of Some Aspects of Tension in the Theology of Paul Tillich," University of Southern California, 1952. Ph.D. Dissertation.

167 Palmer, M. F., "The Problems [sic] of the Historical Jesus in the Theology of Paul Tillich," Durham University, 1973. Ph.D. Dissertation.

168   Palmer, Michael Frank, "The Relevance of Biblical Criticism
       to the Christology of Paul Tillich's Systematic Theology, Vol-
       ume Two, " McMaster University, 1970.   M. A. Thesis.

169   Park, Ha Kyoo, "The Case Against the Ontological Understand-
       ing of Religion in Paul Tillich, " Victoria College, University
       of Toronto, 1969.   Th. M. Thesis.

170   Parrella, Frederick Joseph, "The Role of the Church in the
       Theology of Paul Tillich, " Fordham University, 1974.   Ph. D.
       Dissertation.

171   Patricca, Nicholas A. , "God and the Questioning of Being:
       An Analytical Comparison of the Thinking of Martin Heidegger
       and Paul Tillich, " University of Chicago, 1972.   Ph. D. Dis-
       sertation.

172   Patton, John Hull, "A Theory of Interpersonal Ministry Based
       on the Systematic Theology of Paul Tillich and the Psychologi-
       cal Theory of Harry Stack Sullivan, " University of Chicago,
       1968.   Ph. D. Dissertation.

173   Paul, William Wright, "Paul Tillich's Interpretation of His-
       tory, " Columbia University, 1959.   Ph. D. Dissertation.

174   Peck, Jack Percy, "The Holy Spirit in the Theology of Paul
       Tillich, " McMaster University, 1967.   M. A. Thesis.

175   Perkins, Ronald Wayne, "The Christologies of Friedrich
       Schleiermacher and Paul Tillich, " Boston University, 1968.
       Ph. D. Dissertation.

176   Perry, John M. , "Tillich's Response to Freud's Understanding
       of God and Religion, " Marquette University, 1972.   Ph. D.
       Dissertation.

177   Peters, Eugene Herbert, "Form, Unity, and the Individual:
       A Study of the Concretely Real, " University of Chicago, 1960.
       Ph. D. Dissertation.

178   Piediscalzi, Nicholas, "Paul Tillich and Erik H. Erikson on
       the Origin and Nature of Morality and Ethics, " Boston Univer-
       sity, 1965.   Ph. D. Dissertation.

179   Pitcher, William A. , "Theological Ethics in Paul Tillich and
       Emil Brunner: A Study in the Nature of Protestant Theologi-
       cal Ethics, " University of Chicago, 1955.   Ph. D. Dissertation.

180   Plaskow, Judith E. , "Sex, Sin, and Grace: Women's Experi-
       ence and the Theologies of Reinhold Niebuhr and Paul Tillich, "
       Yale University, 1976.   Ph. D. Dissertation.

181   Porteous, Alvin C. , "The Problem of Religious Immediacy in

Contemporary Theology," Columbia University, 1957. Ph.D. Dissertation.

182 Porter, Bruce Calvin, "An Analysis of the Concepts of the Religious and the Secular in the Thought of Paul Tillich," McMaster University, 1971. M.A. Thesis.

183 Proudfoot, Wayne Lee, "Types of Finite-Infinite Relation and Conceptions of the Unity of Self," Harvard University, 1972. Ph.D. Dissertation.

184 Pratt, Gerald Blount, "Selected Concepts from the Philosophy of Paul Tillich and Their Implications for Education in American Society with Major Emphasis on the Interaction of Teachers and Pupils," North Texas State University, 1967. Ed.D. Dissertation.

185 Randall, Robert L., "A Phenomenology of Self-Transcendence Based on the Works of Paul Tillich and Maurice Merleau-Ponty," University of Chicago, 1973. Ph.D. Dissertation.

186 Reeves, Gene Arthur, "Our Knowledge of God and the Nature of God in the Philosophies of Gabriel Marcel and Paul Tillich," Emory University, 1963. Ph.D. Dissertation.

187 Reeves, M. Frances, "God and History in the Thought of Paul Tillich," Boston University, 1967. Ph.D. Dissertation.

188 Reimer, Bennett, "The Common Dimensions of Aesthetic and Religious Experience," University of Illinois at Urbana-Champaign, 1963. Ed.D. Thesis.

189 Reinberger, Francis E., "A Study of the Thought of Paul Tillich and Medard Boss: Some Major Implications for Pastoral Theology," Union Theological Seminary in the City of New York, 1966. Th.D. Dissertation.

190 Reisz, Frederick, Jr., "Paul Tillich's Doctrine of God as Spirit: A Dynamic View," University of Chicago, 1978. Ph.D. Dissertation.

191 Remick, Oscar Eugene, "Value in the Thought of Paul Tillich," Boston University, 1966. Ph.D. Dissertation.

192 Rich, Maynard Leslie, "Paul Tillich's Utilization of Depth Psychology in the Existential Analysis of the Human Situation," Drew University, 1969. Ph.D. Dissertation.

193 Richards, Glyn, "A Study of the Significance of the History of Religions for the Theology of Paul Tillich," McMaster University, 1970. M.A. Thesis.

194 Riethmiller, Lee K., "The Experience of Nothingness in

Autobiography and Theology: Between 'The Ground' and 'The Underground' of Paul Tillich and Jacob Boehme," Harvard Divinity School, 1971. B.D. Senior Project.

195 Ring, Nancy C., "Doctrine Within the Dialectic of Subject and Object: A Critical Study of the Positions of Paul Tillich and Bernard Lonergan," Marquette University, 1980. Ph.D. Dissertation.

196 Rode, W. A. W., "The Speculative Theology of the 19th Century," Columbia University, 1958. Ph.D. Dissertation.

197 Ross, James Robert, "Towards a Theology of Ephapax: A Comparison of the Claims Made for the Christ Event by Paul Tillich and Gerhard Ebeling," Emory University, 1969. Ph.D. Dissertation.

198 Ross, Robert Reed Newberry, "Tillich on the Existence of God," Harvard University, 1973. Ph.D. Dissertation.

199 Rowe, William Leonard, "An Examination of the Philosophical Theology of Paul Tillich," University of Michigan, 1962. Ph.D. Dissertation.

200 Runyon, Theodore, "The Immediate Awareness of the Unconditioned and the Interpretation of History in the Theology of Paul Tillich," University of Göttingen, 1958. Th.D. Dissertation.

201 Ryan, John D., "The Awareness of God in the Thought of Paul Tillich," Drew University, 1973. Ph.D. Dissertation.

202 Sabin, Raymond Avery, "Tillich's Concept of God," Meadville Theological School, 1944. B.D. Thesis.

203 Satterwhite, John Henry, "The Bearing of Berdyaev's and Tillich's Philosophies of History Upon Theism," Oberlin College, 1938. S.T.M. Thesis.

204 Schlachtenhaufen, Harold D., "Comparison of the Theological Anthropology of Karl Rahner and Paul Tillich," Aquinas Institute of Theology, 1974. Ph.D. Dissertation.

205 Schmidt, Barbara Kugel, "A Dialogical Discussion of Paul Tillich's Theology as Relevant to the Public School Classroom," Wayne State University, 1969. Ph.D. Dissertation.

206 Schrader, Robert William, "The Nature of Theological Argument: A Study of Paul Tillich," Harvard University, 1972. Ph.D. Dissertation. (Published by Scholars Press for Harvard Theological Review, 1975.)

207 Schulz, Otmar, "The Concept of Being in Paul Tillich's Doctrine of God," Baptist Theological Seminary, 1964. B.D. Thesis.

208 Shackelford, James Hubert, "An Analysis of the Utilization of Psychotherapy as a Model in Contemporary Theology Through the Study of Its Use in Thomas C. Oden, Daniel Day Williams, Gregory Baum, and Paul Tillich," University of Chicago, 1974. Ph. D. Dissertation.

209 Shinn, Yu Khill, "Political Religion of the Masses in Korea: A Tillichian Interpretation," Graduate Theological Union, 1981. Ph. D. Dissertation.

210 Shishido, Miles Motoyuki, "Individual and Community in the Systems of Marx and Tillich," University of Chicago, 1968. Ph. D. Dissertation.

211 Smith, Adam Herbert, "The Problem of Theodicy in the Thought of Paul Tillich," School of Theology at Claremont, 1973. Ph. D. Dissertation.

212 Smith, Samuel David, II, "A Study of the Relation Between the Doctrine of Creation and the Doctrine of Revelation through the Created Universe in the Thought of John Calvin, Friedrich Schleiermacher and Paul Tillich," Vanderbilt University, 1965. Ph. D. Dissertation.

213 Snowden, Glen Wenger, "The Relationship of Christianity to Non-Christian Religions in the Theologies of Daniel T. Niles and Paul Tillich," Boston University, 1969. Th. D. Dissertation.

214 Sommer, Guenter Friedrich, "The Significance of the Late Philosophy of Schelling for the Formation and Interpretation of the Thought of Paul Tillich," Duke University, 1960. Ph. D. Dissertation.

215 Song, Choan-Seng, "The Relation of Divine Revelation and Man's Religion in the Theologies of Karl Barth and Paul Tillich," Union Theological Seminary in the City of New York, 1965. Th. D. Dissertation.

216 Spicer, James Edward, "A Critical and Analytical Study of the Concept of the Self as Seen from the Psychological Perspective of Gardner Murphy and Harry Stack Sullivan and from the Theological Perspective of Reinhold Niebuhr and Paul Tillich," University of Chicago, 1966. Ph. D. Dissertation.

217 Sprague, Ruth, "A Study of Early Adolescence from the Perspectives of Paul Tillich's Theology and the Young Person's View of Himself," Columbia University, 1957. Ph. D. Dissertation.

218 Stenger, Mary Ann, "Norms and the Problem of Relativism in Tillich's Theory of Theological Knowledge," University of Iowa, 1977. Ph. D. Dissertation.

219 Stevens, Pearl Ray, "The Idea of God in the Philosophy of
     Paul Tillich," University of Nebraska at Lincoln, 1961.
     Ph. D. Dissertation.

220 Stone, Jerome Arthur, "Secular Experiences of Transcendence:
     The Contributions of Bernard E. Meland, H. Richard Niebuhr,
     and Paul Tillich Towards an Understanding of these Experi-
     ences," University of Chicago, 1973. Ph. D. Dissertation.

221 Streiker, Lowell Dean, "The Mystical A Priori: Paul Tillich's
     Critical Phenomenology of Religion," Princeton University,
     1968. Ph. D. Dissertation.

222 Struzynski, Anthony, "History as Symbol in the Thought of
     Paul Tillich," University of Notre Dame, 1972. Ph. D. Dis-
     sertation.

223 Stumme, John R., "Socialism in Theological Perspective: A
     Study of Paul Tillich, 1918-1933," Union Theological Seminary
     in the City of New York, 1976. Ph. D. Dissertation.

224 Sturdivant, Robert Victor, "Paul Tillich's Protestant Principle
     and Catholic Substance in Recent Catholic Thought," Emory
     University, 1972. Ph. D. Dissertation.

225 Sutphin, John Everett, Sr., "The Sources and Apprehension of
     Values in American Higher Education: A Critique of the Value
     Theories of Ralph Barton Perry, Pitirim A. Sorokin, and Paul
     Tillich," School of Theology at Claremont, 1963. Th. D. Dis-
     sertation.

226 Sutphin, Stanley Terrance, "A Critique of the Premises of
     Rogerian Psychotherapy in the Light of Paul Tillich's Doctrine
     of Man," Pacific School of Theology, 1965. Th. D. Disserta-
     tion.

227 Takei, Franklin Shunji, "Existence and the New Being: A
     Study of Paul Tillich's Theological System," The Pennsylvania
     State University, 1966. Ph. D. Dissertation.

228 Tarbox, Everett Jacob, Jr., "The Referent of God Language
     in the Thought of Paul Tillich," University of Chicago, 1969.
     Ph. D. Dissertation.

229 Taylor, Larry Michael, "The Role of General Revelation in
     American Neo-Orthodoxy: Reinhold Niebuhr, Paul Tillich, and
     H. Richard Niebuhr," Southwestern Baptist Theological Semi-
     nary, 1972. Ph. D. Dissertation.

230 Templeman, Andrew D., "The Conditions of Intelligible Ana-
     logical God-Language in the Theologies of Paul Tillich, Eric
     Mascall, and Karl Barth," University of Chicago, 1972.
     Ph. D. Dissertation.

231 Terry, Ronald Franklin, "The Problem of Evil in the Theolo-
     gies of Paul Tillich and Henry Nelson Wieman," Iliff School
     of Theology, 1962. Ph. D. Dissertation.

232 Thatcher, A. P. A., "The Ontology of Paul Tillich," Oxford
     University, 1973. D. Phil. Dissertation.

233 Thomas, J. Mark, "Towards a Theonomous Technology: An
     Inquiry into the Social Ethics of Technology in Parsons, Mar-
     cuse, and Heidegger Based on Paul Tillich's Theology of Cul-
     ture," University of Chicago, Ph. D. Dissertation in progress
     as of July 1981.

234 Thompson, M. R., "A Critical Analysis of Tillich's Idea of
     the Religious Symbol," London University, 1973. M. Phil.
     Thesis.

235 Thompson, Raymond Duane, "Maritain and Tillich: Art and
     Religion," Boston University, 1962. Ph. D. Dissertation.

236 Towne, Edgar A., "Ontological and Theological Dimensions of
     God in the Thought of Paul Tillich and Charles Hartshorne,"
     University of Chicago, 1968. Ph. D. Dissertation.

237 Tritenbach, David L., "Reason and Revelation: A Discussion
     on Their Relationship in Christian Thinking in the Light of the
     Writings of Tillich and of Brunner," San Francisco Theologi-
     cal Seminary, 1964. Ph. D. Dissertation.

238 Truesdale, Albert L., "A Tillichian Analysis of White Racism
     in the South," Emory University, 1976. Ph. D. Dissertation.

239 Tsambassis, Alexander Nicholas, "Evil and the Abysmal Na-
     ture of God in the Thought of Brightman, Berdyaev, and Til-
     lich," Northwestern University, 1957. Ph. D. Dissertation.

240 Unhjem, Arne, "Justification in the Development of Tillich's
     Philosophy," Boston University, 1964. Ph. D. Dissertation.

241 Van Hook, Jay Martin, "Paul Tillich's Conception of the Re-
     lation Between Philosophy and Theology," Columbia University,
     1966. Ph. D. Dissertation.

242 Vaught, Carl Gray, "Contemporary Conceptions of the Nature
     and Existence of God: A Study of Tillich and Hartshorne,"
     Yale University, 1966. Ph. D. Dissertation.

243 Visick, Vernon M., "Between Theory and Practice: Paul
     Tillich and the University," University of Chicago, Ph. D.
     Dissertation in progress as of July 1981.

244 Vunderink, Ralph William, "The Nature of Being in the
     Thought of Paul Tillich and Martin Heidegger," University of
     Chicago, 1969. Ph. D. Dissertation.

245 Wade, Ben Frank, "God as Transpersonal and Personal in the Thought of Paul Tillich and L. Harold DeWolf," The Hartford Seminary Foundation, 1966. Ph.D. Dissertation.

246 Walker, William Glassford, "Paul Tillich's Doctrine of the New Man and Its Relation to Rollo May's Concept of Selfhood with Specific Emphasis on the Demonic, Anxiety, Courage, and Grace," University of St. Michael's College (Toronto School of Theology), 1982. Ph.D. Dissertation.

247 Wardlaw, H. R., "The Problem of the Theological Method: A Study of Kierkegaard and Tillich," University of Glasgow, 1963. Ph.D. Dissertation.

248 Wiesbaker, Dimis Taylor, "The Place of Aesthetics in the Theology of Paul Tillich," Emory University, 1971. Ph.D. Dissertation.

249 Weisbaker, Donald Robert, "The Concept of Salvation in the Theology of Paul Tillich," University of Chicago, 1966. Ph.D. Dissertation.

250 Welch, Gerald Douglas, "A Model for Parish Ministry Based on Virginia Satir's Family Therapy and Paul Tillich's Doctrine of Salvation," School of Theology at Claremont, 1976. D.Min. Dissertation.

251 Weston, Hugh W., "A Comparative Study of Four Modern Philosophies of History: Christopher Dawson, Benedetto Croce, Ortega y Gasset, and Paul Tillich," Meadville Theological School, Chicago, 1942. B.D. Thesis.

252 Wettstein, Adelbert Arnold, "The Concept of Participation in Paul Tillich's Thought: With Studies in Its Historical Background and Present Significance," McGill University, 1968. Ph.D. Dissertation.

253 White, Frank Tobbit, "Systematic Theological Principles of Friedrich Schleiermacher and Paul Tillich," Columbia University, 1966. Ph.D. Dissertation.

254 White, James Harold, "Personal and Transpersonal Aspects of Tillich's Concept of God," School of Theology at Claremont, 1978. Ph.D. Dissertation.

255 Whitehurst, J. E., "The Christian Interpretation of History in Paul Tillich and Christopher Dawson," University of Edinburgh, 1954. Ph.D. Dissertation.

256 Whitehurst, James Emerson, "The Significance of Christ for the Meaning of History in the Philosophies of Paul Tillich and Nicholas Berdyaev," Northwestern University, 1950. M.A. Thesis.

257   Whitney, Ruth, "An Understanding of Person in the Tillichian Dialectic and Its Implications for Women in American Society: An Interdisciplinary Study," The Catholic University of America, 1973. Ph.D. Dissertation.

258   Whittemore, Paul Baxter, "The 'Fundamental Theology' of Paul Tillich: Revelation and Anthropology in His Writings," Vanderbilt University, 1978. Ph.D. Dissertation.

259   Wiebe, Paul G., "The Theological Hermeneutics of Paul Tillich," University of Chicago, 1975. Ph.D. Dissertation.

260   Wiley, George Bell, "Paul Tillich: A Comparison of Certain Personal and Theological Themes and Their Relation to His Christology," Emory University, 1978. Ph.D. Dissertation.

261   Williams, George Huntston, "Sin in the Theology of Paul Tillich," Meadville Theological Seminary, 1939. B.D. Thesis.

262   Williams, John Rodman, Jr., "The Doctrine of the Imago Dei in Contemporary Theology: A Study in Karl Barth, Emil Brunner, Reinhold Niebuhr, and Paul Tillich," Columbia University, 1954. Ph.D. Dissertation.

263   Wirt, Shirley Jean, "Evolution and Ethics: An Interdisciplinary Approach Through the Works of Theodosius Dobzhansky, John Dewey, and Paul Tillich," Columbia University, 1978. Ed.D. Dissertation.

264   Wolf, Herbert Christian, "The Inadequacy of Personalistic Language Regarding God: A Study Based on the Theologies of Barth, Tillich, and Farmer," Harvard University, 1968. Ph.D. Dissertation.

265   Wood, Eugene Eager, Jr., "The Psychology of Personality in the Thought of Paul Tillich," Boston University, 1955. Ph.D. Dissertation.

266   Woodbury, William Clair, "The Theme of Unity in the Theology of Paul Tillich Evaluated on the Boundary Between His Theology and the Science of Percey Bridgeman," Drew University, 1971. Ph.D. Dissertation.

267   Zabala, Albert J., "Myth and Symbol: An Analysis of Myth and Symbol in Paul Tillich," Institut Catholique de Paris (Jesuit School, The University of San Francisco), 1959. Ph.D. Dissertation.

268   Zietlow, Harold H., "The Living God: The Existential Systems of F. W. J. Schelling and Paul Tillich," University of Chicago, 1962. Ph.D. Dissertation.

3. REVIEWS OF WRITINGS BY OR ABOUT PAUL TILLICH IN ENGLISH

1   Adams, James Luther, Review of Paul Tillich: His Life and Thought, Vol. I, by Wilhelm Pauck and Marion Pauck, Union Seminary Quarterly Review, vol. 32 (Fall, 1976), pp. 36-46.

2   Aldwinckle, R., Review of Ultimate Concern: Tillich in Dialogue, ed. by D. MacKenzie Brown, Interpretation, vol. 20 (July, 1966), pp. 351-352.

3   Allan, D., Review of The Future of Religions, by Paul Tillich, Interpretation, vol. 22 (January, 1968), p. 112.

4   Allison, C., Review of A History of Christian Thought, by Paul Tillich, Interpretation, vol. 26 (January, 1972), pp. 108-110.

5   Amelung, E., Review of My Travel Diary: 1936; Between Two Worlds, by Paul Tillich, Lutheran World, vol. 18, no. 4 (1971), pp. 388-389.

6   Anderson, B., Review of Ultimate Concern: Tillich in Dialogue, ed. by D. MacKenzie Brown, Scottish Journal of Theology, vol. 20 (March, 1967), pp. 104-106.

7   Anonymous, Review of A History of Christian Thought, by Paul Tillich, Bulletin from Virginia Kirkus Bookshop Service, vol. 36 (June 1, 1968), p. 591.   Also in New Yorker, vol. 44, November 9, 1968, p. 239; Library Journal, vol. 93, July 1968, p. 2661; and Publishers Weekly, vol. 194, July 1, 1968, p. 49.

8   Anonymous, Review of Biblical Religion and the Search for Ultimate Reality, by Paul Tillich, Booklist, vol. 52 (November 1, 1955), p. 91.

9   Anonymous, Review of The Christian Answer, ed. by H. P. Van Deusen, America, vol. 74 (October 13, 1945), p. 49.

10 Anonymous, Review of The Construction of the History of Religion in Schelling's Positive Philosophy: Its Presuppositions and

Principles, by Paul Tillich, Library Journal, vol. 100 (May 1, 1975), p. 863. Also in Choice, vol. 12, June 1975, p. 520.

11 Anonymous, Review of The Courage To Be, by Paul Tillich, United States Quarterly Book Review, vol. 9 (June, 1953), p. 174.

12 Anonymous, Review of Dynamics of Faith, by Paul Tillich, Bulletin from Virginia Kirkus Bookshop Service, vol. 25 (February 1, 1957), p. 118. Also in Booklist, vol. 53, March 1, 1957, p. 346.

13 Anonymous, Review of The Eternal Now, by Paul Tillich, Times Literary Supplement (London), February 13, 1964, p. 13.

14 Anonymous, Review of From Time to Time, by Hannah Tillich, Bestsellers, vol. 33 (November 15, 1973), p. 370. Also in Choice, vol. 11, May 1974, p. 460; Kirkus Reviews, vol. 41, August 1, 1973, p. 873; Library Journal, vol. 98, July 1973, p. 3010; National Observer, vol. 12, November 3, 1973, p. 23; Publishers Weekly, vol. 204, August 13, 1973; Time, vol. 102, October 8, 1973; Booklist, vol. 70, December 15, 1973, p. 407; Publishers Weekly, vol. 206, October 21, 1974; Village Voice, vol. 19, January 31, 1974, p. 29; Books and Bookmen, vol. 20, June 1975, p. 46; Observer, June 1975, p. 23; and Times Literary Supplement (London), August 29, 1975, p. 977.

15 Anonymous, Review of The Future of Religions, by Paul Tillich, Bulletin from Virginia Kirkus Bookshop Service, vol. 34 (March 15, 1966), p. 365. Also in Choice, vol. 3, November 1966, p. 802, and Booklist, vol. 62, July 15, 1966, p. 1066.

16 Anonymous, Review of The Interpretation of History, by Paul Tillich, Catholic Historical Review, vol. 24 (April, 1938), p. 71.

17 Anonymous, Review of The Interpretation of History, by Paul Tillich, New York Times, January 24, 1937, p. 6.

18 Anonymous, Review of Love, Power, and Justice, by Paul Tillich, Bulletin from Virginia Kirkus Bookshop Service, vol. 22 (March 15, 1954), p. 192. Also in Chicago Sunday Tribune, August 15, 1954, p. 2; Manchester Guardian, April 13, 1954, p. 4; and Times Literary Supplement, London, June 4, 1954, p. 365.

19 Anonymous, Review of Morality and Beyond, by Paul Tillich, New Yorker, vol. 39 (February 1, 1964), p. 97.

20 Anonymous, Review of My Search for Absolutes, by Paul Tillich, Bulletin from Virginia Kirkus Bookshop Service, vol. 35 (July 1, 1967), p. 794. Also in Publishers Weekly, vol. 192, July 17, 1967, p. 67; Booklist, vol. 64, March 1, 1968, p.

755; and Review of Metaphysics, vol. 22, September 1968, p. 155.

21 Anonymous, Review of My Travel Diary, 1936: Between Two Worlds, by Paul Tillich, Times Literary Supplement (London), December 4, 1970, p. 1426. Also in Publishers Weekly, vol. 199, April 5, 1971, p. 48; New Yorker, vol. 46, July 11, 1970; Choice, vol. 8, May 1971, p. 412; and Kirkus Reviews, vol. 39, March 15, 1971, p. 310.

22 Anonymous, Review of Mysticism and Guilt Consciousness in Schelling's Philosophical Development, by Paul Tillich, Library Journal, vol. 100 (May 1, 1975), p. 863. Also in Choice, vol. 12, June 1975, p. 520.

23 Anonymous, Review of The New Being, by Paul Tillich, Bulletin from Virginia Kirkus Bookshop Service, vol. 23 (February 15, 1955), p. 166. Also in Booklist, vol. 51, July 15, 1955, p. 458; Wisconsin Library Bulletin, vol. 51, May 1955, p. 4; and Expository Times, vol. 67, August 1956, pp. 322-323.

24 Anonymous, Review of On the Boundary: An Autobiographical Sketch, by Paul Tillich, Bulletin from Virginia Kirkus Bookshop Service, vol. 34 (April 15, 1966), p. 440. Also in Critic, vol. 25, August 1966, p. 62; New Yorker, vol. 42, July 9, 1966, p. 91; Choice, vol. 3, January 1967, p. 1030; and Publishers Weekly, vol. 192, July 17, 1967, p. 72.

25 Anonymous, Review of Paulus: Reminiscences of a Friendship, by Rollo May, Choice, vol. 10 (July-August, 1973), p. 855.

26 Anonymous, Review of Perspectives on 19th and 20th Century Theology, by Paul Tillich, Bulletin from Virginia Kirkus Bookshop Service, vol. 35 (February 1, 1967), p. 123. Also in Booklist, vol. 64, September 1, 1967, p. 10, and Choice, vol. 5, March 1968, p. 72.

27 Anonymous, Review of Political Expectation, by Paul Tillich, Commonweal, vol. 95 (November 26, 1971), p. 212.

28 Anonymous, Review of Political Expectation, by Paul Tillich, Publishers Weekly, vol. 199 (April 5, 1971), p. 48. Also in Choice, vol. 8, January 1972, p. 1463.

29 Anonymous, Review of The Protestant Era, by Paul Tillich, San Francisco Chronicle, January 20, 1948, p. 14. Also in Current History, vol. 15, July 1948, p. 15.

30 Anonymous, Review of The Protestant Era, by Paul Tillich, Journal of Religion, vol. 52 (July, 1972), p. 268.

31 Anonymous, Review of Religion and Culture: Essays in Honour of Paul Tillich, ed. by Walter Leibrecht, Booklist, vol. 55

(July 1, 1959), p. 588. Also in New Statesman, vol. 58, November 21, 1959, p. 722, and Time, vol. 73, March 16, 1959, p. 46.

32 Anonymous, Review of The Religious Situation, by Paul Tillich, Boston Transcript, December 24, 1932, p. 2. Also in World Tomorrow, vol. 15, December 21, 1932, p. 596; Booklist, vol. 29, February 2, 1933, p. 167; International Journal of Ethics, vol. 43, April 1933, p. 375; and Survey Graphic, vol. 22, April 1933, p. 229.

33 Anonymous, Review of Systematic Theology: Volumes I to III, by Paul Tillich, Christian Century, vol. 84 (April 26, 1967), p. 562. Also in Booklist, vol. 63, June 15, 1967, p. 1091.

34 Anonymous, Review of Systematic Theology: Volume I, by Paul Tillich, United States Quarterly Book List, vol. 7 (June 1951), p. 150. Also in Review for Religious, vol. 33, January 1974, p. 253.

35 Anonymous, Review of Systematic Theology: Volume II, by Paul Tillich, Lutheran Quarterly, vol. 11 (February, 1959), pp. 76-78.

36 Anonymous, Review of Systematic Theology: Volume III, by Paul Tillich, Times Literary Supplement, October 29, 1964, p. 982.

37 Anonymous, Review of Theology of Culture, by Paul Tillich, Bulletin from Virginia Kirkus Bookshop Service, vol. 27 (May 1, 1959), p. 353. Also in Booklist, vol. 55, July 15, 1959, p. 620; Times Literary Supplement (London), February 5, 1960, p. 84; and Anglican Theological Review, vol. 42, April 1960, p. 186.

38 Anonymous, Review of Ultimate Concern: Tillich in Dialogue, ed. by D. Mackenzie Brown, Booklist, vol. 61 (July 15, 1965), p. 1041. Also in Choice, vol. 2, November 1965, p. 590; Bulletin from Virginia Kirkus Bookshop Service, vol. 33, May 15, 1965, p. 523; and Times Literary Supplement (London), March 3, 1966, p. 176.

39 Anonymous, Review of What Is Religion? by Paul Tillich, Publishers Weekly, vol. 203 (March 19, 1973), p. 74. Also in Christian Century, vol. 86, July 9, 1969, p. 928, and Choice, vol. 6, February 1970, p. 1766.

40 Anonymous, Review of What Is Religion? by Paul Tillich, Journal of Religion, vol. 52 (July, 1972), p. 268.

41 Ashbrook, J., Review of My Search for Absolutes, by Paul Tillich, Pastoral Psychology, vol. 19 (February, 1968), pp. 73-74.

42 Aubrey, E., Review of The Protestant Era, by Paul Tillich, Crozer Quarterly, vol. 25 (October, 1948), p. 348.

43 Aubrey, E., Review of Systematic Theology: Volume I, by Paul Tillich, Journal of Bible and Religion, vol. 20 (January, 1952), pp. 31-32.

44 Baillie, D., Review of The Protestant Era, by Paul Tillich, Theology Today, vol. 6 (January, 1950), pp. 551-552.

45 Baillie, D., Review of The Shaking of the Foundations, by Paul Tillich, Theology Today, vol. 6 (January, 1950), pp. 551-552.

46 Baillie, J., Review of Systematic Theology: Volume I, by Paul Tillich, Theology Today, vol. 8 (January, 1952), pp. 566-568.

47 Barker, C., Review of The Courage To Be, by Paul Tillich, Church Quarterly Review, vol. 155, no. 314 (1954), pp. 88-89.

48 Barker, C., Review of Dynamics of Faith, by Paul Tillich, Church Quarterly Review, vol. 159 (April-June, 1958), pp. 281-282.

49 Barker, C., Review of Systematic Theology: Volume I, by Paul Tillich, Church Quarterly Review, vol. 154, no. 313 (1953), pp. 462-465.

50 Barrett, M., Review of Biblical Religion and the Search for Ultimate Reality, by Paul Tillich, Library Journal, vol. 80 (September 15, 1955), p. 1911.

51 Baum, Gregory, Review of The Socialist Decision, by Paul Tillich, Canadian Forum, vol. 57 (October, 1977), p. 27.

52 Beard, C., Review of The Interpretation of History, by Paul Tillich, American Journal of Sociology, vol. 43 (January, 1938), p. 666.

53 Bedani, V., Review of Ultimate Concern: Tillich in Dialogue, ed. by D. Mackenzie Brown, New Blackfriars, vol. 47 (April, 1966), p. 390.

54 Benkston, B., Review of Systematic Theology: Volume III, by Paul Tillich, Lutheran World, vol. 12, no. 1 (1965), pp. 65-67.

55 Bennett, J., Review of Political Expectation, by Paul Tillich, Judaism, vol. 21 (Winter, 1972), pp. 116-8.

56 Best, E. E., Review of Tillichean Theology and Educational Philosophy, by Samuel E. Lo, Review of Religious Research, vol. 13, no. 2 (1972), p. 157.

57 Biallas, L. J., Review of The Promise of Tillich, by Leslie G.
    Tait, Review of Politics, vol. 35, no. 1 (1973), p. 93.

58 Bide, P., Review of Paulus: Reminiscences of a Friendship,
    by Rollo May, Frontier (London), vol. 18 (Summer, 1975), pp.
    121-122.

59 Bierstedt, Robert, Review of The Courage To Be, by Paul Til-
    lich, Saturday Review, vol. 36 (February 21, 1953), p. 55.

60 Bohlmann, A., Review of Tillich: A Theological Portrait, by
    David H. Hopper, Christianity Today, vol. 12 (April 12, 1968),
    pp. 29-30.

61 Boozer, J., Review of Dynamics of Faith, by Paul Tillich,
    Journal of Bible and Religion, vol. 25 (July, 1957), pp. 249-250.

62 Borsody, Lajos, Review of Love, Power, and Justice, by Paul
    Tillich, Library Journal, vol. 79 (April 15, 1954), p. 775.

63 Bradley, D., Review of The Future of Religions, by Paul Til-
    lich, Journal for the Scientific Study of Religion, vol. 6 (Spring,
    1967), pp. 161-163.

64 Brezine, D., Review of The Future of Religions, by Paul Til-
    lich, Review for Religious, vol. 25 (November, 1966), pp. 112-
    114.

65 Brisay, M., Review of Systematic Theology: Volume II, by
    Paul Tillich, Hibbert Journal, vol. 56 (July, 1958), p. 414.

66 Brody, Alter, Review of The Religious Situation, by Paul Til-
    lich, New Republic, vol. 76 (October 25, 1933), p. 315.

67 Browning, D., Review of Perspectives on 19th and 20th Century
    Protestant Theology, by Paul Tillich, Pastoral Psychology, vol.
    19 (November, 1968), pp. 56-58.

68 Buehrer, E. T., Review of The Religious Situation, by Paul
    Tillich, Christian Century, vol. 50 (February 1, 1933), p. 155.

69 Burger, H. K., Review of Ultimate Concern: Tillich in Dia-
    logue, ed. by D. MacKenzie Brown, New York Times Book Re-
    view, October 31, 1965, p. 53.

70 Burger, H. K., Review of Religion and Culture: Essays in
    Honour of Paul Tillich, ed. by Walter Leibrecht, New York
    Times Book Review, March 22, 1959, p. 39.

71 Burger, H. K., Review of Christianity and the Encounter of
    the World Religions, by Paul Tillich, New York Times Book
    Review, May 19, 1963, p. 43.

72   Burger, H. K., Review of Dynamics of Faith, by Paul Tillich, New York Times Book Review, January 13, 1957, p. 25.

73   Burger, H. K., Review of My Search for Absolutes, by Paul Tillich, New York Times Book Review, vol. 72 (October 15, 1967), p. 34.

74   Burkholder, J. L., Review of Love, Power, and Justice, by Paul Tillich, Mennonite Quarterly Review, vol. 29 (October, 1955), pp. 304-310.

75   Burnaby, J., Review of Systematic Theology: Volume II, by Paul Tillich, Journal of Theological Studies (New Series), vol. 10 (April, 1959), pp. 192-199.

76   Carey, John J., Review of Tillich's Philosophy of Culture, Science and Religion, by James Luther Adams, Journal of the American Academy of Religion, vol. 39, no. 3 (1971), p. 391.

77   Carr, John, Review of Love, Power, and Justice, by Paul Tillich, Catholic World, vol. 179 (July, 1954), p. 318.

78   Case, S. J., Review of The Interpretation of History, by Paul Tillich, Journal of Religion, vol. 17 (April, 1937), p. 217.

79   Cauthen, K., Review of Political Expectation, by Paul Tillich, Interpretation, vol. 26 (April, 1972), pp. 244-245.

80   Chapman, C. T., Review of Theology of Culture, by Paul Tillich, Church Quarterly Review, vol. 162 (April-June, 1961), p. 251.

81   Clancy, William, Review of Religion and Culture: Essays in Honour of Paul Tillich, ed. by Walter Leibrecht, Commonweal, vol. 71 (December 4, 1959), p. 293.

82   Clark, G. H., Review of Perspectives on 19th and 20th Century Protestant Theology, by Paul Tillich, Christianity Today, vol. 11 (June 23, 1967), p. 28.

83   Clark, J. A., Review of Dynamics of Faith, by Paul Tillich, Library Journal, vol. 82 (January 15, 1957), p. 194.

84   Clark, J. A., Review of The Eternal Now, by Paul Tillich, Library Journal, vol. 88 (November 1, 1963), p. 4226.

85   Clark, J. A., Review of Perspectives on 19th and 20th Century Protestant Theology, by Paul Tillich, Library Journal, vol. 92 (February 15, 1967), p. 781.

86   Clarke, Jack, Review of A History of Christian Thought, by Paul Tillich, Library Journal, vol. 93 (July, 1968), p. 266.

87 Clarke, Jack, Review of What Is Religion? by Paul Tillich, Library Journal, vol. 94 (June 15, 1969).

88 Cleobury, F. H., Review of The Eternal Now, by Paul Tillich, Modern Churchman (new series), vol. 11 (July, 1968), pp. 262-264.

89 Cole, S. G., Review of The Religious Situation, by Paul Tillich, Journal of Religion, vol. 13 (July, 1933), p. 348.

90 Comstock, W. R., Review of Christianity and the Encounter of the World Religions, by Paul Tillich, Union Seminary Quarterly Review, vol. 19 (November, 1963), pp. 65-67.

91 Cooke, G., Review of Christianity and the Encounter of the World Religions, by Paul Tillich, Journal of Ecumenical Studies, vol. 1 (Spring, 1964), pp. 330-337.

92 Cooper, J. C., Review of A History of Christian Thought, by Paul Tillich, Christian Century, vol. 85 (October 16, 1968), p. 1305.

93 Cox, Harvey, Review of Paulus: Reminiscences of a Friendship, by Rollo May, New York Times Book Review, October 14, 1973, p. 31.

94 Cox, Harvey, Review of From Time to Time, by Hannah Tillich, New York Times Book Review, October 14, 1973, p. 31.

95 Cox, Harvey, Review of The Theology of Culture, ed. by Robert C. Kimball, Month, vol. 33 (February, 1965), p. 129.

96 Cranston, M., Review of On the Boundary: An Autobiographical Sketch, by Paul Tillich, Encounter, vol. 29 (December, 1967), p. 85.

97 Davies, A. P., Review of The Courage to Be, by Paul Tillich, New Republic, vol. 127 (December 29, 1952), p. 20.

98 Davis, Charles, Review of Paulus: Reminiscences of a Friendship, by Rollo May, Commonweal, vol. 99 (December 21, 1973), pp. 322-323.

99 Davis, Charles, Review of From Time to Time, by Hannah Tillich, Commonweal, vol. 99 (December 21, 1973), pp. 322-323.

100 Davies, J. G., Review of The Eternal Now, by Paul Tillich, Expository Times, vol. 75 (January, 1964), pp. 103-104.

101 Dayton, D. W., Review of Paulus: Reminiscences of a Friend-

ship, by Rollo May, Library Journal, vol. 98 (October 15, 1973), p. 3010.

102 Dayton, D. W., Review of From Time to Time, by Hannah Tillich, Library Journal, vol. 98 (October 15, 1973), p. 3010.

103 Dean, W. D., Review of The Eternal Now, by Paul Tillich, Journal of Religion, vol. 44 (October, 1964), p. 357.

104 Demant, V. A., Review of The Protestant Era, by Paul Tillich, Journal of Theological Studies (new series), vol. 3 (April, 1952), pp. 137-138.

105 Demos, Raphael, Review of Systematic Theology: Volume I, by Paul Tillich, Journal of Philosophy, vol. 49 (1952), pp. 692-708.

106 Despland, M., Review of Reflection and Doubt in the Thought of Paul Tillich, by Robert P. Scharlemann, Journal of the American Academy of Religion, vol. 39, no. 4 (1971), p. 550.

107 Despland, M., Review of What Is Religion? by Paul Tillich, Journal of The American Academy of Religion, vol. 39 (December, 1971), pp. 550-554.

108 DeWolf, L. H., Review of Systematic Theology: Volume II, by Paul Tillich, Journal of Bible and Religion, vol. 25 (October, 1957), pp. 328-329.

109 Dillistone, F. W., Review of Theology of Culture, by Paul Tillich, Journal of Pastoral Care, vol. 15 (Spring, 1961), p. 48.

110 Driver, Tom F., Review of Paulus: Reminiscences of a Friendship, by Rollo May, New Republic, vol. 169 (November 24, 1973), pp. 27-29.

111 Driver, Tom Faw, Review of From Time to Time, by Hannah Tillich, New Republic, vol. 169 (November 24, 1973), pp. 27-29.

112 Driver, Tom Faw, Review of My Travel Diary, 1936: Between Two Worlds, by Paul Tillich, Union Seminary Quarterly Review, vol. 27 (Spring, 1972), pp. 179-181.

113 Driver, Tom Faw, Review of Political Expectation, by Paul Tillich, Union Seminary Quarterly Review, vol. 27 (Spring, 1972), pp. 179-181.

114 Ebersole, M. C., Review of Christianity and the Encounter of the World Religions, by Paul Tillich, Christian Century, vol. 80 (February 27, 1963), p. 273.

115 Eckardt, A. R., Review of The Protestant Era, by Paul Til-
     lich, Journal of Bible and Religion, vol. 18 (October, 1950),
     pp. 261-262.

116 Egan, J., Review of Systematic Theology: Volume I, by Paul
     Tillich, Thomist, vol. 17 (October, 1954), p. 571.

117 Egan, J., Review of The Theology of Paul Tillich, ed. by
     Charles W. Kegley and Robert W. Bretall, Thomist, vol. 17
     (October, 1954), p. 571.

118 Ellmann, Mary, Review of Paulus: Reminiscences of a Friend-
     ship, by Rollo May, Yale Review, vol. 63 (June, 1974), pp.
     602-605.

119 Ellmann, Mary, Review of From Time To Time, by Hannah
     Tillich, Yale Review, vol. 63 (June, 1974), p. 602.

120 Emmet, D. F., Review of Systematic Theology: Volume I,
     by Paul Tillich, Journal of Theological Studies (new series),
     vol. 4 (October, 1953), pp. 294-298.

121 Emmet, D. F., Review of Theology of Culture, by Paul Til-
     lich, Journal of Theological Studies (new series), vol. 11
     April, 1960), p. 228.

122 Everett, J. R., Review of The Protestant Era, by Paul Til-
     lich, Journal of Philosophy, vol. 45 (October 21, 1948), p.
     610.

123 Farnesworth, D. L., Review of The Courage to Be, by Paul
     Tillich, Journal of Pastoral Care, vol. 11 (Spring, 1957), pp.
     36-37.

124 Fennell, W. O., Review of Love, Power, and Justice, by
     Paul Tillich, Canadian Journal of Theology, vol. 1 (April,
     1955), pp. 55-58.

125 Ferre, Nels F. S., Review of Biblical Religion and the Search
     for Ultimate Reality, by Paul Tillich, Christian Century, vol.
     72 (November 2, 1955), p. 1272.

126 Ferre, Nels F. S., Review of Dynamics of Faith, by Paul
     Tillich, Theology Today, vol. 14 (July, 1957), pp. 276-279.

127 Ferre, Nels F. S., Review of The New Being, by Paul Til-
     lich, Interpretation, vol. 9 (October, 1955), pp. 465-467.

128 Fjellman, C., Review of Morality and Beyond, by Paul Til-
     lich, Lutheran Quarterly, vol. 16 (February, 1964), p. 89.

129 Fjellman, C., Review of Systematic Theology: Volume III,

by Paul Tillich, Lutheran Quarterly, vol. 16 (August, 1964), pp. 275-277.

130   Flint, R. W., Review of The Protestant Era, by Paul Tillich, New York Times, January 27, 1948, p. 6.

131   Ford, Lewis S., Review of The Intellectual Legacy of Paul Tillich, by James R. Lyons, Journal of the American Academy of Religion, vol. 39, no. 2 (1971), p. 266.

132   Ford, Lewis S., Review of Ultimate Concern: Tillich in Dialogue, ed. by D. Mackenzie Brown, Journal of Religion, vol. 46 (January, 1966), p. 56.

133   Forell, G. W., Review of Biblical Religion and the Search for Ultimate Reality, by Paul Tillich, Lutheran Quarterly, vol. 8 (November, 1956), pp. 371-372.

134   Forinelli, J., Review of Christianity and the Encounter of the World Religions, by Paul Tillich, Journal of Bible and Religion, vol. 32 (April, 1964), pp. 184-186.

135   Furgeson, E., Review of Ultimate Concern: Tillich in Dialogue, ed. by D. Mackenzie Brown, Pastoral Psychology, vol. 16 (September, 1965), pp. 62-64.

136   Furgeson, E. H., Review of The Eternal Now, by Paul Tillich, Journal of Theological Studies, vol. 14 (November, 1963), pp. 56-57.

137   Furgeson, E. H., Review of Morality and Beyond, by Paul Tillich, Journal of Theological Studies, vol. 14 (November, 1963), pp. 57-58.

138   Galloway, A. D., Review of A History of Christian Thought, by Paul Tillich, Scottish Journal of Theology, vol. 22 (March, 1969), pp. 96-99.

139   Galloway, A. D., Review of On the Boundary: An Autobiographical Sketch, by Paul Tillich, Scottish Journal of Theology, vol. 21 (June, 1968), pp. 223-224.

140   Galloway, A. D., Review of Perspectives of 19th and 20th Century Protestant Theology, by Paul Tillich, Scottish Journal of Theology, vol. 22 (March, 1969), pp. 96-99.

141   Galloway, A. D., Review of Systematic Theology: Volume III, by Paul Tillich, Journal of Theological Studies (new series), vol. 17 (April, 1966), pp. 250-252.

142   Galloway, A., Review of Ultimate Concern: Tillich in Dialogue, ed. by D. Mackenzie Brown, Expository Times, vol. 77 (June, 1966), pp. 269-270.

143 Gambee, R. R., Review of My Search for Absolutes, by Paul Tillich, Library Journal, vol. 92 (August, 1967), p. 2785.

144 Garnett, A. C., Review of Biblical Religion and the Search for Ultimate Reality, by Paul Tillich, Encounter, vol. 17 (Spring, 1956), pp. 177-180.

145 Garrett, J. L., Review of A History of Christian Thought, by Paul Tillich, Review and Expositor, vol. 69 (Spring, 1972), pp. 235-237.

146 Gill, T. A., Review of The New Being, by Paul Tillich, Christian Century, vol. 72 (October 12, 1955), p. 1176.

147 Gillman, I., Review of Perspectives on 19th and 20th Century Protestant Theology, by Paul Tillich, Reformed Theological Review, vol. 27 (January-April, 1968), pp. 32-33.

148 Gilmore, R. E., Review of The Courage to Be, by Paul Tillich, Christian Century, vol. 70 (March 4, 1953), p. 257.

149 Govig, S. G., Review of My Travel Diary, 1936: Between Two Worlds, by Paul Tillich, Lutheran Quarterly, vol. 23 (February, 1971), p. 91.

150 Gray, D. P., Review of Man in Estrangement, by Guyton B. Hammond, Catholic World, vol. 202 (February, 1966), pp. 312-314.

151 Gray, J. G., Review of Love, Power, and Justice, by Paul Tillich, Journal of Philosophy, vol. 51 (October 14, 1954), p. 644.

152 Green, F. Pratt, Review of From Time to Time, by Hannah Tillich, Expository Times, vol. 86 (August, 1975), p. 352.

153 Greene, T. M., Review of Love, Power, and Justice, by Paul Tillich, Theology Today, vol. 12 (October, 1955), pp. 388-391.

154 Grislis, E., Review of A History of Christian Thought, by Paul Tillich, Duke Divinity Review, vol. 34 (Winter, 1969), pp. 40-43.

155 Hall, C. E., Jr., Review of The Future of Religions, by Paul Tillich, Journal of Pastoral Care, vol. 21 (June, 1967), p. 109.

156 Hamilton, Kenneth M., Review of The Fabric of Paul Tillich's Theology, by David H. Kelsey, Christian Century, vol. 84 (April 12, 1967), p. 473.

157 Hamilton, Kenneth M., Review of Systematic Theology:

Volume III, by Paul Tillich, Interpretation, vol. 18 (July, 1964), pp. 365-368.

158 Hammond, Guyton B., Review of A History of Christian Thought, by Paul Tillich, Encounter, vol. 30 (Fall, 1969), pp. 373-374.

159 Hammond, Guyton B., Review of A History of Christian Thought, by Paul Tillich, Journal of the American Academy of Religion, vol. 38 (June, 1970), pp. 215-217.

160 Hammond, Guyton B., Review of Paul Tillich and Dialectical Humanism: Unmasking the God Above God, by Leonard F. Wheat, Journal of the American Academy of Religion, vol. 39, no. 4 (December, 1971), p. 568.

161 Handlin, O., Review of Systematic Theology: Volumes I to III, by Paul Tillich, Atlantic Monthly, vol. 220 (July, 1967), p. 111.

162 Handspicker, M. B., Review of The Future of Religions, by Paul Tillich, Student World, vol. 59, no. 4 (1966), pp. 428-429.

163 Harkness, R. E. E., Review of The Interpretation of History, by Paul Tillich, Crozer Quarterly, vol. 14 (July, 1937), p. 244.

164 Haroutunian, Joseph, Review of The Courage to Be, by Paul Tillich, Theology Today, vol. 11 (January, 1955), pp. 559-560.

165 Haroutunian, Joseph, Review of Dynamics of Faith, by Paul Tillich, Christian Century, vol. 74 (May 8, 1957), p. 592.

166 Hazelton, Roger, Review of My Search for Absolutes, by Paul Tillich, New Republic, vol. 158 (January 6, 1968), p. 36.

167 Hazelton, Roger, Review of Systematic Theology: Volumes I to III, by Paul Tillich, New Republic, vol. 157 (August 5, 1967), p. 36.

168 Heinecken, R., Review of The Protestant Era, by Paul Tillich, Lutheran Quarterly, vol. 1 (November, 1949), pp. 471-472.

169 Hendricks, W. L., Review of Paulus: Reminiscences of a Friendship, by Rollo May, Southwestern Journal of Theology, vol. 16 (Spring, 1974), pp. 101-102.

170 Hendricks, W. L., Review of From Time to Time, by Hannah Tillich, Southwestern Journal of Theology, vol. 16 (Spring, 1974), pp. 101-102.

171 Hendry, George S., Review of Biblical Religion and the Search for Ultimate Reality, by Paul Tillich, Union Seminary Quarterly Review, vol. 11 (January, 1956), pp. 59-60.

172 Hendry, George S., Review of Systematic Theology: Volume II, by Paul Tillich, Theology Today, vol. 15, no. 1 (April, 1958), pp. 78-83.

173 Herberg, Will, Review of Biblical Religion and the Search for Ultimate Reality, by Paul Tillich, New Republic, vol. 133 (October 24, 1955), p. 19.

174 Herzog, Frederick, Review of Systematic Theology: Volume II, by Paul Tillich, Christian Century, vol. 75 (December 10, 1958), p. 1432.

175 Hicks, John H., Review of Systematic Theology: Volumes I and II, by Paul Tillich, Scottish Journal of Theology, vol. 12 (September, 1959), pp. 286-297.

176 Hiltner, S., Review of Paulus: Reminiscences of a Friendship, by Rollo May, Theology Today, vol. 30 (January, 1974), pp. 382-388.

177 Hiltner, S., Review of From Time to Time, by Hannah Tillich, Theology Today, vol. 30 (January, 1974), pp. 382-388.

178 Hoerr, S., Review of Paul Tillich: Retrospect and Future, ed. by T. A. Kantonen, Review of Metaphysics, vol. 23 (1969), pp. 146.

179 Hoffman, J. O., Jr., Review of Systematic Theology: Volume II, by Paul Tillich, Anglican Theological Review, vol. 40 (April, 1958), pp. 139-144.

180 Hoffman, J. O., Jr., Review of Systematic Theology: Volume III, by Paul Tillich, Anglican Theological Review, vol. 47 (April, 1965), pp. 238-243.

181 Hoggart, Richard, Review of Religion and Culture: Essays in Honour of Paul Tillich, ed. by Walter Leibrecht, Spectator, December 4, 1959, p. 842.

182 Hoggart, Richard, Review of Theology of Culture, by Paul Tillich, Spectator, December 4, 1959, p. 842.

183 Holbert, Cornelia, Review of Paulus: Reminiscences of a Friendship, by Rollo May, Best Sellers, vol. 33 (November 15, 1973), p. 370.

184 Holbert, Cornelia, Review of From Time to Time, by Hannah Tillich, Best Sellers, vol. 33 (November 15, 1973), p. 370.

185 Holmer, P. L., Review of Theology of Culture, by Paul Til-
    lich, Lutheran Quarterly, vol. 12 (May, 1960), pp. 178-179.

186 Holmes, J. H., Review of The Religious Situation, by Paul
    Tillich, New York Herald Tribune Books, January 1, 1933,
    p. 1.

187 Holmes, R. L., Review of Morality and Beyond, by Paul Til-
    lich, Union Seminary Quarterly Review, vol. 19 (March, 1964),
    pp. 265-267.

188 Homrighausen, E. G., Review of Dynamics of Faith, by Paul
    Tillich, Pastoral Psychology, vol. 8 (March, 1957), pp. 55-56.

189 Honduras, B., Review of A History of Christian Thought, by
    Paul Tillich, Theology, vol. 72 (November, 1969), pp. 513-
    514.

190 Hoover, H. D., Review of Love, Power, and Justice, by Paul
    Tillich, Lutheran Quarterly, vol. 6 (August, 1954), pp. 265-
    266.

191 Hopper, M. T., Review of The New Being, by Paul Tillich,
    Pastoral Psychology, vol. 6 (June, 1955), pp. 59-60.

192 Hunt, W. B., Review of Theology of Culture, by Paul Tillich,
    Southwestern Journal of Theology, vol. 1 (April, 1959), pp.
    61-62.

193 Hutchison, J. A., Review of Theology of Culture, by Paul Til-
    lich, Theology Today, vol. 16 (October, 1959), pp. 407-408.

194 Irish, J. A., Review of Paulus: Reminiscences of a Friend-
    ship, by Rollo May, Christian Century, vol. 90 (December 12,
    1973), p. 1236.

195 Jackson, K. G., Review of The Eternal Now, by Paul Tillich,
    Harper's Magazine, vol. 228 (January, 1964), p. 108.

196 Jelly, F. M., Review of Tillich's System, by Wayne W.
    Mahan, Review of Metaphysics, vol. 29, no. 2 (1975), pp.
    346-347.

197 Joad, C. E. M., Review of The Interpretation of History, by
    Paul Tillich, New Statesman and Nation, vol. 13 (March 6,
    1937), p. 374.

198 Jocz, J., Review of Die Judenfrage: Ein Christliches und ein
    Deutsches Problem, by Paul Tillich, International Review of
    Missions, vol. 43 (July, 1954), pp. 344-346.

199 Johnson, C. R., Review of Religion and Culture: Essays in
    Honour of Paul Tillich, ed. by Walter Leibrecht, Library
    Journal, vol. 84 (April 15, 1959), p. 1267.

200 Johnson, C. R., Review of Theology of Culture, by Paul Til-
     lich, Library Journal, vol. 84 (June 1, 1959), p. 1895.

201 Johnson, Shildes, Review of Ultimate Concern: Tillich in Dia-
     logue, ed. by D. Mackenzie Brown, Library Journal, vol. 90
     (June 1, 1965), p. 2560.

202 Johnson, Shildes, Reivew of The Future of Religions, by Paul
     Tillich, Library Journal, vol. 91 (May 15, 1966), p. 2499.

203 Johnson, William, Review of The Protestant Era, by Paul
     Tillich, Canadian Forum, vol. 28 (January, 1949), p. 236.

204 Jurji, E. J., Review of Christianity and the Encounter of the
     World Religions, by Paul Tillich, Princeton Seminary Bulletin,
     vol. 56 (May, 1963), pp. 54-55.

205 Jurji, E. J., Review of The Future of Religions, by Paul
     Tillich, Princeton Seminary Bulletin, vol. 60 (October, 1966),
     pp. 76-77.

206 Jurji, E. J., Review of On the Boundary: An Autobiographi-
     cal Sketch, by Paul Tillich, Princeton Seminary Bulletin, vol.
     59 (June, 1966), pp. 82-83.

207 Kantonen, R., Review of Systematic Theology: Volume I, by
     Paul Tillich, Lutheran Quarterly, vol. 3 (November, 1951),
     pp. 419-420.

208 Kau, I., Review of From Time to Time, by Hannah Tillich,
     Radical Religion, vol. 1 (Spring, 1974), pp. 66-67.

209 Kaufman, G. D., Review of Systematic Theology: Volume III,
     by Paul Tillich, Harvard Divinity Bulletin, vol. 28 (April,
     1964), p. 97.

210 Kean, C. D., Review of The Courage to Be, by Paul Tillich,
     Anglican Theological Review, vol. 35 (October, 1953), pp.
     270-274.

211 Keefe, Donald J., Review of The Protestant Era, by Paul
     Tillich, Review for Religious, vol. 30 (November, 1971), p.
     1153.

212 Kegley, Charles W., Review of Ultimate Concern: Tillich in
     Dialogue, ed. by D. Mackenzie Brown, Christian Century,
     vol. 82 (August 18, 1965), p. 1012.

213 Kegley, Charles W., Review of The New Being, by Paul Til-
     lich, Saturday Review, vol. 38 (July 30, 1955), p. 19.

214 Kegley, Charles W., Review of Political Expectations, by
     Paul Tillich, Theology Today, vol. 28 (October, 1971), pp.
     366-368.

215 Kelsey, D. H., Review of Perspectives on 19th and 20th Century Protestant Theology, by Paul Tillich, Journal of Politics, vol. 30 (August, 1968), p. 113.

216 Kerr, H. T., Review of Biblical Religion and the Search for Ultimate Reality, by Paul Tillich, Princeton Seminary Bulletin, vol. 49 (May, 1956), p. 59.

217 Killinger, J., Review of Paulus: Reminiscences of a Friendship, by Rollo May, Religion in Life, vol. 43 (Summer, 1974), pp. 242-244.

218 Kitching, J., Review of On the Boundary: An Autobiographical Sketch, by Paul Tillich, Publishers Weekly, vol. 189 (April 25, 1966), p. 120.

219 Knitter, Paul, Review of Mysticism and Guilt Consciousness in Schelling's Philosophical Development, by Paul Tillich, Library Journal, vol. 100 (May 1, 1975), p. 863.

220 Knitter, Paul, Review of The Construction of the History of Religion in Schelling's Positive Philosophy: Its Presuppositions and Principles, by Paul Tillich, Library Journal, vol. 100 (May 1, 1975), p. 863.

221 Kucheman, Clark A., Review of Political Expectation and What Is Religion? by Paul Tillich, Journal of Religion, vol. 52 (July, 1972), pp. 268-286. This review is entitled "Religion, Culture, and Religious Socialism."

222 Kysar, R., Review of Paul Tillich's Dialectical Humanism: Unmasking God Above God, by Leonard F. Wheat, Christian Century, vol. 88, no. 36 (September 8, 1971), pp. 1062, 1064.

223 Lake, F., Review of The Courage to Be, by Paul Tillich, Scottish Journal of Theology, vol. 6 (December, 1953), pp. 418-421.

224 Lawson, O. G., Review of The Courage to Be, by Paul Tillich, Library Journal, vol. 77 (December 15, 1952), p. 2174.

225 Lee, E. K., Review of The New Being, by Paul Tillich, Scottish Journal of Theology, vol. 10 (March, 1957), pp. 103-105.

226 LeFevre, P., Review of Theology of Culture, by Paul Tillich, Pastoral Psychology, vol. 10 (March, 1959), pp. 62-64.

227 Leibrecht, Walter, Review of Theology of Culture, by Paul Tillich, Christian Century, vol. 76 (November 4, 1959), p. 1281.

228 Littell, Franklin H., Review of My Travel Diary, 1936: Between Two Worlds, by Paul Tillich, Church History, vol. 40 (September, 1971), p. 350.

229 Lund, L. D., Review of The Eternal Now, by Paul Tillich, Lutheran Quarterly, vol. 16 (August, 1964), p. 277.

130 MacKinnon, D. M., Review of Religion and Culture: Essays in Honour of Paul Tillich, ed. by Walter Leibrecht, Guardian, November 6, 1959, p. 7.

231 Macleod, J., Review of Biblical Religion and the Search for Ultimate Reality, by Paul Tillich, Expository Times, vol. 67 (September, 1956), pp. 359-360.

232 Macleod, J., Review of Dynamics of Faith, by Paul Tillich, Expository Times, vol. 69 (November, 1957), p. 38.

233 MacQuarrie, John, Review of Systematic Theology: Volume III, by Paul Tillich, New York Times Book Review, February 23, 1964, p. 10.

234 MacQuarrie, John, and Randall, John Herman, Review of Systematic Theology: Volume III, by Paul Tillich, Union Seminary Quarterly Review, vol. 19 (May, 1964), pp. 345-349.

235 McCord, J. I., Review of Love, Power, and Justice, by Paul Tillich, Interpretation, vol. 9 (April, 1955), pp. 221-222.

236 McCord, J. I., Review of Perspectives on 19th and 20th Century Protestant Theology, by Paul Tillich, Princeton Seminary Bulletin, vol. 61 (Autumn, 1967), p. 80.

237 McCord, J. I., Review of Systematic Theology: Volume II, by Paul Tillich, Interpretation, vol. 12 (October, 1958), pp. 460-463.

238 McCraken, R. J., Review of The New Being, by Paul Tillich, Union Seminary Quarterly Review, vol. 13 (January, 1956), pp. 60-61.

239 McKelway, A. J., Review of What Is Religion? by Paul Tillich, Interpretation, vol. 25 (April, 1971), pp. 238-240.

240 McLelland, J. C., Review of Systematic Theology: Volume II, by Paul Tillich, Canadian Journal of Theology, vol. 4 (April, 1958), pp. 149-151.

241 Maddocks, Melvin, Review of Dynamics of Faith, by Paul Tillich, Christian Science Monitor, February 21, 1957, p. 7.

242 Markus, R. A., Review of Dynamics of Faith, by Paul Tillich, Scottish Journal of Theology, vol. 11 (June, 1958), pp. 200-202.

243 Marty, Martin E., Review of Paulus: Reminiscences of a

Friendship, by Rollo May, Critic, vol. 32 (November-December, 1973), p. 91.

244 Marty, Martin E., Review of From Time to Time, by Hannah Tillich, Critic, vol. 32 (November-December, 1973), p. 91.

245 Marty, Martin E., Review of The Future of Religions, by Paul Tillich, Book Week, May 29, 1966, p. 3.

246 Marty, Martin E., Review of My Travel Diary, 1936: Between Two Worlds, by Paul Tillich, Critic, vol. 29 (September, 1970), p. 93.

247 Marty, Martin E., Review of On the Boundary: An Autobiographical Sketch, by Paul Tillich, Book Week, May 29, 1966, p. 3.

248 Marty, Martin E., Review of Political Expectation, by Paul Tillich, Commonweal, vol. 95 (November 26, 1971), p. 213.

249 Mayhew, L. F. X., Review of Theology of Culture, by Paul Tillich, Commonweal, vol. 71 (November 6, 1959), p. 187.

250 Mays, Morley, Review of Love, Power, and Justice, by Paul Tillich, Christian Century, vol. 71 (June 2, 1954), p. 671.

251 Miller, K. D., Review of The New Being, by Paul Tillich, New York Herald Tribune Book Review, March 27, 1955, p. 4.

252 Miller, R. C., Review of The Protestant Era, by Paul Tillich, Churchman, vol. 162 (September 1, 1948), p. 17.

253 Miller, S. H., Review of The Courage to Be, by Paul Tillich, Journal of Pastoral Care, vol. 7, no. 3 (1953), pp. 174-177.

254 Mitton, C. L., Review of Paulus: Reminiscences of a Friendship, by Rollo May, Expository Times (London), vol. 86 (March, 1975), pp. 161-162.

255 Mollegen, A. T., Review of The Courage to Be, by Paul Tillich, Journal of Religious Thought, vol. 11, no. 1 (1953-1954), pp. 68-69.

256 Mollegen, A. T., Review of Systematic Theology: Volume II, by Paul Tillich, Union Seminary Quarterly Review, vol. 13 (January, 1958), pp. 53-54.

257 Moore, F. J., Review of Systematic Theology: Volume I, by Paul Tillich, Churchman, vol. 165 (July, 1951), p. 16.

258 Moore, T. W., Review of My Travel Diary, 1936: Between Two Worlds, by Paul Tillich, Christian Century, vol. 87 (September 23, 1970), p. 1126.

259 Mueller, D. L., Review of Perspectives on 19th and 20th Century Protestant Theology, by Paul Tillich, Review and Expositor, vol. 65 (Spring, 1968), pp. 244-245.

260 Mueller, D. L., Review of Political Expectation, by Paul Tillich, Review and Expositor, vol. 69 (Summer, 1972), pp. 389-390.

261 Murchland, Bernard, Review of Morality and Beyond, by Paul Tillich, Commonweal, vol. 80 (April 17, 1964), p. 123.

262 Murphy, John W., Review of The Socialist Decision, by Paul Tillich, Studies in Soviet Thought, vol. 21 (February, 1980), pp. 105-108.

263 Neimark, P. G., Review of The Future of Religions, by Paul Tillich, Books Today, vol. 3 (May 22, 1966), p. 9.

264 Neimark, P. G., Review of Perspectives on 19th and 20th Century Protestant Theology, by Paul Tillich, Books Today, vol. 4 (July 23, 1967), p. 11.

265 Neville, R. C., Review of My Search for Absolutes, by Paul Tillich, Catholic World, vol. 207 (September, 1968), p. 276.

266 Nichols, J. H., Review of The Protestant Era, by Paul Tillich, Christian Century, vol. 65 (July 14, 1948), p. 709.

267 Nickle, K. F., Review of My Search for Absolutes, by Paul Tillich, Review for Religious, vol. 27 (May, 1968), p. 562.

268 Niebuhr, Reinhold, Review of Dynamics of Faith, by Paul Tillich, Union Seminary Quarterly Review, vol. 12 (May, 1957), pp. 111-113.

269 Niebuhr, Reinhold, Review of My Travel Diary: 1936: Between Two Worlds, by Paul Tillich, New York Times Book Review, May 10, 1970, p. 6.

270 Niebuhr, Reinhold, Review of Theology of Culture, by Paul Tillich, Union Seminary Quarterly Review, vol. 15 (January, 1960), pp. 163-164.

271 Nishi, Shunji, Review of Paulus: Reminiscences of a Friendship, by Rollo May, Anglican Theological Review, vol. 57 (April, 1975), pp. 261-262.

272 Noyes, H. D., Review of Paul Tillich in Catholic Thought, ed. by Thomas A. O'Meara and Celestin D. Weisser, Catholic World, vol. 201 (April, 1965), p. 72.

273 Oden, T. C., Review of Systematic Theology of Paul Tillich, by Alexander J. McKelway, Christian Century, vol. 82 (December 1, 1965), p. 1481.

274   O'Hanlon, Daniel J., Review of Paul Tillich and the Christian Message, by Georges Henri Tavard, Commonweal, vol. 76, no. 21 (September 21, 1962), pp. 519-520.

275   Olsen, A. L., Review of A History of Christian Thought, by Paul Tillich, Dialog, vol. 8 (Spring, 1969), pp. 142-144.

276   Olsen, A. L., Review of Perspectives on 19th and 20th Century Protestant Theology, by Paul Tillich, Dialog, vol. 8 (Spring, 1969), pp. 142-144.

277   Osborn, A. D., Review of The New Being, by Paul Tillich, Library Journal, vol. 80 (March 15, 1955), p. 642.

278   Outler, A. C., Review of Dynamics of Faith, by Paul Tillich, Interpretation, vol. 11 (October, 1957), pp. 473-475.

279   Outler, A. C., Review of Systematic Theology: Volume I, by Paul Tillich, Interpretation, vol. 5 (October, 1951), pp. 476-480.

280   Owen, D. R. G., Review of Biblical Religion and the Search for Ultimate Reality, by Paul Tillich, Canadian Journal of Theology, vol. 2 (October, 1956), pp. 242-243.

281   Pannenberg, Wolfhart, Review of Systematic Theology: Volume III, by Paul Tillich, Dialog, vol. 4 (Summer, 1965), pp. 229-232.

282   Parker, T. H. L., Review of The Protestant Era, by Paul Tillich, Scottish Journal of Theology, vol. 7 (December, 1954), pp. 433-435.

283   Paul, W. W., Review of Religion and Culture: Essays in Honour of Paul Tillich, ed. by Walter Leibrecht, Journal of Philosophy, vol. 56 (October 8, 1959), p. 837.

284   Paul, W. W., Review of Christianity and the Encounter of the World Religions, by Paul Tillich, Christianity Today, vol. 7 (July 19, 1963), pp. 38-39.

285   Peel, Robert, Review of Theology of Culture, by Paul Tillich, Christian Science Monitor, May 21, 1959, p. 13.

286   Pennington, C. A., Review of The Eternal Now, by Paul Tillich, Journal of Bible and Religion, vol. 32 (July, 1964), p. 290.

287   Perkins, R. L., Review of Morality and Beyond, by Paul Tillich, Library Journal, vol. 88 (December 15, 1963), p. 4767.

288   Perkins, R. L., Review of On the Boundary: An Autobio-

graphical Sketch, by Paul Tillich, Library Journal, vol. 91 (June 1, 1966), p. 2850.

289 Perkins, R. L., Review of Systematic Theology: Volume III, by Paul Tillich, Library Journal, vol. 89 (January 1, 1964), p. 116.

290 Piepkorn, Arthur Carl, Review of Biblical Religion and the Search for Ultimate Reality, by Paul Tillich, Concordia Theological Monthly, vol. 28, no. 10 (October, 1957), pp. 780-781.

291 Piepkorn, Arthur Carl, Review of Love, Power, and Justice, by Paul Tillich, Concordia Theological Monthly, vol. 28, no. 10 (October, 1957), pp. 780-781.

292 Pike, N., Review of Religious Symbols and God: A Philosophical Study of Tillich's Theology, William L. Rowe, Philosophical Review, vol. 79, no. 3 (1970), p. 424.

293 Pittenger, N., Review of Perspectives on 19th and 20th Century Protestant Theology, by Paul Tillich, Journal of Theological Studies (new series), vol. 19 (April, 1968), pp. 385-386.

294 Pittenger, W. N., Review of The Courage to Be, by Paul Tillich, New York Times Book Review, January 4, 1953, p. 10.

295 Pittenger, W. N., Review of The New Being, by Paul Tillich, New York Times Book Review, July 31, 1955, p. 10.

296 Pittenger, W. N., Review of Systematic Theology: Volume III, by Paul Tillich, Modern Churchman (new series), vol. 8 (January, 1965), pp. 138-141.

297 Poling, David, Review of The Future of Religions, by Paul Tillich, Saturday Review, vol. 49 (May 14, 1966), p. 30.

298 Porter, L. E., Review of On the Boundary: An Autobiographical Sketch, by Paul Tillich, Evangelical Quarterly, vol. 41 (July-September, 1969), pp. 177-178.

299 Ramsey, Paul, Review of Biblical Religion and the Search for Ultimate Reality, by Paul Tillich, New York Times Book Review, September 18, 1955, p. 14.

300 Ramsey, Paul, Review of The Eternal Now, by Paul Tillich, Book Week, February 23, 1964, p. 1.

301 Ramsey, Paul, Review of Morality and Beyond, by Paul Tillich, Book Week, February 23, 1964, p. 1.

302 Ramsey, Paul, Review of Systematic Theology: Volume III, by Paul Tillich, Book Week, February 23, 1964, p. 1.

303 Ramsey, Paul, Review of Theology of Culture, by Paul Tillich, New York Times Book Review, July 26, 1959, p. 10.

304 Randall, J. H., Review of Systematic Theology: Volume III, by Paul Tillich, Union Seminary Quarterly Review, vol. 19 (May, 1964), pp. 351-359.

305 Reese, G. C., Review of Paulus: Reminiscences of a Friendship, by Rollo May, Lutheran Quarterly, vol. 26 (May, 1974), pp. 243-244.

306 Rice, Philip Blair, Review of Biblical Religion and the Search for Ultimate Reality, by Paul Tillich, Perspectives USA, vol. 15 (Spring, 1956), pp. 204-209.

307 Riemer, N., Review of Political Expectation, by Paul Tillich, Anglican Theological Review, vol. 54 (January, 1972), pp. 58-60.

308 Robinson, J. M., Review of Dynamics of Faith, by Paul Tillich, Journal of Bible and Religion, vol. 27 (July, 1959), pp. 233-242.

309 Rolo, C. J., Review of Love, Power, and Justice, by Paul Tillich, Atlantic Monthly, vol. 193 (June, 1954), p. 82.

310 Rowe, William L., Review of The Fabric of Tillich's Theology, by D. H. Kelsey, Philosophical Review, vol. 78, no. 4 (1969), p. 552.

311 Rowe, William L., Review of Systematic Theology: Volume III, by Paul Tillich, Philosophical Review, vol. 75 (April, 1966), p. 260.

312 Rupp, G., Review of Systematic Theology: Volume III, by Paul Tillich, Expository Times, vol. 76 (April, 1965), p. 211.

313 Rust, E. C., Review of Biblical Religion and the Search for Ultimate Reality, by Paul Tillich, Review and Expositor, vol. 54 (January, 1957), pp. 125-127.

314 Saliers, D. E., Review of Language, Existence, and God: Interpretations of Moore, Russell, Ayer, Wittgenstein, Wisdom, Oxford Philosophy and Tillich, by Edward Cell, Journal of the American Academy of Religion, vol. 40, no. 4 (1972), p. 582.

315 Sanborn, Sara, Review of Paulus: Reminiscences of a Friendship, by Rollo May, Nation, vol. 217 (December 31, 1973), pp. 730-732.

316 Sanborn, Sara, Review of From Time to Time, by Hannah Tillich, Nation, vol. 217 (December 31, 1973), pp. 730-732.

317 Sanderson, J. W., Jr., Review of What Is Religion? by Paul Tillich, Westminster Theological Journal, vol. 34 (November, 1971), pp. 103-106.

318 Sasse, H., Review of A History of Christian Thought, by Paul Tillich, Reformed Theological Review, vol. 28 (January-April, 1969), pp. 36-38.

319 Scharlemann, Robert P., Review of The Construction of the History of Religion in Schelling's Positive Philosophy, by Paul Tillich, Journal of Religion, vol. 56 (January, 1976), pp. 105-112.

320 Scharlemann, Robert P., Review of Mysticism and Guilt Consciousness in Schelling's Philosophical Development, by Paul Tillich, Journal of Religion, vol. 56 (January, 1976), pp. 105-112.

321 Seaburg, Alan, Review of My Travel Diary, 1936: Between Two Worlds, by Paul Tillich, Library Journal, vol. 94 (December 15, 1969), p. 4521.

322 Sherrard, Jani, Review of From Time to Time, by Hannah Tillich, The Drew Gateway, vol. 44 (Winter-Spring, 1974), pp. 142-145.

323 Smith, H., Review of The Future of Religions, by Paul Tillich, Journal of Religion, vol. 47 (April, 1967), p. 184.

324 Smith, J. E., Review of Morality and Beyond, by Paul Tillich, Saturday Review, vol. 47 (January 4, 1964), p. 80.

325 Smith, J. E., Review of Systematic Theology: Volume II, by Paul Tillich, Christian Century, vol. 75 (December 3, 1958), p. 1399.

326 Smith, J. E., Review of The Theology of Paul Tillich, ed. by Charles W. Kegley and Robert W. Bretall, Journal of Philosophy, vol. 50, no. 21 (October 8, 1953), pp. 638-646.

327 Spitz, L. W., Review of Systematic Theology: Volume II, by Paul Tillich, Concordia Theological Monthly, vol. 29 (August, 1958), p. 630.

328 Spitzer, A., Review of The Protestant Era, by Paul Tillich, American Catholic Sociological Review, vol. 18 (December, 1957), p. 336.

329 Stanley, C. L., Review of Systematic Theology: Volume I, by Paul Tillich, Anglican Theological Review, vol. 33 (October, 1951), pp. 247-250.

330 Steimle, E. A., Review of The Eternal Now, by Paul Tillich, Union Seminary Quarterly Review, vol. 19 (March, 1964), pp. 280-283.

331 Stewart, D., Review of Theology of Culture, by Paul Tillich, Baptist Quarterly, vol. 18 (January, 1960), pp. 230-232.

332 Streiker, L. D., Review of The Future of Religions, by Paul Tillich, Christian Century, vol. 83 (August 17, 1966), p. 1012.

333 Streiker, L. D., Review of On the Boundary: An Autobiographical Sketch, by Paul Tillich, Christian Century, vol. 83 (August 17, 1966), p. 1012.

334 Streiker, L. D., Review of The Future of Religions, by Paul Tillich, Journal of Ecumenical Studies, vol. 4 (Spring, 1967), p. 317.

335 Streiker, L. D., Review of Perspectives on 19th and 20th Century Protestant Theology, by Paul Tillich, Christian Century, vol. 84 (July 12, 1967), p. 920.

336 Sykes, S. W., Review of Ultimate Concern: Tillich in Dialogue, ed. by D. Mackenzie Brown, Modern Churchman (new series), vol. 10 (January, 1967), pp. 173-174.

337 Tavard, G. H., Review of A History of Christian Thought, by Paul Tillich, Theological Studies, vol. 30 (March, 1969), pp. 131-133.

338 Tavard, G. H., Review of Perspectives on 19th and 20th Century Protestant Theology, by Paul Tillich, Theological Studies, vol. 28 (December, 1967), pp. 855-856.

339 TeSelle, E., Review of A History of Christian Thought, by Paul Tillich, Theology Today, vol. 25 (January, 1955), pp. 501-502.

340 Thomas, I., Review of Systematic Theology: Volume I, by Paul Tillich, Dominican Studies, vol. 7 (1954), p. 281.

341 Thomas, John Heywood, Review of Love, Power, and Justice, by Paul Tillich, Hibbert Journal, vol. 52 (July, 1954), p. 415.

342 Thomasma, D., Review of The Future of Religions, by Paul Tillich, Dominicana, vol. 51 (Fall, 1966), p. 279.

343 Trilling, Diana, Review of From Time to Time, by Hannah Tillich, Partisan Review, vol. 41 (Winter, 1974), pp. 120-127.

344 Vahanian, Gabriel, Review of Theology of Culture, by Paul Tillich, Nation, vol. 189 (September 5, 1959), p. 117.

345 Van Ackeren, G., Review of The Courage to Be, by Paul Tillich, America, vol. 88 (March 21, 1953), p. 683.

346 Van Buren, Paul, Review of The Eternal Now, by Paul Tillich, Christian Century, vol. 81 (February 5, 1964), p. 177.

347 Van Buren, Paul, Review of Morality and Beyond, by Paul Tillich, Christian Century, vol. 81 (February 5, 1964), p. 177.

348 Van Buren, Paul, Review of Systematic Theology: Volume III, by Paul Tillich, Christian Century, vol. 81 (February 5, 1964), p. 177.

349 Van Den Heuvel, A. H., Review of Ultimate Concern: Tillich in Dialogue, ed. by D. Mackenzie Brown, Ecumenical Review, vol. 18 (July, 1966), p. 399.

350 Van Harvey, A., Review of Morality and Beyond, by Paul Tillich, Theology Today, vol. 21 (October, 1964), pp. 379-382.

351 Van Harvey, A., Review of Systematic Theology: Volume III, by Paul Tillich, Theology Today, vol. 21 (October, 1964), pp. 379-382.

352 Van Til, C., Review of Systematic Theology: Volume II, by Paul Tillich, Westminster Theological Journal, vol. 20 (November, 1957), pp. 93-99.

353 Watt, R. J. G., Review of Ultimate Concern: Tillich in Dialogue, ed. by D. Mackenzie Brown, Student World, vol. 60, no. 2 (1967), p. 198.

354 Weisberg, Harold, Review of Dynamics of Faith, by Paul Tillich, New Republic, vol. 136 (April, 1957), p. 20.

355 Welsh, C., Review of Love, Power, and Justice, by Paul Tillich, Anglican Theological Review, vol. 37 (April, 1955), pp. 155-156.

356 White, V., Review of Biblical Religion and the Search for Ultimate Reality, by Paul Tillich, Blackfriars, vol. 38 (March, 1957), p. 137.

357 White, V., Review of Dynamics of Faith, by Paul Tillich, Blackfriars, vol. 39 (May, 1958), p. 233.

358 White, V., Review of Systematic Theology, by Paul Tillich, Blackfriars, vol. 39 (May, 1958), p. 233.

359 Whitehouse, W. A., Review of The Religious Situation, by Paul Tillich, Congregational Quarterly, vol. 35 (April, 1957), pp. 171-172.

360 Wildung, B., Review of Ultimate Concern: Tillich in Dialogue, ed. by D. Mackenzie Brown, Union Seminary Quarterly Review, vol. 21 (March, 1966), pp. 369-370.

361 Williams, D. D., Review of Systematic Theology: Volume I, by Paul Tillich, Christian Century, vol. 68 (August 1, 1951), p. 893.

362 Williams, D. D., Review of Systematic Theology: Volume III, by Paul Tillich, Christian Century, vol. 81 (April 22, 1964), p. 518.

363 Williams, Robert R., Review of The Construction of the History of Religion in Schelling's Positive Philosophy, by Paul Tillich, Religious Studies Review, vol. 5, no. 2 (April, 1979), pp. 116-123.

364 Williams, Robert R., Review of Mysticism and Guilt Consciousness in Schelling's Philosophical Development, by Paul Tillich, Religious Studies Review, vol. 5, no. 2 (April, 1979), pp. 116-123.

365 Williamson, C. M., Review of Morality and Beyond, by Paul Tillich, Journal of Religion, vol. 45 (January, 1965), p. 58.

366 Williamson, C. M., Review of On the Boundary: An Autobiographical Sketch, by Paul Tillich, Encounter, vol. 28 (Winter, 1967), pp. 89-90.

367 Williamson, C. M., Review of Perspectives on 19th and 20th Century Protestant Theology, by Paul Tillich, Church History, vol. 37 (June, 1968), p. 224.

368 Williamson, C. M., Review of Systematic Theology: Volume III, by Paul Tillich, Journal of Religion, vol. 46 (April, 1966), p. 301.

369 Williamson, C. M., Review of What Is Religion? by Paul Tillich, Encounter, vol. 31 (Spring, 1970), pp. 207-208.

370 Wilson, K., Review of A History of Christian Thought, by Paul Tillich, Church Quarterly, vol. 1 (January, 1969), p. 247.

371 Wilson, P. W., Review of The Religious Situation, by Paul Tillich, Saturday Review of Literature, vol. 9 (January 14, 1933), p. 379.

372 Witherspoon, Frances, Review of The Courage to Be, by Paul Tillich, New York Herald Tribune Book Review, December 28, 1952, p. 10.

373 Witherspoon, Frances, Review of Love, Power, and Justice, by Paul Tillich, New York Herald Tribune Book Review, May 2, 1954, p. 8.

374 Woods, G. F., Review of Love, Power, and Justice, by Paul Tillich, Journal of Theological Studies (new series), vol. 6 (April, 1955), pp. 150-153.

375 Wren-Lewis, John, Review of Paulus, by Rollo May, and From Time to Time, by Hannah Tillich, Psychology Today, vol. 7, no. 11 (1974), pp. 14-15.

376 Wright, C. J., Review of The Protestant Era, by Paul Tillich, Modern Churchman, vol. 42 (December, 1952), pp. 365-366.

377 Yielde, H., Review of Theology of Culture, by Paul Tillich, Harvard Divinity Bulletin, vol. 24 (July, 1960), p. 21.

378 Young, W., Review of The Religious Situation, by Paul Tillich, Westminster Theological Journal, vol. 19 (May 1957), pp. 230-235.

379 Zuck, J. E., Review of Thomism and the Ontological Theology of Paul Tillich: A Comparison of Systems, by D. J. Keefe, Journal of the American Academy of Religion, vol. 41, no. 2 (1973), p. 271.

380 Zuver, D. D., Review of The Interpretation of History, by Paul Tillich, Churchman, vol. 151 (February 1, 1937), p. 19.

4. ARTICLES ABOUT OR RELATED TO PAUL TILLICH IN ENGLISH

1   Abelson, Raziel, "The Logic of Faith and Belief," Religious Experience and Truth, Sidney Hook, ed. New York: New York University Press, 1961, pp. 116-130.

2   Adams, James Luther, "Introduction," Political Expectation, Paul Tillich. New York: Harper and Row, 1971, pp. vi-xx.

3   Adams, James Luther, "Paul Tillich on Luther," Interpretation of Luther: Essays in Honour of Wilhelm Pauck, Jaroslav Pelikan, ed. Philadelphia: Fortress Press, 1968, pp. 304-334.

4   Adams, James Luther, "Tillich's Concept of the Protestant Era," The Protestant Era, Paul Tillich. Chicago: University of Chicago Press, 1948. This article does not appear in the abridged edition of this book.

5   Adams, James Luther, "Tillich's Interpretation of History," The Theology of Paul Tillich, Charles W. Kegley and Robert W. Bretall. New York: The Macmillan Company, 1964, pp. 294-312.

6   Adams, James Luther, "Tribute," Prospect (Harvard Divinity School), vol. 5, no. 7 (November 4, 1965).

7   Ahern, E., "Enigma of Paul Tillich: Nature and Method of Systematic Theology," Homiletic and Pastoral Review, vol. 63 (March, 1963), pp. 477-484.

8   Akahoshi, Susumu, "Fundamental Problems of the Relationship of Religion and Medicine Sought in Paul Tillich's Theology," Ministerium Medici, no. 2 (1961), pp. 23-30.

9   Albrecht, Renate, "Right Thinking and the Church," Faith and Freedom, vol. 17 (part 2), no. 50 (1964), pp. 79-84.

10 Aldrich, Virgil C., "The Outsider," Religious Experience and

Truth, Sidney Hook, ed. New York: New York University Press, 1961, pp. 27-39. A paper prompted by Tillich's essay, "The Religious Symbol."

11 Aldwinckle, R. F., "Tillich's Theory of Religious Symbolism," Canadian Journal of Theology, vol. 10, no. 2 (April, 1964), pp. 110-117.

12 Allchin, F. R., "Religious Symbols and Indian Thought," Symbols of Power, Hilda Roderick Ellis Davidson. Cambridge, England: D. S. Brewer (for the Folklore Society), 1977, pp. 1-34.

13 Alston, William P., "Tillich on Idolatry," Journal of Religion, vol. 38 (October, 1958), pp. 263-267.

14 Alston, William P., "Tillich's Conception of a Religious Symbol," Symposium on Religious Experience and Truth, New York, New York University Institute of Philosophy, 1960, pp. 12-26.

15 Amelung, E., "Life and Selfhood in Tillich's Theology," Kairos and Logos: Studies in the Roots and Implications of Tillich's Theology, John J. Carey, ed. Cambridge, Massachusetts: North American Paul Tillich Society, 1978.

16 Anderson, Reymond Kemp, "Barth on Tillich: Neo-Gnosticism?" The Christian Century, vol. 87, no. 49 (December 9, 1970), pp. 1477-1481. Recollections revealing what was behind the tension that developed between Barth and Tillich.

17 Anonymous, "A Man of Ultimate Concer," Time, vol. 86 (October 29, 1965), pp. 80-82.

18 Anonymous, "A Theology for Protestants," Time, vol. 73, no. 11 (March 16, 1959).

19 Anonymous, "Between Mountain and Plain," Time, vol. 60 (October 20, 1952), pp. 69-72.

20 Anonymous, "Brain to Science: Theologian Tillich Succumbs," Christian Advocate, vol. 9 (November 4, 1965), p. 23.

21 Anonymous, "Courage to Be," Christian Century, vol. 82 (November 3, 1965), p. 1340.

22 Anonymous, "Great Radical Theologian was Apostle to the Skeptics," Life, vol. 59 (November 5, 1965), p. 40.

23 Anonymous, "Harvard's Theologian," Newsweek, vol. 43 (May 17, 1954), p. 66.

24 Anonymous, "In Memoriam: Paul Tillich," Christ und Sozialist, no. 4 (1965).

25 Anonymous, "Jewish Influences on Contemporary Christian Theology," Cross Currents, vol. 2 (Spring, 1952), pp. 35-42.

26 Anonymous, "The Mind and the Heart," Time, vol. 66 (October 17, 1955), p. 54.

27 Anonymous, "Molder of Modern Theology Is Gone," Christianity Today, vol. 10 (November 19, 1965), pp. 30-31.

28 Anonymous, "Much Church Teaching Irrelevant: Tillich," Christian Advocate, vol. 5 (February 16, 1961), p. 21.

29 Anonymous, "Obituary," Publisher's Weekly, vol. 188 (November 1, 1965), p. 39.

30 Anonymous, "Passionate Protestant," Newsweek, vol. 66 (November 1, 1965), p. 60.

31 Anonymous, "Paul Tillich and Christian Realism," America, vol. 113 (November 6, 1965), p. 514.

32 Anonymous, "Paul Tillich: Lover," Time, vol. 102 (October 8, 1973), pp. 73-74.

33 Anonymous, "Paul Tillich: Lutheran and Catholic," Dialogue, vol. 5 (Winter, 1966), pp. 6-7.

34 Anonymous, "Portrait of Paul Tillich," Saturday Night, vol. 83 (May, 1968), p. 27.

35 Anonymous, "A Protestant Message," Newsweek, vol. 45 (May 2, 1955), pp. 89-90.

36 Anonymous, "Tillich on Revivalism," Christian Century, vol. 74, no. 19 (May 8, 1957), pp. 582-583.

37 Anonymous, "Tillich, Paul," Life, vol. 39 (December 26, 1955), p. 141.

38 Anonymous, "Tillich, Paul," Time, vol. 67 (June 11, 1956), p. 67.

39 Anonymous, "Tillich, Paul," Newsweek, vol. 49 (January 14, 1957), p. 74.

40 Anonymous, "Tillich's Lost Dimension," Catholic World, vol. 187 (August, 1958), pp. 324-325.

41 Anonymous, "Tillich's 79-Year Quest," Christianity Today, vol. 10 (November 19, 1965), p. 46.

42 Anonymous, "Tillich to Chicago," Christian Century, vol. 79 (July 4, 1962), p. 832.

43 Anonymous, "Tillich to Join Harvard," Christian Century, vol. 71 (May 12, 1954), p. 574.

44 Anonymous, "To Be or Not to Be," Time, vol. 73 (March 16, 1959), pp. 46-48.

45 Anonymous, "TV Theology," Time, vol. 67 (January 9, 1956), p. 40.

46 Anonymous, "Westward Ho!" Newsweek, vol. 59 (June 25, 1962), p. 82.

47 Ariga, Tetsutaro, "A Christian-Buddhist Encounter," Frontier (London), vol. 4 (1961), pp. 50-54.

48 Arnett, William Melvin, "Existentialism in the Thought of Bultmann and Tillich," Asbury Seminarian, vol. 20 (June, 1966), pp. 28-39.

49 Arnett, William Melvin, "Tillich's Doctrine of God," Asbury Seminarian, vol. 13 (Spring, 1959), pp. 10-17.

50 Aubrey, Edwin E., "Letter to the Editor," Journal of Liberal Religion, vol. 2 (Spring, 1941), pp. 201-202.

51 Ayers, R. H., "Biblical Criticism and Faith in Tillich and Niebuhr," Journal of Bible and Religion, vol. 31 (October, 1963), pp. 311-319.

52 Ayers, R. H., "Myth in Theological Discourse: A Profusion of Confusion," Anglican Theological Review, vol. 48 (April, 1966), pp. 200-217.

53 Bagnell, Kenneth, "Paul Tillich: Dangerous Theologian?" The Observer (Toronto), November 1, 1965, pp. 24-26.

54 Baldridge, William E. and Gleason, John J., "A Theological Framework for Pastoral Care," Journal of Pastoral Care, vol. 32, no. 4 (1978), pp. 232-238.

55 Barnhart, J., "An Anthropocentric Starting Point," Philosophy Today, vol. 8 (Fall, 1964), pp. 190-196.

56 Barnhouse, D. G., "What About Paul Tillich?" Eternity, vol. 10 (June, 1959), pp. 15-18.

57 Barth, Markus, "On God's Existence," Religious Experience and Truth, Sidney Hook, ed. New York: New York University Press, 1961, pp. 220-224.

58 Basescu, Sabert, "Human Nature and Psychotherapy," Humanitas, vol. 3 (Fall, 1967), pp. 127-138.

59 Beck, Samuel J., "Implications for Ego in Tillich's Ontology of Anxiety," Philosophy and Phenomenological Research, vol. 18 (June, 1958), pp. 451-470.

60 Bense, Walter F., "Tillich's 'Kairos' and Hitler's Seizure of Power: The Tillich-Hirsch Exchange of 1934-1935," Tillich Studies: 1975, John J. Carey, ed. Tallahassee, Florida (Florida State University): The Second North American Consultation on Paul Tillich Studies, 1975, pp. 39-51. A paper prepared for a consultation sponsored by the American Academy of Religion at its meeting in Chicago, October 30-November 2, 1975.

61 Bernard, Johannes, "Deification and Alienation: Non-Biblical Terms in the Light of Biblical Revelation," Studia Biblica 1978, E. Livingstone. Oxford: Sixth International Congress on Biblical Studies, vol. 1 (1979), pp. 27-39.

62 Bertocci, P., "An Impasse in Philosophical Theology," International Philosophical Quarterly, vol. 5 (Spring, 1965), pp. 379-396.

63 Beyer, C. W., "Creation and Fall in Tillich's Ontology (Reply to Scharlemann)," Dialog, vol. 4 (Winter, 1965), pp. 62-65.

64 Bird, Michael, "Film as Heirophany," Horizons, vol. 6 (Spring, 1979), pp. 81-97.

65 Blanshard, Brand, "Symbolism," Religious Experience and Truth, Sidney Hook, ed. New York: New York University Press, 1961, pp. 48-55. A paper prompted by Tillich's essay, "The Religious Symbol."

66 Bloy, M. B., "Counterculture and Academic Reform," Christianity and Crisis, vol. 30, no. 7 (April 27, 1970), pp. 85-90.

67 Boas, George, "Being and Existence," Journal of Philosophy, vol. 53 (November, 1956), pp. 748-758.

68 Bochenski, J. M., "Some Problems for a Philosophy of Religion," Religious Experience and Truth, Sidney Hook, ed. New York: New York University Press, 1961, pp. 39-48. A paper prompted by Tillich's essay, "The Religious Symbol."

69 Bokser, Ben Z., "Atheism as a Religious Phenomenon," Perspectives on Jews and Judaism: Essays in Honor of Wolfe Kelman, Arthur A. Chiel. New York: Rabinical Assembly, 1978, pp. 25-29.

70 Boozer, J. S., "Religion and Culture: An Essay on Essays in Appreciation of Paul Tillich," Journal of Bible and Religion, vol. 28 (April, 1960), pp. 229-239.

71   Bowker, John W., "Can Differences Make a Difference? A
     Comment on Tillich's Proposals for Dialogue Between Reli-
     gions," Journal of Theological Studies, vol. 24 (April, 1973),
     pp. 158-188.

72   Bowman, L., "Living on the Boundary," Presbyterian Life,
     September 1, 1966, p. 17.

73   Boyd, Malcolm, "Point of Contact: A Doctrinal Examination of
     Revelation," Anglican Theological Review, vol. 39 (January,
     1957), pp. 70-81.

74   Braaten, Carl E., "Paul Tillich as a Lutheran Theologian,"
     The Chicago Lutheran Theological Seminary Record, vol. 67
     (August, 1962).

75   Braaten, Leif J., "Tillich and the Art of Healing: A Thera-
     pist's View," Journal of Existential Psychiatry, vol. 4, no. 13
     (Summer, 1963), pp. 3-14.

76   Brauer, Jerald C., "Preface (Paul Tillich in Memoriam)," The
     Journal of Religion, vol. 46, no. 1, part 2 (January, 1966),
     pp. 89-91.

77   Brauer, Jerald C., "Paul Tillich's Impact on America," The
     Future of Religions, Paul Tillich. New York: Harper and
     Row, 1966, pp. 15-22.

78   Brauer, Jerald C., "Tribute (to Paul Tillich)," Criterion,
     vol. 5, no. 1 (1966).

79   Brown, R. M., "Lenten Troika: Off-Beat Devotional Reading,"
     Christianity and Crisis, vol. 37 (March 7, 1977), pp. 42-44.

80   Brown, R. M., "Paul Tillich," Commonweal, vol. 83 (January
     21, 1966), pp. 471-473.

81   Browning, Don, "Analogy, Symbol, and Pastoral Theology in
     Tillich's Thought," Pastoral Psychology, vol. 19, no. 181
     (February, 1968), pp. 41-54.

82   Bryant, R. H., "An Evaluation of the Christological Dimen-
     sions of Tillich's Theology of Culture," Kairos and Logos:
     Studies in the Roots and Implications of Tillich's Theology,
     John J. Carey, ed. Cambridge, Massachusetts: North Amer-
     ican Paul Tillich Society, 1978.

83   Bulman, R. F., "Theonomy and Technology," Kairos and Lo-
     gos: Studies in the Roots and Implications of Tillich's Theol-
     ogy, John J. Carey, ed. Cambridge, Massachusetts: North
     American Paul Tillich Society, 1978.

84   Burkle, Horst, "Paul Tillich," Theologians of Our Time,

Leonhard Reinisch, ed. Notre Dame, Indiana: University of Notre Dame Press, 1964, pp. 65-77.

85 Burkle, Horst, "Paul Tillich: An Ecumenical Theologian," African Ecclesiastical Review (Nairobi), April, 1967, pp. 114-123.

86 Burkle, Howard R., "Tillich's 'Dynamic-Typological' Approach to the History of Religions," Journal of the American Academy of Religion, vol. 49, no. 2 (June, 1981), pp. 175-185.

87 Burnaby, John, "Towards Understanding Paul Tillich," Journal of Theological Studies (new series), vol. 5 (October, 1954), pp. 195-205.

88 Burns, Patrick J., "Apologetic of Liberation and Fulfillment," International Catholic Review: Communio, vol. 2 (Winter, 1975), pp. 323-342.

89 Burrill, Donald R., "The Meaning of Religious Symbols: Paul Tillich and His Critics," Personalist, vol. 54 (Summer, 1973), pp. 274-282.

90 Buschmann, Harold, "Contemporary Thought Around the World XIV: Paul Tillich," The Christian Leader, vol. 9 (December, 1933), pp. 1553-1556.

91 Buschmann, Harold, "Paul Tillich and American Humanism," The New Humanist, vol. 6 (November-December, 1933), pp. 13-21.

92 Cairns, Grace E., "The New Being," Main Currents in Modern Thought, vol. 19 (March-April, 1963), pp. 90-94.

93 Calvert, D. G. A., "Paul Tillich and Biblical Theology," Scottish Journal of Theology, vol. 29, no. 6 (1976), pp. 517-534.

94 Cameron, Bruce J. R., "Hegelian Christology of Paul Tillich," Scottish Journal of Theology, vol. 29, no. 1 (1976), pp. 27-48.

95 Cameron, Bruce J. R., "Historical Problem in Paul Tillich's Christology," Scottish Journal of Theology, vol. 18, no. 3 (September, 1965), pp. 257-272.

96 Campbell, T. C., "Theology of Social Change," Review and Expositor, vol. 68 (Summer, 1971), pp. 317-325.

97 Carey, John J., "Life on The Boundary: The Paradoxical Models of Tillich and Pike," Duke Divinity Review, vol. 42 (Fall, 1977), pp. 149-164.

98 Carey, John J., "Morality and Beyond: Tillich's Ethics in Life and Death," Tillich Studies: 1975, John J. Carey, ed. Talla-

hassee, Florida: (Florida State University), The Second North
American Consultation on Paul Tillich Studies, 1975, pp. 104-
115. A paper prepared for a consultation sponsored by the
American Academy of Religion at its meeting in Chicago, October 30-November 2, 1975.

99 Carey, John J., "Theological Relevance of the Early Tillich,"
Religion in the Life, vol. 41 (Summer, 1972), pp. 186-195.

100 Carey, John J., "Tillich Archives: A Bibliographical and Research Report," Theology Today, vol. 32 (April, 1975), pp.
46-55.

101 Case, Shirley Jackson, "The Christian Philosophy of History,"
Chicago (University of Chicago Press), 1943, pp. 104-107.

102 Casserley, J. W. L., "Event-Symbols and Myth-Symbols,"
Cross Currents, vol. 8, no. 4 (1958), pp. 315-326.

103 Cauthen, W. K., "Biblical Truths and Rational Knowledge,"
Review and Expositor, vol. 53 (October, 1956), pp. 467-476.

104 Cell, Edward, "A Tillichian Analysis of 'God Acts in History,'" Language, Existence, and God: Interpretations of
Moore, Russell, Ayer, Wittgenstein, Wisdom, Oxford Philosophy, and Tillich, Edward Cell. Nashville: Abingdon Press,
1971, pp. 337-382.

105 Chapey, F., "The Principle of Correlation in the Theology of
Paul Tillich," Theological Digest, vol. 20 (Spring, 1972), pp.
58-66.

106 Cherbonnier, E., "Biblical Metaphysics and Christian Philosophy," Theology Today, vol. 9 (October, 1952), pp. 360-375.

107 Cherbonnier, E., "Jerusalem and Athens," Anglican Theological Review, vol. 36 (October, 1954), pp. 251-271.

108 Cherbonnier, E., "Mystical Versus Biblical Symbolism,"
Christian Scholar, vol. 39 (March, 1956), pp. 32-44.

109 Cherbonnier, E., "The Theology of the Word of God," Journal of Religion, vol. 33 (January, 1953), pp. 16-30.

110 Chiles, Robert E., ed., "Glossary of Tillich Terms," Theology Today, vol. 17, no. 1 (April, 1960), pp. 77-89.

111 Christian, C. W., "The Significance of Paul Tillich for Today," Catalyst, vol. 8, no. 4 (April, 1976).

112 Clark, W. R., "Christian Images of Fulfillment: Healing
Within Anticipation," Religion in Life, vol. 46 (Summer,
1977), pp. 186-197.

113   Clarke, Bowman L., "God and the Symbolic in Tillich,"
      Anglican Theological Review, vol. 43, no. 3 (July, 1961),
      pp. 302-311.

114   Clarke, Bowman L., "Religion and the Human Situation,"
      The Philosophy Forum (DeKalb), vol. 8 (June, 1970), pp.
      3-31.

115   Clarke, W. Norris, "On Professors Ziff, Niebuhr, and Til-
      lich," Religious Experience and Truth: A Symposium, Sidney
      Hook, ed.   New York: New York University Press, 1961, pp.
      224-231.

116   Clayton, John Powell, "Is Jesus Necessary for Christology?
      An Antinomy in Tillich's Theological Method," Christ, Faith,
      and History, Stephen Sykes and John P. Clayton, eds.   New
      York: Cambridge University Press, 1972, pp. 147-162.
      From the Cambridge Studies in Christology.

117   Clayton, John Powell, "Questioning, Answering and Tillich's
      Concept of Correlation," Kairos and Logos: Studies in the
      Roots and Implications of Tillich's Theology, John J. Carey,
      ed.   Cambridge, Massachusetts: North American Paul Til-
      lich Society, 1978.

118   [No entry]

119   Clift, Wallace B., "Tillich and Jung: A New Mythology of
      'Salvation'?" The Iliff Review, vol. 32 (Winter, 1975), pp.
      3-15.

120   Cohen, Robert S., "Contemporary Marxism," Review of Meta-
      physics, vol. 4 (December, 1950), pp. 291-310.

121   Colm, H., "Healing as Participation: Tillich's Therapeutic
      Theology," The Human Dialogue: Perspectives on Communi-
      cation, Floyd W. Matson and Ashley Montagu, eds.   New
      York: The Free Press of Glencoe Inc., 1967, pp. 267-
      284.

122   Comstock, W. Richard, "Two Ontologies of Power: A Com-
      parison of Santayana and Tillich," The Harvard Theological
      Review, vol. 60, no. 1 (January, 1967), pp. 39-67.

123   Cooper, John C., "The Epistemological Order of Value and
      Fact," Ohio Journal of Religious Studies, vol. 5 (April,
      1977), pp. 78-83.   The relation between Aristotle and Tillich
      is addressed in this article.

124   Cooper, John C., "The Eternal and the Present: The Wit-
      ness of Paul Tillich," Resource, vol. 7 (March, 1966), pp.
      31-33.

125 Craighead, Houston, "Paul Tillich's Argument for God's Reality," Thomist, vol. 39 (April, 1975), pp. 309-318.

126 Cranston, M., "Teilhard and Tillich," Encounter, vol. 29 (December, 1967), pp. 83-86. Review article.

127 Crean, Hugh F., "Faith and Doubt in the Theology of Paul Tillich," Sylloge Excerptorum E Dissertationibus, Edmund J. Dobbin, et al., vol. 48 (1976), pp. 145-164.

128 Cross, Wilford O., "Some Notes on the Ontology of Paul Tillich," Anglican Theological Review, vol. 39, no. 1 (October, 1957), pp. 297-311.

129 Curtis, C. J., "Existentialist Theology: Tillich and Bultmann," Contemporary Protestant Thought, C. J. Curtis, ed. Beverly Hills, California: Benziger, Bruce and Glencoe, 1970, pp. 150-165. Contemporary Theology Series.

130 Cushman, Robert E., "The Christology of Paul Tillich," The Heritage of Christian Thought, Robert E. Cushman and Egil Grislis, eds. New York: Harper and Row, 1965, pp. 166-181.

131 Dalles, A. R., "Paul Tillich and the Bible," Theological Studies, vol. 17 (September, 1956), pp. 345-367.

132 Danto, Arthur C., "Faith, Language, and Religious Experience: A Dialogue," Religious Experience and Truth, Sidney Hook, ed. New York: New York University Press, 1961, pp. 137-150.

133 D'Arcy, M. C., "A Protestant 'Summa Theologica,'" Month, vol. 10 (November, 1953), pp. 270-281.

134 Daubney, R. H., "A Preface to Paul Tillich," Church Quarterly Review, vol. 150, no. 150 (April-June, 1950), pp. 1-36.

135 Daubney, R. H., "Some Notes on the Work of Paul Tillich," Christendom, vol. 14 (June, 1949), pp. 61-65.

136 Daubney, R. H., "Some Structural Concepts in Tillich's Thought and the Pattern of the Liturgy," The Theology of Paul Tillich, Charles W. Kegley and Robert W. Bretall, eds. New York: The Macmillan Company, 1964, pp. 268-294.

137 Davies, Alan T., "Paul Tillich on Judaism and Martin Buber on Christianity," Studies in Religion, Sciences Religieuses, vol. 5, no. 1 (1975-76), pp. 66-74.

138 Davis, J., "Tillich: Accurate Aims, Alien Assumptions," Christianity Today, vol. 20 (August 27, 1976), pp. 6-8.

104 / Paul Tillich

139   Dayton, W. T., "Tillich and the New Being," Asbury Seminarian, vol. 13 (Spring, 1959), pp. 27-33.

140   Dean, W. D., "The Universal and the Particular in the Theology of Paul Tillich," Encounter, vol. 32 (Autumn, 1971), pp. 278-285.

141   Demos, Raphael, "Religious Faith and Scientific Faith," Religious Experience and Truth, Sidney Hook, ed. New York: New York University Press, 1961, pp. 130-137.

142   Demos, Raphael, "Religious Symbols and/or Religious Beliefs," Religious Experience and Truth, Sidney Hook, ed. New York: New York University Press, 1961, pp. 55-59. A paper prompted by Tillich's essay, "The Religious Symbol."

143   Demos, Raphael, "Reply to Mr. H. M. Tiebout, Jr's. 'Demos on Tillich,'" Philosophy and Phenomenological Research, vol. 20 (September, 1959), pp. 113-115.

144   Demos, Raphael, "Tillich's Philosophical Theology," Philosophical and Phenomenological Research, vol. 19 (September, 1958), pp. 74-85.

145   Detweiler, Robert, "Langer and Tillich: Two Backgrounds of Symbolic Thought," The Personalist, vol. 46 (Spring-April, 1965), pp. 171-192.

146   Deugd, Cornelius de, "Old Wine in New Bottles? Tillich and Spinoza," Talk of God, Royal Institute of Philosophy. New York: St. Martin's Press, 1969, pp. 133-151. From the Royal Institute of Philosophy Lectures, vol. 2, 1967-1968.

147   Dicken, Thomas M., "Biblical Picture of Jesus as the Christ in Tillich's Theology," Journal of Religious Thought, vol. 25, no. 1 (1968-1969), pp. 27-41.

148   Dillenberger, John, "Paul Tillich: Theologian of Culture," Paul Tillich: Retrospect and Future, T. A. Kantonen, ed. Nashville: Abingdon, 1966, pp. 31-41.

149   Dillenberger, John, "Paul Tillich: Theologian of Culture," Religion in Life, vol. 35 (Winter, 1967), pp. 686-696.

150   Dillenberger, John, "Tillich's Use of the Concept 'Being,'" Christianity and Crisis, vol. 13, no. 4 (1953), pp. 30-31.

151   Diogenes, "Wake Up and Dream," Time and Tide, vol. 38 (1957), p. 959.

152   Dixon, John, Jr., "Is Tragedy Essential to Knowing? A Critique of Dr. Tillich's Aesthetics," Journal of Religion, vol. 43 (October, 1963), pp. 271-284.

153 Dobsevage, A. P., "Existential Values Are Humanistic, and Moral Too," Philosophy and Phenomenological Research, vol. 23 (June, 1963), pp. 610-615.

154 Dourley, John P., "God, Life and the Trinity in the Theologies of Paul Tillich and St. Bonaventure," St. Bonaventura 1274-1974, W. Dettloff, et al., 1974, pp. 271-282.

155 Dourley, John P., "Jung, Tillich, and Aspects of the Western Christian Development," Thought, vol. 52 (March, 1977), pp. 18-49.

156 Dourley, John P., "Tillich's Evaluation of the Development of Western Christian Thought: Ontologism or Schizophrenia," Tillich Studies: 1975, John J. Carey, ed. Tallahassee, Florida: (Florida State University), The Second North American Consultation on Paul Tillich Studies, 1975, pp. 2-14. A paper prepared for a consultation sponsored by the American Academy of Religion at its meeting in Chicago, October 30-November 2, 1975.

157 Dourley, John P., "Trinitarian Models and Human Integration: Jung and Tillich Compared," Journal of Analytical Psychology, vol. 19, no. 2 (1974), pp. 131f.

158 Dowey, Edward A., Jr., "Tillich, Barth, and the Criteria of Theology," Theology Today, vol. 15, no. 1 (April, 1958), pp. 43-58.

159 Dreisbach, Donald F., "Essence, Existence, and the Fall: Paul Tillich's Analysis of Existence," The Harvard Theological Review, vol. 73 (July-December, 1980), pp. 521-538.

160 Dreisbach, Donald F., "Paul Tillich's Doctrine of Religious Symbols," Encounter, vol. 37 (Autumn, 1976), pp. 326-343.

161 Dreisbach, Donald F., "Paul Tillich's Hermeneutic," Journal of the American Academy of Religion, vol. 43, no. 1 (March, 1975), pp. 84-94.

162 Dreisbach, Donald F., "The Unity of Paul Tillich's Existential Analysis," Encounter, vol. 41 (Autumn, 1980), pp. 365-380.

163 Driver, Tom Faw, "Form and Energy: An Argument with Paul Tillich," Union Seminary Quarterly Review, vol. 31 (Winter, 1976), pp. 102-112.

164 Driver, Tom Faw, "A Legacy of Paul Johannes Tillich," ARC Directions, New York, June, 1966, pp. 1-2.

165 Driver, Tom Faw, "Paul Tillich, 1886-1965," Christianity and Crisis, vol. 25 (November 29, 1965), pp. 252-253.

166 Dulles, Avery R., "Paul Tillich and the Bible," Theological Studies, vol. 17 (1956), pp. 345-367. Included in Paul Tillich in Catholic Thought, edited by Thomas F. O'Meara and Donald M. Weisser (Doubleday & Company, Inc., 1969).

167 Durfee, Harold A., "The Reformulation of the Question as to the Existence of God," Philosophy and Phenomenological Research, vol. 28, no. 3 (March, 1968), pp. 385-391.

168 Edwards, Paul, "Professor Tillich's Confusions," Mind, vol. 74 (April, 1965), pp. 192-214.

169 Edwards, Paul, "Some Notes on Anthropomorphic Theology," Religious Experience and Truth, Sidney Hook, ed. New York: New York University Press, 1961, pp. 241-251.

170 Edwards, Paul, "Tillich, Paul," The Encyclopedia of Philosophy. New York: The Macmillan Company, vol. 8 (1967).

171 Ehrlich, L. H., "Tillich's 'Symbol,' vis-à-vis Jaspers' 'Cipher,'" Harvard Theological Review, vol. 66 (January, 1973), pp. 153-156.

172 Eliade, Mircea, "Paul Tillich and the History of Religions," The Future of Religions, Paul Tillich. New York: Harper and Row, 1966, pp. 31-36.

173 Eliade, Mircea, "Tribute To Paul Tillich," Criterion, vol. 5, no. 1 (1966).

174 Emmet, Dorothy M., "Ambiguities in the Concept of God," Religious Experience and Truth, Sidney Hook, ed. New York: New York University Press, 1961, pp. 251-254.

175 Emmet, Dorothy M., "Epistemology and the Idea of Revelation," The Theology of Paul Tillich, Charles W. Kegley and Robert W. Bretall. New York: The Macmillan Company, 1964, pp. 198-216.

176 Emmet, Dorothy M., "The Ground of Being," Journal of Theological Studies (new series), vol. 15 (October, 1964), pp. 280-292.

177 Enquist, Roy J., "A Tillichian Analysis of Afrikanerdom," Dialog, vol. 18 (Spring, 1959), pp. 125-131.

178 Enquist, Roy J., "Utopia and the Search for a Godly Future," Dialog, vol. 19 (Spring, 1980), pp. 131-140.

179 Erikson, Erik, Tribute (to Paul Tillich)," Prospect (Harvard Divinity School), vol. 5, no. 7 (November 4, 1965).

180 Ettinger, Ronald F., and Walker, C. Eugene, "Behaviorism

and Existentialism: Views of Skinner and Tillich," Journal of Religion and Health, vol. 5, no. 2 (April, 1966), pp. 151-157.

181 Fagre, Ivan B., "Revelation in the Thought of Paul Tillich: A Study of Tillich's Concept of Revelation in Volume I of His Systematic Theology," Theological Journal of Japan Lutheran Theological College, no. 2 (1967), pp. 44-70.

182 Fancher, Robert, "Whitehead and The Courage to Be," Encounter, vol. 38 (Autumn, 1977), pp. 347-361.

183 Feldstein, Grace Cali, "Paul Tillich and My Religious Search," World Order (Wilmette, Illinois), vol. 5 (Summer, 1971), pp. 5-13.

184 Fenton, John Y., "Being-Itself and Religious Symbolism," Journal of Religion, vol. 45, no. 2 (April, 1965), pp. 73-86.

185 Fenton, John Y., "Faith and Facts," Journal of Religious Thought, vol. 23, no. 2 (1966-1967), pp. 105-118.

186 Ferre, Nels F. S., "Contemporary Theology in the Light of 100 Years," Theology Today, vol. 15 (October, 1958), pp. 366-376.

187 Ferre, Nels F. S., "Fabric of Paul Tillich's Theology," Scottish Journal of Theology, vol. 21 (June, 1968), pp. 157-169.

188 Ferre, Nels F. S., "Honest to God," Expository Times, vol. 74 (July, 1963), pp. 308-309. Reply to C. L. Mitton.

189 Ferre, Nels F. S., "Place and Power of Existentialism and Neo-naturalism," Moravian Theological Seminary Bulletin, 1959, pp. 49-64.

190 Ferre, Nels F. S., "Tillich and the Nature of Transcendence," Religion in Life, vol. 35 (Winter, 1966), pp. 662-673. Included in Paul Tillich: Retrospect and Future, edited by T. A. Kantonen (Abingdon Press, 1966), pp. 7-18.

191 Ferre, Nels F. S., "The Theological Doctrine of Man," Religion in Life, vol. 11, no. 4 (1942), pp. 571-583.

192 Ferre, Nels F. S., "Three Critical Issues in Tillich's Philosophical Theology," Scottish Journal of Theology, vol. 10 (September, 1957), pp. 223-258.

193 Ferre, Nels F. S., "Tillich's View of the Church," The Theology of Paul Tillich, Charles W. Kegley and Robert W. Bretall, eds. New York: The Macmillan Company, 1964, pp. 248-268.

194   Fisher, James V., "The Politicizing of Paul Tillich: The
       First Phase," Tillich Studies: 1975, John J. Carey, ed.
       Tallahassee, Florida: (Florida State University), The Second
       North American Consultation on Paul Tillich Studies, 1975,
       pp. 27-39.   A paper prepared for a consultation sponsored by
       the American Academy of Religion at its meeting in Chicago,
       October 30-November 2, 1975.

195   Fisher, James V., "Tillich's Early Use of 'Gestalt' and Its
       Implications for the Meaning of 'Meaning,'" Philosophy of Re-
       ligion and Theology: 1976 Proceedings, American Academy of
       Religion.   Missoula, Montana: Scholars Press, 1976, pp.
       265-284.

196   Fitch, Robert E., "The Social Philosophy of Paul Tillich,"
       Religion in Life, vol. 27 (Spring, 1958), pp. 247-256.

197   Fitzer, Joseph, "Paul Tillich on Natural Theology," God in
       Contemporary Thought: A Philosophical Perspective, Sebastian
       A. Matczak, ed.   New York: Learned Publications, 1977, pp.
       643-664.

198   Fletcher, Joseph, "Tillich and Ethics: The Negation of Law,"
       Pastoral Psychology, vol. 19, no. 181 (February, 1968), pp.
       33-40.

199   Foley, Grover, E., "Paul Tillich and the Bible," Interpreta-
       tion, vol. 18 (October, 1964), pp. 463-478.

200   Ford, Lewis S., "The Appropriation of Dynamics and Form
       for Tillich's God," Harvard Theological Review, vol. 68 (Jan-
       uary, 1975), pp. 35-51.

201   Ford, Lewis S., "The Three Strands of Tillich's Theory of
       Religious Symbols," Journal of Religion, vol. 46, no. 1, part
       2 (January, 1966), pp. 104-130.

202   Ford, Lewis S., "Tillich and Thomas Aquinas: The Analogy
       of Being," The Journal of Religion, vol. 46, no. 2 (April,
       1966), pp. 229-245.

203   Ford, Lewis S., "Tillich's Implicit Natural Theology," Scot-
       tish Journal of Theology, vol. 24 (August, 1971), pp. 257-270.

204   Ford, Lewis S., "Tillich's One Nonsymbolic Statement: A
       Propos of a Recent Study by William Rowe," Journal of the
       American Academy of Religion, vol. 38, no. 2 (June, 1970),
       pp. 176-182.

205   Ford, Lewis S., "Tillich's Tergiversations Toward the Power
       of Being," Scottish Journal of Theology, vol. 28, no. 4
       (1975), pp. 323-340.   Review article.

206 Forstman, H. F., "Paul Tillich and His Critics," Encounter, vol. 25 (Autumn, 1964), pp. 476-481.

207 Foster, Kenelm, "Paul Tillich and St. Thomas," Blackfriars, vol. 41 (September, 1960), pp. 306-313. Included in Paul Tillich in Catholic Thought, edited by Thomas F. O'Meara and Donald M. Weisser (Doubleday & Company, Inc., 1969).

208 Fox, Charles, "Tillich's Advice to Thomists," Listening, vol. 9 (Winter-Spring, 1974), pp. 144-152.

209 Fox, Marvin, "Tillich's Ontology and God," Anglican Theological Review, vol. 43, no. 3 (July, 1961), pp. 260-267.

210 Franklin, Mitchell, "On Hegel's Theory of Alienation and Its Historic Force," Tulane Studies in Philosophy, vol. 9 (1960), pp. 50-100.

211 Freeman, D. H., "Paul Tillich's Doctrine of Revelation," Christianity Today, vol. 2 (July 21, 1958), pp. 12-15.

212 Friedlander, Albert Hoschander, "A Final Conversation with Paul Tillich," The Reconstructionist, vol. 31, no. 14 (November 12, 1965).

213 Friedman, Lawrence, "Psychoanalysis, Existentialism, and the Esthetic Universe," Journal of Philosophy, vol. 55 (July, 1958), pp. 617-630.

214 Furuya, Yasuo Carl, "Apologetic or Kerygmatic Theology," Theology Today, vol. 16, no. 4 (January, 1960), pp. 471-480.

215 Garnett, A. Campbell, "Is Modern Theology Atheistic?" Christian Century, vol. 78 (May 31, 1961), pp. 680-682.

216 Gaughan, James, "An Ecumenical Philosopher of Religious Experience: Paul Tillich," Philosophy Today, vol. 18 (Winter, 1974), pp. 330-337.

217 Giannini, R., "Paul Tillich's Understanding of Mysticism," Cistercian Studies, vol. 10, nos. 3 and 4 (1975), pp. 139-172.

218 Gill, Jerry H., "Paul Tillich's Religious Epistemology," Religious Studies, vol. 3 (April, 1968), pp. 477-498.

219 Godwin, Gene, "Paul Tillich: Boundary-line Theologian," Union Seminary Quarterly Review, vol. 10, no. 4 (May, 1955), pp. 19-25.

220 Goff, Robert Allen, "The Tillichian Symbol: An Essay in Philosophical Methodology," Journal of Existentialism, vol. 6 (Summer, 1966), pp. 439-448.

221 Graber, Glenn, "Metaethics of Paul Tillich," Journal of Religious Ethics, vol. 1 (Fall, 1973), pp. 113-133.

222 Gragg, Alan, "Paul Tillich's Existential Questions and Their Theological Answers: A Compendium," The Journal of Bible and Religion, vol. 34 (January, 1966), pp. 4-17.

223 Grant, F. C., "Paul Tillich," Anglican Theological Review, vol. 43 (July, 1961), pp. 241-244.

224 Gray, Wallace, "Final Appraisal of Paul Tillich (1886-1965) vis-à-vis Nels Ferre (1908-1971), Part One," Communio Viatorum, vol. 19 (1976), pp. 195-216.

225 Gray, Wallace, "Final Appraisal of Paul Tillich (1886-1965) vis-à-vis Nels Ferre (1908-1971), Part Two," Communio Viatorum, vol. 20 (1977), pp. 63-87.

226 Gray, Wallace, "Is God Personal? Some Final Reflections from Tillich on Ferre," Religion in Life, vol. 47, no. 4 (Winter, 1978), pp. 401-414. An imaginary discussion between Tillich and Nels Ferre.

227 Green, William B., "Theologians of Our Time: Paul Tillich," Expository Times, vol. 75 (August, 1964), pp. 324-327.

228 Greene, Theodore M., "Paul Tillich and Our Secular Culture," The Theology of Paul Tillich, Charles W. Kegley and Robert W. Bretall. New York: The Macmillan Company, 1964, pp. 50-68.

229 Greenlaw, W. A., "Second Look at Reinhold Niebuhr's Biblical-Dramatic Worldview," Encounter, vol. 37 (Autumn, 1976), pp. 344-355.

230 Grene, Marjorie G., "The German Existentialists," Chicago Review, vol. 13 (Summer, 1959), pp. 49-58. Included in Philosophy In and Out of Europe, Marjorie Grene. University of California Press, 1976, pp. 71-78.

231 Grounds, Vernon C., "Pacesetters for the Radical Theologians of the 60's and 70's," Journal of the Evangelical Theological Society, vol. 18 (Summer, 1975 and Fall, 1975), pp. 151-171, 255-283. Included in Tensions in Contemporary Theology, edited by S. Gundry and A. Johnson (Moody Press, 1976).

232 Hall, Richard C., "Tillich's Apparent Inconsistency: A Reply to Santoni," Anglican Theological Review, vol. 52 (January, 1970), pp. 52-55.

233 Halsey, B., "Paul Tillich on Religion and Art," Lexington Theological Quarterly, vol. 9 (October, 1974), pp. 100-112.

234 Halverson, William H., "Freedom and the Self," The Journal of Religion, vol. 43, no. 2 (1963), pp. 139-150.

235 Hamilton, Kenneth M., "Homo Religiosus and Historical Faith," Journal of Bible and Religion, vol. 33 (July, 1965), pp. 213-222. Reply by D. L. Miller, vol. 34, October 1966, pp. 305-315.

236 Hamilton, Kenneth M., "New Dogma of Religious Symbolism: A Critique of the Viewpoints of Tillich and Jaspers," Encounter, vol. 25 (Summer, 1964), pp. 368-377.

237 Hamilton, Kenneth M., "On Having Nothing to Worship: The Divine Abyss in Paul Tillich and Richard Rubenstein," God and the Good: Essays in Honor of Henry Stob, Clifton Orlebeke and Lewis Smedes, eds. Grand Rapids: Eerdmans Publishing Company, 1975, pp. 150-164.

238 Hamilton, Kenneth M., "Paul Tillich," Creative Minds in Contemporary Theology: A Guidebook to the Principal Teachings of Karl Barth and Others, Philip Edgcumbe Hughes, ed. Grand Rapids, Michigan: Eerdmanns, 1966, pp. 451-479.

239 Hamilton, Kenneth M., "Paul Tillich and the Idealistic Appraisal of Christianity," Scottish Journal of Theology, vol. 13 (March, 1960), pp. 33-44.

240 Hamilton, Kenneth M., "Tillich's Method of Correlation," Canadian Journal of Theology, vol. 5, no. 2 (April, 1959), pp. 87-95.

241 Hammett, J. Y., "God 'As': Image vs. Idol in Current Liberation Theology," Religion in Life, vol. 45 (Winter, 1976), pp. 403-410.

242 Hammond, Guyton B., "Examination of Tillich's Method of Correlation," Journal of Bible and Religion, vol. 32, no. 3 (July, 1964), pp. 248-251.

243 Hammond, Guyton B., "Paul Tillich's Critique of Humanism," Religious Humanism, vol. 6 (Winter, 1972), pp. 10-14.

244 Hammond, Guyton B., "Paul Tillich's Impact on American Life," Motive, vol. 26 (May, 1966), pp. 26-30.

245 Hammond, Guyton B., "Tillich on the Personal God," Journal of Religion, vol. 44 (October, 1964), pp. 289-293.

246 Haroutunian, Joseph, "The Question Tillich Left Us," Religion in Life, vol. 35 (Winter, 1966), pp. 706-718. Included in Paul Tillich: Retrospect and Future, edited by T. A. Kantonen (Abingdon Press, 1966), pp. 51-63.

247 Harris, Ishwar, "The Dilemma of the Universal and the Particular Nature of Religion," The Journal of Religious Thought, vol. 37 (Summer, 1980), pp. 42-49.

248 Hart, R. L., "Recent Tillichiana: A Review Article," Drew Gateway, vol. 31 (Winter, 1961), pp. 98-106.

249 Hartshorne, Charles, "God's Existence: A Conceptual Problem," Religious Experience and Truth, Sidney Hook, ed. New York: New York University Press, 1961, pp. 211-220.

250 Hartshorne, Charles, "Process as Inclusive Category: A Reply," Journal of Philosophy, vol. 52 (February, 1955), pp. 94-102.

251 Hartshorne, Charles, "Tillich and the Nontheological Meanings of Theological Terms," Religion in Life, vol. 35 (Winter, 1966), pp. 674-685. Included in Paul Tillich: Retrospect and Future, edited by T. A. Kantonen (Abingdon Press, 1966), pp. 19-30.

252 Hartshorne, Charles, "Tillich and the Other Great Tradition," Anglican Theological Review, vol. 43, no. 3 (July, 1961), pp. 245-259.

253 Hartshorne, Charles, "Tillich's Doctrine of God," The Theology of Paul Tillich, Charles W. Kegley and Robert W. Bretall, eds. New York: The Macmillan Company, 1964, pp. 164-198.

254 Hashimoto, Hideo, "Christian Theology and the Challenge of Non-Christian Religions," The Journal of Bible and Religion (Philadelphia), vol. 28, no. 3 (1960), pp. 299-307.

255 Hay, E. R., "Tillich's View of Miracle," The Modern Churchman (new series), vol. 15 (July, 1972), pp. 246-257.

256 Hebblethwaite, Peter, "The Way of the Theologian," Times Literary Supplement, July 15, 1977, p. 876.

257 Hecht, W. H., "Tillich's Non-symbolic Doctrine of God," The Springfielder, vol. 30, no. 3 (Autumn, 1966), pp. 5-18.

258 Hefner, Philip, "The Relocation of the God Question," Lutheran Quarterly, vol. 21 (1969), pp. 329-341.

259 Heinmann, Eduard, "Tillich's Doctrine of Religious Socialism," The Theology of Paul Tillich, Charles W. Kegley and Robert W. Bretall, eds. New York: The Macmillan Company, 1964, pp. 312-329.

260 Hendrix, H., "Ontological Character of Anxiety," Journal of Religion and Health, vol. 6 (January, 1967), pp. 46-65.

261 Henry, C. F. H., "Justification by Ignorance: A Neo-Protestant Motif?" Christianity Today, vol. 14 (January 2, 1970), pp. 10-15.

262 Herberg, Will, "Can Faith and Reason be Reconciled?" New Republic, vol. 133 (October 24, 1955), p. 19.

263 Herberg, Will, "Three Dialogues of Man," New Republic, vol. 132 (May 16, 1955), pp. 30-31.

264 Hess, M. W., "Paul Tillich: Last of the German Idealists," Catholic World, vol. 189 (September, 1959), pp. 421-426.

265 Hick, John, "Meaning and Truth in Theology," Religious Experience and Truth, Sidney Hook, ed. New York: New York University Press, 1961, pp. 203-211.

266 Hick, John, "Some Recapitulation Theories of Immortality," The Visvabharati Journal of Philosophy, vol. 6 (February, 1970), pp. 71-79.

267 Hill, Brennan, "Schleiermacher and Tillich: From Feeling of Absolute Dependence to Ultimate Concern," Discourse (Moorhead, Minnesota), vol. 13 (Autumn, 1970), pp. 453-462.

268 Hill, David, "Paul's Second Adam and Tillich's Christology," Union Seminary Quarterly Review, vol. 21, no. 1 (November, 1965), pp. 13-25. Replies by D. D. Williams, T. F. Driver, and W. D. Davies, pp. 27-34.

269 Hiltner, Seward, "Pastoral Psychology after Paul Tillich," Pastoral Psychology, vol. 19, no. 181 (February, 1968), p. 5. This whole volume is focused on Paul Tillich.

270 Hiltner, Seward, "Paul Tillich and Pastoral Psychology," Pastoral Psychology, vol. 16 (December, 1965), pp. 5-10.

271 Hiltner, Seward, "Tillich and Pastoral Psychology," Pastoral Psychology, vol. 3, no. 29 (1952), pp. 9-10, 66.

272 Hiltner, Seward, "Tillich the Person: A Review Article," Theology Today, vol. 30, no. 4 (January, 1974), pp. 382-388.

273 Hintz, Howard W., "On Defining the Term 'God,'" Religious Experience and Truth, Sidney Hook, ed. New York: New York University Press, 1961, pp. 254-261.

274 Hobart, Charles W. and Warne, Nanci, "On Sources of Alienation," Journal of Existentialism, vol. 5 (Fall, 1964), pp. 183-198.

275 Hoitenga, D., "Tillich's Religious Epistemology," God and the Good: Essays in Honor of Henry Stob, Clifton Orlebeke and

Lewis Smedes, eds. Grand Rapids: Eerdmans Publishing Company, 1975.

276   Holder, Fred L., "Bultmann, Tillich, and Mephistopheles," Encounter, vol. 29, no. 3 (Summer, 1968), pp. 235-245.

277   Holmer, Paul L., "Paul Tillich and the Language About God," Journal of Religious Thought, vol. 22, no. 1 (1965-1966), pp. 35-50.

278   Holmer, Paul L., "Paul Tillich: Language and Meaning," Journal of Religious Thought, vol. 22, no. 2 (1965-1966), pp. 85-106.

279   Holmes, Arthur F., "The Role of Philosophy in Tillich's Theology," Journal of the Evangelical Theological Society, vol. 10, no. 3 (Summer, 1967), pp. 161-171.

280   Homans, Peter, "Protestant Theology and Dynamic Psychology: New Thoughts on an Old Problem," Anglican Theological Review: Supplementary Series, no. 7 (November, 1976), pp. 125-138.

281   Homans, Peter, "Toward a Psychology of Religion: By Way of Freud and Tillich," The Dialogue Between Theology and Psychology, Peter Homans, ed. Chicago: University of Chicago Press, 1968, pp. 53-81. Appears also in Zygon, vol. 2, no. 1, March 1967, pp. 97-119.

282   Homans, Peter, "Transference and Transcendence: Freud and Tillich on the Nature of Personal Relatedness," The Journal of Religion, vol. 46, no. 1, part 2 (January, 1966), pp. 148-164.

283   Hook, Sidney, "The Atheism of Paul Tillich," Institute of Philosophy (New York: New York University), vol. 4 (1960). Included in Religious Experience and Truth, edited by Sidney Hook (New York University Press, 1961), pp. 59-65.

284   Hook, Sidney, "Modern Knowledge and the Idea of God," Commentary (New York), vol. 29, no. 3 (1960), pp. 205-216.

285   Hopkin, C. E., "Basic Principles of Systematic Theology," Anglican Theological Review, vol. 43 (January, 1961), pp. 17-31.

286   Hopper, David H., "Towards Understanding the Thought of Paul Tillich," Princeton Seminary Bulletin, vol. 55 (April, 1962), pp. 36-43.

287   Hordern, William, "Recent Trends in Systematic Theology," Canadian Journal of Theology, vol. 7, no. 2 (1961), pp. 82-90.

288 Hordern, William, "Theology in Prospect," Journal of Bible and Religion, vol. 28 (April, 1960), pp. 222-228.

289 Horne, James R., "Tillich's Rejection of Absolute Mysticism," Journal of Religion, vol. 58 (April, 1978), pp. 130-139.

290 Horton, Walter M., "Tillich's Role in Contemporary Theology," The Theology of Paul Tillich, Charles W. Kegley and Robert W. Bretall, eds. New York: The Macmillan Company, 1964, pp. 26-50.

291 Housley, J., "Paul Tillich and Christian Education," Religious Education, vol. 62 (July-August, 1967), pp. 307-315.

292 Howe, Leroy T., "Is History a Theological Problem?" Journal of Religious Thought, vol. 26, no. 2 (1969), pp. 81-99.

293 Howe, Leroy T., "Tillich on the Trinity," Christian Scholar, vol. 49 (Fall, 1966), pp. 206-213.

294 Hunter, Howard E., "Tillich and Tennant: Two Types of Philosophical Theology," The Crane Review, vol. 1, no. 3 (1959), pp. 100-110.

295 Hutchison, John A., "Some Recent Theology," Review of Metaphysics, vol. 11 (September, 1957), pp. 94-107.

296 Huxtable, John, "Paul Tillich on the Christian Church Today: An Interview," Listener, vol. 66 (December 14, 1961), pp. 1025-1026.

297 Idinopoulos, T. A., "The Theology of Correlation: Paul Tillich," The Erosion of Faith: An Inquiry into the Origins of the Contemporary Crisis in Religious Thought, T. A. Idinopoulos. New York: Quadrangle Books, 1971, pp. 90-121.

298 Inbody, T., "Paul Tillich and Process Theology," Theological Studies, vol. 36 (September, 1975), pp. 472-492.

299 Irwin, I. E. G., "Paul Tillich's Concept of Prayer," Colloquium (The Australian and New Zealand Theological Review), vol. 3, no. 3 (1969), pp. 249-255.

300 Irwin, John E. G., "Psychoanalysis and Christian Thought: In Search of Man Through the 'Gestaltkreis,'" The Drew Gateway, vol. 46, nos. 1-3 (1975-1976), pp. 107-108. A dissertation abstract.

301 James, R. B., "Tillichian Analysis of James Cone's Black Theology," Perspectives in Religious Studies, vol. 1 (Spring, 1974), pp. 15-28.

302 Johnson, Robert Clyde, "The Contextual Approach," Authority

in Protestant Theology, Robert Clyde Johnson. Philadelphia: Westminster Press, 1959, pp. 111-143.

303 Johnson, Robert Clyde, "A Theologian of Synthesis," Theology Today, vol. 15 (April, 1958), pp. 36-42. From a symposium on Tillich's theology.

304 Johnson, W. A., "Tillich's Religious Symbol," Encounter, vol. 23 (Summer, 1962), pp. 325-342.

305 Johnson, W. H., "Tillich's Science of Being," Princeton Seminary Bulletin, vol. 56 (October, 1962), pp. 52-62.

306 Johnson, Wayne G., "Martin Luther's Law-Gospel Distinction and Paul Tillich's Method of Correlation: A Study in Parallels," The Lutheran Quarterly, vol. 23 (August, 1971), pp. 274-288.

307 Jones, W. P., "Art as the Creator of Lived Meaning," Journal of Bible and Religion, vol. 31 (July 1963), pp. 225-232.

308 Kantzer, K. S., "Evangelical Theology and Paul Tillich," Asbury Seminarian, vol. 13 (Spring, 1959), pp. 3-9.

309 Kaufman, Gordon D., "Can a Man Serve Two Masters? ... Philosophy and Theology in the Thought of Tillich," Theology Today, vol. 15 (April, 1958), pp. 59-77.

310 Kaufmann, Walter, "Theology," Self, Religion and Metaphysics: Essays in Memory of James Bissett Pratt, Gerald E. Myers. New York: Macmillan, 1961, pp. 83-109.

311 Keady, Richard E., "Depression, Psychophysiology and Concepts of God," Encounter, vol. 41 (Summer, 1980), pp. 263-277.

312 Keene, J. C., "Existential Theology," Journal of Religious Thought, vol. 10, no. 1 (1952-1953), pp. 56-73.

313 Kegley, Charles W., "Meat of Truth," Saturday Review, vol. 39 (July 30, 1955), p. 19.

314 Kegley, Charles W., "Paul Tillich on the Philosophy of Art," Journal of Aesthetics and Art Criticism, vol. 19 (Winter, 1960), pp. 175-184.

315 Keiper, R. L., "The Passing of a Theologian," Eternity, vol. 17 (January, 1966), p. 30.

316 Kennedy, Gail, "Some Meanings of Faith," Religious Experience and Truth, Sidney Hook, ed. New York: New York University Press, 1961, pp. 109-116.

317 Kennick, William E., "On Proving That God Exists," Religious Experience and Truth, Sidney Hook, ed. New York: New York University Press, 1961, pp. 261-270.

318 Kiesling, Christopher, "A Translation of Tillich's Idea of God," Journal of Ecumenical Studies, vol. 4, no. 4 (Fall, 1967), pp. 700-715.

319 Kiesling, Christopher, "The Life of the New Being," Paul Tillich in Catholic Thought, Thomas F. O'Meara and Donald M. Weisser, eds. Garden City, New York: Doubleday & Company, Inc., 1969, pp. 321-344.

320 Kik, J. M., "The King's Existential Garments ... with Ardent Apologies to Hans Christian Andersen," Christianity Today, vol. 2 (September 29, 1958), pp. 15-16.

321 Killen, R. Allen, "Tillich, The Trinity, and Honest to God," Bulletin of the Evangelical Theological Society, vol. 7, no. 1 (Winter, 1964), pp. 22-27.

322 Kim, Jong-Won, "Paul Tillich and Daisetsu T. Suzuki: A Comparative Study of Their Thoughts on Ethics in Relation to Being," Japan Review, vol. 10, no. 2 (1978), pp. 42-67.

323 King, R. H., "Tillich at New Harmony," Christian Century, vol. 89 (March 1, 1972), pp. 252-253.

324 King, W. L., "Negation as a Religious Category," Journal of Religion, vol. 37 (April, 1957), pp. 111-112.

325 King-Farlow, J., "Miracles: Nowell-Smith's Analysis and Tillich's Phenomenology," International Philosophical Quarterly, vol. 2, no. 2 (May, 1962), pp. 265-294.

326 Kitagawa, J. M., "Theology and the Science of Religion," Anglican Theological Review, vol. 39 (January, 1957), pp. 33-52.

327 Klass, D., "Beneath the Boundary Theme: An Inquiry into Paul Tillich's Autobiography and Theology," Encounter, vol. 34 (Summer, 1973), pp. 222-232.

328 Knudsen, Robert D., "The Ambiguity of Human Autonomy and Freedom in the Thought of Paul Tillich," Philosophical Reform, vol. 34 (1969), pp. 38-51. Appears also in Philosophia Reformata, vol. 37, 1972, pp. 3-25.

329 Kohak, Erazim, "Religious Knowledge and Religious Reality," Philosophical Forum (Boston), vol. 19 (1961-1962), pp. 56-72.

330 Krishna, Daya, "Religious Experience, Language, and Truth,"

Religious Experience and Truth, Sidney Hook, ed. New York: New York University Press, 1961, pp. 231-241.

331 Krueger, Stephen, "Challenge from Paul Tillich--and a Lutheran Response," Currents in Theology and Mission, vol. 4 (June, 1977), pp. 168-174.

332 Kucheman, Clark A., "Morality Versus Economic Science in Religious Socialism," Belief and Ethics: Essays in Ethics, the Human Sciences, and Ministry in Honor of W. Alvin Pitcher, W. Widick Schroeder. Chicago: Center for the Scientific Study of Religion, 1978, pp. 199-216.

333 Kucheman, Clark A., "Professor Tillich: Justice and the Economic Order," The Journal of Religion, vol. 46, no. 1, part 2 (January, 1966), pp. 165-183.

334 Kuhn, H. B., "Anthropology of Paul Tillich," Asbury Seminarian, vol. 13 (Spring, 1959), pp. 18-26.

335 Kuntz, Paul Grimley, "The Sense and Nonsense of Omnipotence," Religious Studies, vol. 3 (April, 1968), pp. 525-538.

336 Lam, Elizabeth P., "Tillich's Reconstruction of the Concept of Ideology," Christianity and Society (New York), vol. 5, no. 5 (1940), pp. 11-15.

337 Langford, J. J., "Tillich on Tradition," Catholic World, vol. 209 (August, 1969), pp. 233-234.

338 Lansing, John W., "A Philosopher and a Theologian Compared: Tillich and Whitehead on God," Philosophy of Religion and Theology: 1976 Proceedings, Peter Slater, compiler. Missoula, Montana: Scholars Press (American Academy of Religion), 1976, pp. 92-103.

339 Lee, John Park, "Paul Tillich at Harvard," Presbyterian Life, vol. 10, no. 24 (1957), pp. 22-23, 35-38.

340 Lehmann, H. T., "Books Beyond Boundaries: Frankfurt Book Trade Annual Fair," Christian Century, vol. 79 (November 14, 1962), pp. 1391-1392.

341 Leibrecht, Walter, "The Life and Mind of Paul Tillich," Religion and Culture: Essays in Honor of Paul Tillich, Walter Leibrecht, ed. New York: Harper & Brothers, 1959, pp. 3-31.

342 Leslie, John, "The Value of Time," American Philosophical Quarterly, vol. 13 (April, 1976), pp. 109-121.

343 Lewis, Douglass, "The Conceptual Structure of Tillich's Method of Correlation," Encounter, vol. 28 (Summer, 1967), pp. 263-274.

344 Lindbeck, G. A., "Natural Law in the Thought of Paul Tillich," Natural Law Forum, vol. 7 (1962), pp. 84-96.

345 Livergood, Norman, "A Critique of Tillich's Theology," The
Crane Review, vol. 4, no. 3 (Spring, 1962), pp. 153-163.

346 Livingston, James C., "Tillich's Christology and Historical
Research," Religion in Life, vol. 35 (Winter, 1966), pp. 697-
705. Included in Paul Tillich: Retrospect and Future, edited
by T. A. Kantonen (Abingdon Press, 1966), pp. 42-50.

347 Loomer, B. M., "Tillich's Theology of Correlation," Journal
of Religion, vol. 36, no. 7 (May, 1956), pp. 150-156.

348 Loomis, E. A., "The Psychiatric Legacy of Paul Tillich,"
The Intellectual Legacy of Paul Tillich, James R. Lyons, ed.
Detroit: Wayne State University Press, 1969.

349 Losee, J. P., "Biblical Religion and Ontology: Has Tillich
Established a Point of Identity?" Journal of Bible and Religion,
vol. 33 (July, 1965), pp. 223-228.

350 Lounibos, John B., "Paul Tillich's Structures of Liberation,"
Tillich Studies: 1975, John J. Carey, ed. Tallahassee,
Florida: (Florida State University), The Second North Amer-
ican Consultation on Paul Tillich Studies, 1975, pp. 63-76. A
paper prepared for a consultation sponsored by the American
Academy of Religion at its meeting in Chicago, October 30-
November 2, 1975.

351 Lukacs, J., "A German Inheritance," Triumph, vol. 9 (June,
1974), pp. 32-34.

352 Mackey, J., "Notes on the Nature and Scope of the Philosophy
of Religion," Philosophical Studies, vol. 14 (1965), pp. 94-118.

353 Madden, Edward H., and Hare, Peter H., "On the Difficulty
of Evading the Problem of Evil," Philosophy and Phenomenological Research, vol. 28, no. 1 (September, 1967), pp. 58-
69.

354 Magmer, James, "Why Protestant Theologians Use Existentialism," Catholic World, vol. 182, no. 1087 (October, 1955),
pp. 19-24.

355 Margolis, Joseph, "Existentialism Reclaimed," The Personalist, vol. 42 (January, 1962), pp. 14-20.

356 Martin, B., "Paul Tillich and Judaism," Judaism, vol. 15
(Spring, 1966), pp. 180-188.

357 Martin, James A., Jr., "St. Thomas and Tillich on the
Names of God," Journal of Religion, vol. 37 (October, 1957),
pp. 253-259.

358   Marty, Martin E., "American Protestant Theology Today,"
       Thought, vol. 41 (June, 1966), pp. 165-180.

359   Marty, Martin E., "Eros and the Theologian," Christian Cen-
       tury, vol. 90 (September 26, 1973), pp. 959f.

360   Mathers, Donald, "Biblical and Systematic Theology," Canadi-
       an Journal of Theology, vol. 5 (1959), pp. 15-24.

361   Matthews, A. W., "Philosophical Concepts and Religious Con-
       cepts: Some Problems Illustrated on St. Aurelius Augustine
       and Professor Paul Tillich," Revue des Etudes Augustiniennes
       (Paris), vol. 17 (1971), pp. 143-154.

362   Matthews, Thomas F., "Tillich on Religious Content in Mod-
       ern Art," College Art Journal, vol. 27 (Fall, 1967), pp. 16-
       19.

363   Maus, Cyrin, "The Possibility of Knowing God Naturally:
       Paul Tillich and Duns Scotus--A Contrast," Scotus Speaks To-
       day, P. Ramstetter, et al., Southfield, Michigan: Duns Scotus
       College, 1968, pp. 270-289. This material was drawn from a
       seventh centenary symposium at Duns Scotus College on April
       21-23, 1966.

364   May, Rollo, "Memorial Talk at the Interment of Paul Tillich,"
       Review of Existential Psychology and Psychiatry, vol. 5, no.
       3 (Fall, 1965).

365   May, Rollo, "Paul Tillich: In Memoriam," Pastoral Psychol-
       ogy, vol. 19, no. 181 (February, 1968), pp. 7-10.

366   Mays, M. J., "The Language of Faith," Brethren Life and
       Thought, vol. 5 (Summer, 1960), pp. 5-12.

367   McChesney, Donald, "Tillich and His Critics," Month, vol. 38
       (September, 1967), pp. 137-145.

368   McClendon, James W., "Tillich: The Boundary Theologian,"
       The Baptist Student, vol. 39, no. 6 (March, 1960), pp. 38-41.

369   McCollough, T. E., "Ontology of Tillich and Biblical Person-
       alism," Scottish Journal of Theology, vol. 15 (September,
       1962), pp. 266-281.

370   McDonald, H. D., "Symbolic Theology of Paul Tillich," Scot-
       tish Journal of Theology, vol. 17, (December, 1964), pp. 414-
       430.

371   McEachran, F., "The Theological Debate: The Ideas Behind
       'Honest to God,'" The Hibbert Journal, vol. 62 (Summer,
       1964), pp. 165-169.

372 McKelway, Alexander J., "New Perspectives on Paul Tillich,"
Perspectives in Religious Studies, vol. 4 (Summer, 1977), pp.
174-186.

373 McKirachan, J. F., "The Preaching of Paul Tillich," Princeton Seminary Bulletin, vol. 53, no. 3 (January, 1960), pp.
33-42.

374 McLean, George Francis, "Paul Tillich: Philosopher of Contemporary Protestantism," Twentieth-Century Thinkers: Studies in the Work of Seventeen Modern Philosophers, John Kenneth Ryan, ed. New York: Alba House, 1965, pp. 385-399.

375 McLean, George Francis, "Paul Tillich's Existential Philosophy of Protestantism," Thomist, vol. 28 (January, 1964), pp.
1-50. Included in Paul Tillich in Catholic Thought, edited by
Thomas F. O'Meara and Donald M. Weisser (Doubleday &
Company, Inc., 1969).

376 McLean, George Francis, "Symbol and Analogy: Tillich and
Thomas," Revue de l'Université d'Ottawa, vol. 28 (October-
December, 1958), pp. 193-233. Included in Paul Tillich in
Catholic Thought, edited by Thomas F. O'Meara and Donald
M. Weisser (Doubleday & Company, Inc., 1969).

377 Mehta, V., "Profiles: Concerning 'Honest to God' by J.
Robinson," New Yorker, vol. 41 (November 13, 1965), p. 64.

378 Meitzen, Manfred Otto, "From the Editor's Corner," Rocky
Mountain Review (Billings, Montana), vol. 3 (1966), pp. 4-6.

379 Meland, Bernard E., "Prolegomena to Inquiry into the Reality
of God," American Journal of Theology and Philosophy, vol.
1, no. 3 (1980), pp. 71-82.

380 Meland, Bernard E., "The Significance of Paul Tillich," The
Christian Register, vol. 112, no. 48 (1933), p. 797.

381 Merritt, D. R., "Tillich's Method of Correlation," Reformed
Theological Review, vol. 21 (October, 1962), pp. 65-75.

382 Meserve, H. C., "Buber, Schweitzer, Tillich: Editorial,"
Journal of Religion and Health, vol. 5 (January, 1966), pp.
3-6.

383 Mews, S., "Paul Tillich and the Religious Situation of American Intellectuals," Religion: A Journal of Religion and Religions, vol. 2 (Autumn, 1972), pp. 122-140.

384 Meynell, Hugo, "Tillich's Theological Method," The New Theology and Modern Theologians, Hugo Meynell. London/Mel-
bourne: Sheed and Ward, 1967, pp. 137-156.

385 Midgley, Louis Casper, "Paul Tillich's New Science of Values," Western Political Quarterly, vol. 15, no. 2 (June, 1962), pp. 235-253.

386 Midgley, Louis Casper, "Religion and Ultimate Concern: An Encounter with Paul Tillich's Theology," Dialogue: A Journal of Mormon Thought, vol. 1, no. 2 (1966), pp. 55-71.

387 Midgley, Louis Casper, "Ultimate Concern and Politics: A Critical Examination of Paul Tillich's Political Theology," Western Political Quarterly, vol. 20, no. 1 (March, 1967), pp. 31-50.

388 Migliore, Daniel L., "How Historical Is the Resurrection: A Dialogue," Theology Today, vol. 33 (April, 1976), pp. 5-14.

389 Miller, Allen O., and Arther, Donald E., "Paul Tillich's Systematic Theology: A Philosophical Analysis of Being Human (essence, existence, life/history, ... questions arising out of living on the boundary) in Correlation with an Apologetic Theology of the Divine Life (God-Christ, Spirit/Kingdom of God, ... answers derived from the Christian revelation)," The Journal of Ecumenical Studies, vol. 12, no. 1 (Winter, 1975). Also appears as a book published by Eden Publishing House, St. Louis, 1975.

390 Misra, R. S., "The Concept of Reason in the Systematic Theology of Paul Tillich," Religion and Society (Bangalore, India), vol. 13, no. 2 (1966), pp. 15-33.

391 Mitchell, Kenneth R., "Paul Tillich's Contributions to Pastoral Care and Counseling," Pastoral Psychology, vol. 19, no. 181 (February, 1968), p. 24.

392 Mollegen, A. T., "Christology and Biblical Criticism in Tillich," The Theology of Paul Tillich, Charles W. Kegley and Robert W. Bretall. New York: The Macmillan Company, 1964, pp. 230-248.

393 Mondin, Battista, "Tillich's Doctrine of Religious Symbolism," The Principles of Analogy in Protestant and Catholic Theology, Battista Mondin. The Hague: Martinus Nijhoff, 1968.

394 Montgomery, John Warwick, "Tillich's Philosophy of History: The Bearing of His Historical Understanding on His Theological Commitment," The Lutheran Scholar, vol. 25, no. 1 (1968), pp. 8-22. Also appears in The Gordon Review, vol. 10, no. 3, Summer, 1967, pp. 130-149.

395 Morgan, John H., "The Concept of Meaning in Religion and Culture: A Dialogue Between Theology and Anthropology," Understanding Religion and Culture: Anthropological and Theological Perspectives, John H. Morgan, ed. Washington, D.C.: University Press of America, 1979, pp. 87-140.

396 Morgan, John H., "Religion and Culture as Meaning Systems: A Dialogue Between Geertz and Tillich," Journal of Religion, vol. 57 (October, 1977), pp. 363-375.

397 Morris, J. S., "The Philosophical Basis of Tillich's Apologetic Theology," Christian Scholar, vol. 47 (Fall, 1964), pp. 233-242.

398 Morrison, Roy D., "Tillich and the Space-Time Conflicts," Scottish Journal of Theology, vol. 26 (August, 1973), pp. 312-326.

399 Morrison, Roy D., II, "Tillich's Appropriation of Jacob Boehme," Tillich Studies: 1975, John J. Carey, ed. Tallahassee, Florida: (Florida State University), The Second North American Consultation on Paul Tillich Studies, 1975, pp. 14-27. A paper prepared for a consultation sponsored by the American Academy of Religion at its meeting in Chicago, October 30-November 2, 1975.

400 Morrison, Roy D., "Tillich's Telescoping of Ontology and Naturalism," Kairos and Logos: Studies in the Roots and Implications of Tillich's Theology, John J. Carey, ed. Cambridge, Massachusetts: North American Paul Tillich Society, 1978.

401 Muilenburg, J., "A Man for Our Season," Convenant Companion, May 20, 1966, p. 12.

402 Muilenburg, J., "A Neighbor Remembers Tillich," United Church Herald, March 1, 1966, p. 19.

403 Myers, E., "The Gospel According to Tillich," Priest, vol. 24 (March, 1968), pp. 187-194.

404 Nakhnikian, George, "On the Cognitive Import of Certain Consciousness States," Religious Experience and Truth, Sidney Hook, ed. New York: New York University Press, 1961, pp. 156-165.

405 Nelson, John Wiley, "Inquiry into the Methodological Structure of Paul Tillich's 'Systematic Theology,'" Encounter, vol. 35 (Summer, 1974), pp. 171-183.

406 Neville, R. C., "Life Richer than Intellect," Catholic World, vol. 207 (September, 1968), pp. 276-277.

407 Niebuhr, H. Richard, "On the Nature of Faith," Religious Experience and Truth, Sidney Hook, ed. New York: New York University Press, 1961, pp. 93-103.

408 Niebuhr, Reinhold, "Biblical Thought and Ontological Speculation in Tillich's Theology," The Theology of Paul Tillich,

Charles W. Kegley and Robert W. Bretall, eds. New York: The Macmillan Company, 1964, pp. 216-230.

409   Niebuhr, Reinhold, "The Contribution of Paul Tillich," Religion in Life, vol. 6, no. 4 (1937), pp. 574-581.

410   Niebuhr, Reinhold, "Faith as the Sense of Meaning in Human Existence," Christianity and Crisis, vol. 26 (June 13, 1966), pp. 127-131.

411   Niebuhr, Reinhold, "Paul Tillich in Memoriam," Union Seminary Quarterly Review, vol. 21 (November, 1965), p. 11.

412   Nielsen, Kai, "Is God So Powerful that He Doesn't Even Have to Exist?" Religious Experience and Truth, Sidney Hook, ed. New York: New York University Press, 1961, pp. 270-282.

413   Nielsen, Kai, "Tillich and Niebuhr and Facing Anxiety," Religious Humanism, vol. 9 (Winter, 1975), pp. 29-30.

414   Northcott, C., "Paul Tillich's Germany," Christian Century, vol. 79 (October 10, 1962), p. 1219.

415   Northwell, J., "Tillich's Concern for Preaching the Gospel," Preaching, vol. 4 (May-June, 1969), pp. 24-27.

416   Novak, Michael, "The Religion of Paul Tillich," Commentary, vol. 43 (April, 1967), pp. 53-65.

417   Nuovo, Victor L., "The Early/Late Tillich and the History of Religions," Philosophy of Religion and Theology: 1973 Papers, David Griffin, compiler. Tallahassee, Florida: American Academy of Religion, 1973, pp. 213-219.

418   Nuovo, Victor L., "On Revising Tillich: An Essay on the Principles of Theology," Kairos and Logos: Studies in the Roots and Implications of Tillich's Theology, John J. Carey, ed. Cambridge, Massachusetts: North American Paul Tillich Society, 1978, pp. 45-73.

419   O'Connor, Edward D., "Paul Tillich, An Impression," Thought, Fordham University Quarterly, vol. 30, no. 119 (Winter, 1955), pp. 507-524. Included in Paul Tillich in Catholic Thought, edited by Thomas F. O'Meara and Donald M. Weisser (Doubleday & Company, Inc., 1969).

420   O'Meara, T., "Marian Theology and the Contemporary Problem of Myth," Marian Studies, vol. 15 (1964), pp. 127-156.

421   O'Meara, Thomas A., "Paul Tillich and Ecumenism," Reality (Dubuque, Iowa), 1962, pp. 151-180.

422   O'Meara, Thomas F., "Art and Music as Illustrators of The-

ology," Anglican Theological Review, vol. 55 (July, 1973), pp. 267-277.

423 O'Meara, Thomas F., "Discussion (of Cyrin Maus' Article, 'The Possibility of Knowing God Naturally')," Scotus Speaks Today, 1266-1966, P. Ramstetter, et al., Southfield, Michigan: Duns Scotus College, 1968, pp. 291-294. The material is drawn from a seventh centenary symposium at Duns Scotus College on April 21-23, 1966.

424 O'Meara, Thomas F., "Paul Tillich and the Problem of God," Paul Tillich in Catholic Thought, Thomas F. O'Meara and Donald M. Weisser, eds. Garden City, New York: Doubleday & Company, Inc., 1969, pp. 345-368.

425 O'Meara, Thomas F., "Tillich and Heidegger: A Structural Relationship," Harvard Theological Review, vol. 61, no. 2 (April, 1968), pp. 249-261.

426 Oates, Wayne E., "The Contribution of Paul Tillich to Pastoral Psychology," Pastoral Psychology, vol. 19, no. 181 (February, 1968), p. 11.

427 Palmer, Michael F., "A Reply to Some Interpretations of Tillich's Christology," Heythrop Journal, vol. 17 (April, 1976), pp. 169-177.

428 Palmer, Michael F., "The Certainty of Faith and Tillich's Concept of the 'Analogia Imaginis,'" Scottish Journal of Theology, vol. 25 (August, 1972), pp. 279-295.

429 Palmer, Michael F., "Correlation and Ontology: A Study in Tillich's Christology," The Downside Review, vol. 96, no. 323 (April, 1978), pp. 120-131.

430 Palmer, Michael F., "Hartshorne's Critique of Tillich's Theory of Religious Symbolism," Heythrop Journal, vol. 17 (October, 1976), pp. 379-394.

431 Palmer, Michael F., "Paul Tillich's Critique of Bultmann's Christology," Heythrop Journal, vol. 20, no. 3 (1979), pp. 279-289.

432 Partin, H. B., "Theology and History of Religions: Issues in Some Recent Literature," Anglican Theological Review, vol. 53 (October, 1971), pp. 270-278.

433 Patterson, Charles H., "The Religious Philosophy of Paul Tillich," The Life Review, vol. 20, no. 1 (1963), pp. 21-31.

434 Patton, John H., "Theological Interpretation of Pastoral Supervision," The New Shape of Pastoral Theology: Essays in Honor of Seward Hiltner, William B. Oglesby. Nashville: Abingdon Press, 1969, pp. 234-247.

435 Pauck, Wilhelm, "Paul Tillich, 1889-1965," Theology Today, vol. 23 (April, 1966), pp. 1-11.

436 Pauck, Wilhelm, "The Sources of Paul Tillich's Richness," Union Seminary Quarterly Review, vol. 21, no. 1 (November, 1965), pp. 3-9. Included in The Future of Religions, edited by Jerald C. Brauer (Harper and Row, 1966).

437 Pauck, Wilhelm, "Tribute to Paul Tillich," Criterion, vol. 5, no. 1 (1966).

438 Paul, William Wright, "Interplay Between Philosophy and Theology in Tillich's Thought," Bulletin of the Evangelical Theological Society, vol. 11, no. 2 (Spring, 1968), pp. 93-102.

439 Paul, William Wright, "What Can Religion Say to Its Cultured Despisers? A Comparison of Schleiermacher (1799) and Tillich (1959)," Reformed Review, vol. 23 (Summer, 1970), pp. 208-216.

440 Pemberton, John, "Ontology and Christology: The Apologetic Theology of Paul Tillich," A Miscellany of American Christianity, H. S. Smith and A. C. Outler, eds. Durham, North Carolina: Duke University Press, 1963, pp. 248-291.

441 Peters, Eugene H., "Tillich's Doctrine of Essence, Existence, and the Christ," Journal of Religion, vol. 43 (October, 1963), pp. 295-302.

442 Piediscalzi, N., "Comments on Friedman's 'The Transmoral Morality,'" Journal for the Scientific Study of Religion, vol. 4 (April, 1965), pp. 237-242. Rejoinder on pp. 242-246.

443 Pittenger, W. Norman, "Paul Tillich as a Theologian: An Appreciation," Anglican Theological Review, vol. 43, no. 3 (July, 1961), pp. 268-286.

444 Pittenger, W. Norman, "Some Comments on Paul Tillich," Modern Churchman, New Series, vol. 11, no. 2 (January, 1968), pp. 107-110.

445 Pittenger, W. Norman, "Tillich: The Prophet from America," Modern Churchman, vol. 8 (January, 1965), pp. 138-141.

446 Porteus, Alvin C., "Is Doubt a Sin?" Christian Herald, November, 1966, p. 48.

447 Posey, L., "Paul Tillich's Gift of Understanding," Christian Century, vol. 98 (September 30, 1981), pp. 967-969.

448 Price, Bob, "Homiletical Hermeneutics in Paul Tillich," The Drew Gateway, vol. 50, no. 1 (1979), pp. 15-24.

449 Progoff, Ira, "The Man Who Transforms Consciousness: The Inner Myths of Martin Buber, Paul Tillich and C. G. Jung," Eranos-Jahrbuch, vol. 35 (1966), pp. 99-144.

450 Proudfoot, Wayne, "Conceptions of God and the Self," Journal of Religion, vol. 55 (January, 1975), pp. 57-75.

451 Przywara, Erich, "Christian Root-Terms: Kerygma, Mysterium, Kairos, Oikonomia," Paul Tillich in Catholic Thought, Thomas F. O'Meara and Donald M. Weisser, eds. Garden City, New York: Doubleday & Company, Inc., 1969, pp. 256-265.

452 Pusey, N. M., "Words for Paul Tillich," Harvard Divinity Bulletin, vol. 30 (January, 1966), pp. 1-21.

453 Putnam, L. J., "Tillich on the Sacraments," Theology and Life, vol. 8 (Summer, 1965), pp. 108-116.

454 Putnam, L. J., "Tillich, Revelation, and Miracle," Theology and Life, vol. 9 (Winter, 1966), pp. 355-370.

455 Quinney, Richard, "The Theology of Culture: Marx, Tillich and the Prophetic Tradition in the Reconstruction of Social and Moral Order," Union Seminary Quarterly Review, vol. 34, no. 4 (1979), pp. 203-214.

456 Ralls, Anthony, "Ontological Presuppositions in Religion," Sophia, vol. 2 (April, 1964), pp. 3-11.

457 Ramm, B., "Inscrutable Dr. Tillich," Eternity, vol. 14 (November, 1963), pp. 28f.

458 Ramsey, Paul, "Paul Tillich and Emil Brunner: Christ Transforming Natural Justice," Nine Modern Moralists, Paul Ramsey, ed. New York: Prentice-Hall, 1962, pp. 181-208.

459 Randall, John Herman, Jr., "On Being Rejected," Journal of Philosophy, vol. 50 (December, 1953), pp. 797-804.

460 Randall, John Herman, Jr., "The Ontology of Paul Tillich," The Theology of Paul Tillich, Charles W. Kegley and Robert W. Bretall. New York: The Macmillan Company, 1964, pp. 132-164.

461 Randall, John Herman, Jr., "The Philosophical Legacy of Paul Tillich," The Intellectual Legacy of Paul Tillich, James R. Lyons, ed. Detroit: Wayne State University Press, 1969.

462 Rathbun, John W., "Martin Luther King: The Theology of Social Action," American Quarterly, vol. 20 (Spring, 1968), pp. 38-53.

463   Rathbun, John W., and Burwick, Fred, "Paul Tillich and the
       Philosophy of Schelling," International Philosophy Quarterly,
       vol. 4, no. 3 (September, 1964), pp. 373-393.

464   Reardon, Bernard M. G., "Tillich and Anglicanism," Anglican
       Theological Review, vol. 43, no. 3 (July, 1961), pp. 287-302.

465   Reese, William L., "Analogy, Symbolism, and Linguistic
       Analysis," Review of Metaphysics, vol. 13 (March, 1960), pp.
       447-468.

466   Reimer, A. James, "Theological Method and Political Ethics:
       The Paul Tillich-Emmanuel Hirsch Debate," Journal of the
       American Academy of Religion, vol. 47, no. 1 (March, 1979),
       pp. 171-192.

467   Reisz, H. Frederick, Jr., "Ambiguities in the Use of the
       Theological Symbol 'Spirit' in Paul Tillich's Theology," Tillich
       Studies: 1975, John J. Carey, ed.   Tallahassee, Florida:
       (Florida State University), The Second North American Con-
       sultation on Paul Tillich Studies, 1975, pp. 89-104.   A paper
       prepared for a consultation sponsored by the American Acad-
       emy of Religion at its meeting in Chicago, October 30-
       November 2, 1975.

468   Reisz, H. Frederick, Jr., "Liberation Theology of Culture:
       A Tillichian Perspective," Kairos and Logos: Studies in the
       Roots and Implications of Tillich's Theology, John J. Carey,
       ed.   Cambridge, Massachusetts: North American Paul Til-
       lich Society, 1978.

469   Reyna, Ruth, "On the Ontology of Paul Tillich--Its Structure
       and Meaning," Journal of the Philosophical Association, vol.
       7 (July, 1960), pp. 85-98.

470   Rich, M. L., "Paul Tillich's Utilization of Depth Psychology
       in the Existential Analysis of the Human Situation," The Drew
       Gateway, vol. 41 (Fall, 1970), pp. 40-41.   An abstract of a
       dissertation.

471   Richards, G., "Paul Tillich and the Historical Jesus," Studies
       in Religion, Sciences Religieuses, vol. 4, no. 2 (1974-1975),
       pp. 120-128.

472   Richardson, Cyril C., "Do the Gods Exist?" Religious Ex-
       perience and Truth, Sidney Hook, ed.   New York: New York
       University Press, 1961, pp. 282-290.

473   Roberts, David E., "The Man of the Month: Paul Tillich,"
       Pastoral Psychology, vol. 3, no. 29 (1952), pp. 8, 66.

474   Roberts, David E., "Tillich's Doctrine of Man," The Theology
       of Paul Tillich, Charles W. Kegley and Robert W. Bretall.
       New York: The Macmillan Company, 1964, pp. 108-132.

475 Robertson, J., Jr., "Tillich and the Transcendental Method,"
Theology Digest, vol. 24 (Spring, 1976), pp. 50-56. Con-
densed from The Journal of Religion, April, 1975.

476 Robertson, John C., "Tillich's 'Two Types' and the Transcendental Method," The Journal of Religion, vol. 55 (April,
1975), pp. 199-219.

477 Robinson, Daniel S., "Tillich and Marcel: Theistic Existentialists," The Personalist (Los Angeles), vol. 34, no. 3
(1953), pp. 237-250.

478 Rogers, Carl, "Paul Tillich and Carl Rogers: A Dialogue,"
Pastoral Psychology, vol. 19, no. 181 (February, 1968), pp.
55-64.

479 Rohr, John A., "Paul Tillich: A Critical Evaluation," The
American Ecclesiastical Review, vol. 157, no. 5 (November,
1967), pp. 333-339.

480 Romero, Joan Arnold, "The Protestant Principle: A Woman's
Eye-View of Barth and Tillich," Religion and Sexism: Images
of Woman in the Jewish and the Christian Traditions, Rose-
mary Radford Ruether. New York: Simon & Schuster, 1974,
pp. 319-340.

481 Rose, D. R., "Paul Tillich, An Existential Theologian,"
Asbury Seminarian, vol. 11 (Summer, 1957), pp. 15-20.

482 Rosenthal, Klaus, "Myth and Symbol," Scottish Journal of
Theology, vol. 18, no. 4 (December, 1965), pp. 411-434.

483 Ross, Robert R. N., "A Form of Ontological Argument,"
Harvard Theological Review, vol. 70 (January-April, 1977),
pp. 115-135.

484 Ross, Robert N., "God and Singular Existence," International
Journal for Philosophy and Religion, vol. 8, no. 2 (1977), pp.
127-141.

485 Ross, Robert R. N., "Hegel, Tillich and the Theology of
Culture: A Response to Professor Thomas," Kairos and Logos:
Studies in the Roots and Implications of Tillich's Theology,
John J. Carey, ed. Cambridge, Massachusetts: North
American Paul Tillich Society, 1978, pp. 229-235.

486 Ross, Robert R. N., "Non-Being and Being in Taoist and
Western Traditions," Religious Traditions (Brisbane, Australia), vol. 2 (October, 1979), pp. 24-38.

487 Ross, Robert R. N., "Non-Existence of God: Tillich, Aquinas,
and the Pseudo-Dionysius," Harvard Theological Review, vol.
68 (April, 1975), pp. 141-166.

488 Ross, Robert R. N., "Tillich and Plato," Sophia (Australia), vol. 15 (October, 1976), pp. 26-29.

489 Rowe, William L., "The Meaning of God in Tillich's Theology," Journal of Religion, vol. 42 (October, 1962), pp. 274-286.

490 Rowe, William L., "Tillich's Theory of Signs and Symbols," The Monist, vol. 50, no. 4 (October, 1966), pp. 593-610.

491 Royster, James E., "Paul Tillich's Ethical Thought," Ohio Journal of Religious Studies, vol. 5 (April, 1977), pp. 35-51.

492 Rubenstein, Richard Lowell, "Religious Naturalism and Human Evil," Reconstructionist, vol. 24 (January 23, 1959), pp. 6-10.

493 Runia, K., "The Christology of Paul Tillich," Vox Reformata (Geelong, Victoria, Australia), vol. 7 (1966), pp. 1-33.

494 Runia, K., "Dangerous Trends in Modern Theological Thought," Concordia Theological Monthly, vol. 35 (June, 1964), pp. 331-342. This article is continued in the September 1964 issue (see next entry).

495 Runia, K., "Dangerous Trends in Modern Theological Thought," Concordia Theological Monthly, vol. 35 (September, 1964), pp. 470-481.

496 Rupp, E. G., "Caviare for the General: Professor Paul Tillich's Second Volume," Expository Times (Edinburgh), vol. 69 (1958), pp. 272-273.

497 Ryan, J. D., "Awareness of God in the Thought of Paul Tillich," The Drew Gateway, vol. 44 (Fall, 1973), pp. 33-34. A dissertation abstract.

498 Salzman, Leon, "Observations on Dr. Tillich's Views on Guilt, Sin, and Reconciliation," The Journal of Pastoral Care, vol. 11, no. 1 (Spring, 1957), pp. 14-19.

499 Sanderson, John W., Jr., "Historical Fact or Symbol? The Philosophies of History of Paul Tillich and Reinhold Niebuhr," Westminster Theological Journal, vol. 20 (May, 1958), pp. 158-169. This article is continued in the November 1958 issue (see next entry).

500 Sanderson, John W., Jr., "Historical Fact or Symbol? The Philosophies of History of Paul Tillich and Reinhold Niebuhr," Westminster Theological Journal, vol. 21, no. 1 (November, 1958), pp. 58-74.

501 Santoni, Ronald E., "Symbolism and Ultimate Concern: A

Problem," Anglican Theological Review, vol. 49 (January, 1967), pp. 90-94.

502 Scharlemann, Robert P., "After Tillich, What?" Christian Century, vol. 82 (December 1, 1965), pp. 1478-1480. From an address given October 22, 1965.

503 Scharlemann, Robert P., "The Argument from Faith to History," Religion in Life, vol. 43, no. 2 (Summer, 1974), pp. 137-149.

504 Scharlemann, Robert P., "Concepts, Symbols, and Sentences," Theology Today, vol. 22 (January, 1966), pp. 513-527. A reply to this article is given by J. H. Hick on pp. 528-529. A further rejoinder by R. Scharlemann appears in the April 1966 issue, pp. 139-140.

505 Scharlemann, Robert P., "Critical and Religious Consciousness: Some Reflections on the Questions of Truth in the Philosophy of Religion," Kairos and Logos: Studies in the Roots and Implications of Tillich's Theology, John J. Carey, ed. Cambridge, Massachusetts: North American Paul Tillich Society, 1978.

506 Scharlemann, Robert P., "Scope of Systematics: An Analysis of Tillich's Two Systems," Journal of Religion, vol. 48 (April, 1968), pp. 136-149.

507 Scharlemann, Robert P., "The Theology of the University," Dialog (Minneapolis), vol. 8, no. 2 (Spring, 1969), pp. 102-107.

508 Scharlemann, Robert P., "Tillich on Schelling and the Principle of Identity: A Review," Journal of Religion, vol. 56 (January, 1975), pp. 105-112.

509 Scharlemann, Robert P., "Tillich's Method of Correlation," The Journal of Religion, vol. 46, no. 1, part 2 (January, 1966), pp. 92-103.

510 Schepers, Maurice B., "Paul Tillich on the Church," Paul Tillich in Catholic Thought, Thomas F. O'Meara and Donald M. Weisser, eds. Garden City, New York: Doubleday & Company, Inc., 1969, pp. 304-320.

511 Schick, Thomas, "Reason and Knowledge in the Epistemology of Paul Tillich," The Thomist, vol. 30, no. 1 (January, 1966), pp. 66-79.

512 Schmidt, Paul F., "Frustrating Strategies in Religious Discussion," Religious Experience and Truth, Sidney Hook, ed. New York: New York University Press, 1961, pp. 290-301.

513 Schrader, R., "The Nature of Theological Argument: A Study
     of Paul Tillich," Harvard Theological Review, vol. 65 (Octo-
     ber, 1972), pp. 604-605. A dissertation abstract.

514 Schrag, Calvin O., "Religion and Culture in the Thought of
     Paul Tillich," The Lutheran Scholar, vol. 25, no. 1 (1968),
     pp. 3-7.

515 Schulweis, Harold, "Theodicy and the Ground of Being: Paul
     Tillich," Philosophy Today, vol. 18 (Winter, 1974), pp. 338-
     342.

516 Scott, D., "The Gospel and History in the Thought of Paul
     Tillich," The Indian Journal of Theology (Calcutta), vol. 14,
     no. 4 (1965), pp. 184-193.

517 Scott, Nathan A., Jr., "The Collaboration of Vision in the
     Poetic Act: Its Establishment of the Religious Dimension,"
     The Christian Scholar, vol. 40 (December, 1957), pp. 277-
     295.

518 Seah, Ingram S., "On the Fascinations of Being and Non-
     Being," Southeast Asia Journal of Theology, vol. 20, no. 2
     (1979), pp. 1-11.

519 Sellers, James E., "Five Approaches to the Human Situation,"
     Theology Today, vol. 15 (January, 1959), pp. 521-530.

520 Sharpe, Eric J., "Spirit and the Religions," The Church Cross-
     ing Frontiers: Essays on the Nature of Mission in Honor of
     Bengt Sundkler, P. Beyerhaus. Lund: Gleerup, 1969, pp.
     111-123.

521 Sherman, Franklin, "New Ethic for a New Age?" Dialog,
     vol. 14 (Winter, 1975), pp. 33-37.

522 Sherman, Franklin, "Tillich on 'Morality and Beyond,'" Com
     mon Factor, vol. 1 (October, 1964), pp. 41-43.

523 Sherman, Franklin, "Tillich's Social Thought: New Perspec-
     tives," Christian Century, vol. 93 (February 25, 1976), pp.
     168-172.

524 Shiner, Roger A., "The Ontological Necessity of Sin in Til-
     lich's Theology," Southern Journal of Philosophy, vol. 15
     (Summer, 1977), pp. 215-225.

525 Shinn, Roger L., "Lover's Quarrel of the Church with the
     World," Crisis in the Church: Essays in Honor of Truman B.
     Douglass, Everett C. Parker. Philadelphia: Pilgrim Press,
     1968, pp. 15-27.

526 Shinn, Roger L., "Paul Tillich as Contemporary Theologian,"

The Intellectual Legacy of Paul Tillich, James R. Lyons, ed. Detroit: Wayne State University Press, 1969.

527 Siegfried, Theodor, "The Significance of Paul Tillich's Theology for the German Situation," The Theology of Paul Tillich, Charles W. Kegley and Robert W. Bretall, eds. New York: The Macmillan Company, 1964, pp. 68-86.

528 Simmons, James R., "Super-, Sub-, or Pseudo-Naturalism?" Journal of Philosophy, vol. 52 (March, 1955), pp. 128-130.

529 Simpson, Michael, "The 'Death of God' Theology: Some Philosophical Reflections," Heythrop Journal, vol. 10 (October, 1969), pp. 371-389.

530 Simpson, Michael, "Paul Tillich: Symbolism and Objectivity," Heythrop Journal, vol. 8 (July, 1967), pp. 293-309.

531 Skinner, John E., "Being, Selfhood, and Presence," Lutheran Quarterly, vol. 12 (November, 1960), pp. 292-302.

532 Skinner, John E., "Critique of Tillich's Ontology," Anglican Theological Review, vol. 39, no. 1 (January, 1957), pp. 53-61.

533 Smart, R. N., "Being and the Bible: A Dialogue Between 'Mild' and 'Violent,'" Review of Metaphysics, vol. 9 (June, 1956), pp. 589-607.

534 Smith, B. L., "What Price Tillich?" Christianity Today, vol. 16 (December 17, 1971), pp. 16-18. This article is continued in the January 7, 1972 issue.

535 Smith, B. L., "What Price Tillich?" Christianity Today, vol. 16 (January 7, 1972), pp. 13-15.

536 Smith, D. Moody, Jr., "The Historical Jesus in Paul Tillich's Christology," The Journal of Religion, vol. 46, no. 1, part 2 (January, 1966), pp. 131-147.

537 Smith, Huston and Tillich, Paul, "Human Fulfillment," The Search for America, Huston Smith, ed. Englewood Cliffs, New Jersey: Prentice-Hall, 1959, pp. 164-174. The ideas in this essay are Tillich's. The formulations of the ideas are Huston Smith's.

538 Smith, J., "Paul Tillich and Catholic Theology," Politics, Religion and Modernity, Charles W. Kegley, ed. Quezon City (The Philippines): University of the Philippines Press, 1969.

539 Smith, John E., "The Present Status of Natural Theology," Journal of Philosophy, vol. 55 (October, 1958), pp. 925-935.

540   Smith, John E., "Ultimate Concern and the Really Ultimate,"
      Religious Experience and Truth, Sidney Hook, ed.   New York:
      New York University Press, 1961, pp. 65-70.   A paper
      prompted by Tillich's essay, "The Religious Symbol."

541   Smith, J. R., "Creation, Fall and Theodicy in Paul Tillich's
      Systematic Theology," Kairos and Logos: Studies in the Roots
      and Implications of Tillich's Theology, John J. Carey, ed.
      Cambridge, Massachusetts: North American Paul Tillich So-
      ciety, 1978.

542   Smith, J. W. D., "The Resurrection of Christ: Myth or
      History?" Expository Times, vol. 72 (September, 1961), pp.
      370-375.

543   Smith, R. V., "Radical Protestantism: The Apologetic Task,"
      Journal of Bible and Religion, vol. 26 (January, 1958), pp.
      29-33.

544   Smith, Raymond, "Paul Tillich's Concept of Faith," Catholic
      World, vol. 200 (December, 1964), pp. 162-163, 166-171.
      Included in Paul Tillich in Catholic Thought, edited by Thomas
      O'Meara and Donald M. Weisser (Doubleday and Company,
      1969), as "Faith Without Belief," pp. 180-191.

545   Smolik, J., "God--The Depth of Being: Paul Tillich," World
      Student Christian Federation Books, vol. 1, no. 2 (1971), pp.
      63-67.

546   Sontag, Frederick E., "Biblical Authority and Tillich's Search
      for the Ultimate," Journal of Bible and Religion, vol. 30
      (October, 1962), pp. 278-283.

547   Sontag, Frederick E., "Continuity and Change in Theological
      Formulation," Heythrop Journal, vol. 7 (January, 1966), pp.
      43-51.

548   Sontag, Frederick E., "Ontological Possibility and the Nature
      of God: A Reply to Tillich," Journal of Religion, vol. 36
      (October, 1956), pp. 234-240.

549   Sontag, Frederick E., "Why Language About God Cannot Be
      Final," Heythrop Journal, vol. 9 (October, 1968), pp. 371-
      383.

550   Soper, D. W., "Beyond Religion and Irreligion," Major Voices
      in American Theology, D. W. Soper.   Philadelphia: West-
      minster Press, 1953, pp. 107-152.

551   Sparks, Hale, "Common Ground," Sunrise (Pasadena, Califor-
      nia), vol. 12 (June, 1963), pp. 259-264.

552   Sprague, Elmer, "How to Avoid Being Professor Tillich,"

Journal of Philosophy, vol. 56 (November, 1959), pp. 969-970.

553 Sprague, Elmer, "Professor Tillich's Ontological Question," International Philosophical Quarterly, vol. 2, no. 1 (February, 1962), pp. 81-91.

554 Stanley, Michael W., "Tillich and the Human Situation," New Church Magazine, vol. 89 (July-September, 1970), pp. 82-90.

555 Stewart, Claude Y., "Process Theology and the Protestant Principle," Foundations (Baptist), vol. 21 (October-December, 1978), pp. 356-364.

556 Stiernotte, Alfred P., "Paul Tillich: Mystic, Rationalist, Universalist," The Crane Review, vol. 4, no. 3 (Spring, 1962), pp. 164-180.

557 Stiernotte, Alfred P., "Tillich Rounds Out His System," The Journal of the Liberal Ministry (Rockford, Illinois), vol. 4, no. 3 (1964), pp. 130-142.

558 Stone, Jerome A., "Tillich and Schelling's Later Philosophy," Kairos and Logos: Studies in the Roots and Implications of Tillich's Theology, John J. Carey, ed. Cambridge: Massachusetts: North American Paul Tillich Society, 1978, pp. 11-14.

559 Stone, Ronald, "Christian Ethics and the Socialist Vision of Paul Tillich," Tillich Studies: 1975, John J. Carey, ed. Tallahassee, Florida: (Florida State University), The Second North American Consultation on Paul Tillich Studies, 1975, pp. 51-63. A paper prepared for a consultation sponsored by the American Academy of Religion at its meeting in Chicago, October 30-November 2, 1975.

560 Stone, Ronald, "Tillich: Radical Political Theologian," Religion in Life, vol. 46 (Spring, 1977), pp. 44-53.

561 Stone, Ronald, "Tillich's Critical Use of Marx and Freud in the Social Context of the Frankfort School," Union Seminary Quarterly Review, vol. 33 (Fall, 1977), pp. 3-9.

562 Streiker, L. D., "Boundary Lines," Christian Century, vol. 83 (August 17, 1966), p. 1012.

563 Stumme, J. R., "Theonomy and Paradox: A Response to Professor Bulman," Kairos and Logos: Studies in the Roots and Implications of Tillich's Theology, John J. Carey, ed. Cambridge, Massachusetts: North American Paul Tillich Society, 1978.

564 Sulzbach, M. F., "The Place of Christology in Contemporary

Protestantism," Religion in Life, vol. 23 (Winter, 1953-1954), pp. 206-215.

565 Tait, L. G., "Paul Tillich on the Dynamics of Hope," Perspective, vol. 13, no. 3 (1972), pp. 213-222.

566 Talley, Joseph E., "Psychological Separation-Individuation and Spiritual Reunion," Journal of Psychology and Theology, vol. 8 (Summer, 1980), pp. 97-106.

567 Taubes, Jacob, "The Copernican Turn of Theology," Religious Experience and Truth, Sidney Hook, ed. New York: New York University Press, 1961, pp. 70-76. A paper prompted by Tillich's essay, "The Religious Symbol."

568 Taubes, Jacob, "On the Nature of the Theological Method: Some Reflections on the Methodological Principles of Tillich's Theology," Toward a New Christianity: Readings on the Death of God Theology, Jacob Taubes. New York: Harcourt, Brace, and World, 1967. Appears also in The Journal of Religion, vol. 34, 1954, pp. 12-25.

569 Tavard, George Henri, "Christianity and the Philosophies of Existence," Theological Studies, vol. 18 (March, 1957), pp. 1-16.

570 Tavard, George Henri, "Christology as Symbol," Paul Tillich in Catholic Thought, Thomas F. O'Meara and Donald M. Weisser, eds. Garden City, New York: Doubleday & Company, Inc., 1969, pp. 269-288. An excerpt from Paul Tillich and the Christian Message, by George H. Tavard (Charles Scribner's Sons, 1962).

571 Tavard, George Henri, "Paul Tillich's System," Commonweal, vol. 79 (February 7, 1964), pp. 566-568.

572 Tavard, George Henri, "The Protestant Principle and the Theological System of Paul Tillich," Paul Tillich in Catholic Thought, Thomas F. O'Meara and Donald M. Weisser, eds. Garden City, New York: Doubleday & Company, Inc., 1969, pp. 126-139.

573 Tavard, George Henri, "Tillich: Christ as the Answer to Existential Anguish," Continuum (Chicago), vol. 4, no. 1 (1966), pp. 3-12. Included in Paul Tillich in Catholic Thought, edited by Thomas F. O'Meara and Donald M. Weisser (Doubleday & Company, Inc., 1969).

574 Tavard, George Henri, "Tillich's Christology," Jubilee, vol. 10 (June, 1962), pp. 16-19. Excerpt from Paul Tillich and the Christian Message, by George H. Tavard (Charles Scribner's Sons, 1962).

575 Tavard, George Henri, "The Unconditioned Concern: The Theology of Paul Tillich," Thought (Fordham University Quarterly), vol. 28, no. 109 (Summer, 1953), pp. 234-246.

576 Taylor, Richard, "Faith," Religious Experience and Truth, Sidney Hook, ed. New York: New York University Press, 1961, pp. 165-170.

577 Thatcher, Adrian, "Concepts of Deity: A Criticism of H. P. Owen," Anglican Theological Review, vol. 58 (July, 1976), pp. 294-306.

578 Thatcher, Adrian, "Existence and Life in Tillich," Scottish Journal of Theology, vol. 27 (August, 1974), pp. 306-312.

579 Thie, Marilyn C., "The 'Broken' World of Myth: An Analysis," The New Scholasticism, vol. 45 (Winter, 1971), pp. 38-55.

580 Thiselton, A. C., "Theology of Paul Tillich," The Churchman, vol. 88 (April-June, 1974), pp. 86-107.

581 Thomas, George F., "The Method and Structure of Tillich's Theology," The Theology of Paul Tillich, Charles W. Kegley and Robert W. Bretall. New York: The Macmillan Company, 1964, pp. 86-108.

582 Thomas, George F., "Philosophical Theology: Tillich," Religious Philosophies of the West, George F. Thomas. New York: Charles Scribner's Sons, 1965, pp. 390-423.

583 Thomas, John Heywood, "Article Review: Tillich as a Philosopher of Religion," Scottish Journal of Theology, vol. 31, no. 4 (1978), pp. 365-371.

584 Thomas, John Heywood, "Catholic Criticism of Tillich," Scottish Journal of Theology, vol. 16 (March, 1963), pp. 32-49.

585 Thomas, John Heywood, "The Correlation of Philosophy and Theology in Tillich's System," London Quarterly and Holborn Review, vol. 184 (January, 1959), pp. 47-54.

586 Thomas, John Heywood, "Introducing Paul Tillich," London Quarterly and Holborn Review, vol. 181 (January, 1956), pp. 40-47.

587 Thomas, John Heywood, "Metaphysician Seeking the Nature of Self," Times, February 3, 1968, p. 10.

588 Thomas, John Heywood, "Philosophical Influences on Tillich's Development of a Theology of Culture," Kairos and Logos: Studies in the Roots and Implications of Tillich's Theology,

John J. Carey, ed. Cambridge, Massachusetts: North American Paul Tillich Society, 1978.

589 Thomas, John Heywood, "The Problem of Defining a Theology of Culture with Reference to the Theology of Paul Tillich," Creation, Christ and Culture: Studies in Honour of T. F. Torrance, R. McKinney, ed. Edinburgh: T. & T. Clark, 1976, pp. 272-287.

590 Thomas, John Heywood, "Some Aspects of Tillich's Systematic Theology," Canadian Journal of Theology, vol. 9 (July, 1963), pp. 157-165.

591 Thomas, John Heywood, "Some Comments on Tillich's Doctrine of Creation," Scottish Journal of Theology, vol. 14 (June, 1961), pp. 113-118.

592 Thomas, John Heywood, "Some Critical Notes on the Theology of Paul Tillich," Hibbert Journal, vol. 57 (April, 1959), pp. 252-258.

593 Thomas, O. C., "Barth and Tillich: A Conversation on Contemporary Theology," Religion in Life, vol. 32 (Fall, 1963), pp. 508-520.

594 Thompson, R. Duane, "Tillich's Aesthetics of Ultimate Meaning," Continuum (Chicago), vol. 3, no. 1 (Spring, 1965), pp. 68-74.

595 Thomson, James Sutherland, "Paul Tillich," Architects of Modern Thought. Toronto: Canadian Broadcasting Corporation, 1955, pp. 75-82. Part of a transcription from a radio broadcast.

596 Tiebout, Harry M., Jr., "Demos on Tillich," Philosophy and Phenomenological Research, vol. 20 (September, 1959), pp. 109-112.

597 Tiebout, Harry M., Jr., "Tillich and Freud on Sin," Religion in Life, vol. 28 (Spring, 1959), pp. 223-235.

598 Tiebout, Harry M., Jr., "Tillich, Existentialism, and Psychoanalysis," The Journal of Philosophy, vol. 56, no. 14 (July 2, 1959), pp. 605-612.

599 Tomas, Vincent, "Darkness or Light," Religious Experience and Truth, Sidney Hook, ed. New York: New York University Press, 1961, pp. 76-83. A paper prompted by Tillich's essay, "The Religious Symbol."

600 Tonne, Herbert A., "A Communication," Religious Humanism, vol. 10 (Summer, 1976), pp. 116-117.

601 Tonne, Herbert A., "Humanism and Tillich's Existentialism," The Humanist, vol. 20, no. 6 (November-December, 1960), pp. 346-349.

602 Tracy, D. W., "The Task of Fundamental Theology," Journal of Religion, vol. 54 (January, 1974), pp. 13-34.

603 Tully, John, "Tillich--Meeting the Christ," Record (St. Mary's of the West), vol. 16 (Winter, 1965), pp. 5-8.

604 Turner, Geoffrey, "Tillich and Bonhoeffer: Exile and Death," New Blackfriars, vol. 58 (September, 1977), pp. 428-433.

605 Urban, Linwood, "On Theological Definition," Religious Experience and Truth, Sidney Hook, ed. New York: New York University Press, 1961, pp. 170-180.

606 Urban, Wilbur M., "Professor Tillich's Theory of Religious Symbol," The Journal of Liberal Religion, vol. 2, no. 1 (1940), pp. 34-36.

607 Vahanian, G. A., "Doubt as Corollary to Faith," Nation, vol. 189 (September 5, 1959), pp. 117-119.

608 Van Buren, Paul, "Tillich as Apologist," Christian Century, vol. 81 (February 5, 1964), pp. 177-179. A discussion of this article is found in the March 11, 1964 issue, pp. 343-344.

609 Van den Haag, Ernest, "On Faith," Religious Experience and Truth, Sidney Hook, ed. New York: New York University Press, 1961, pp. 150-156.

610 Van Hook, Jay M., "Tillich on the Relation Between Philosophy and Theology," Journal of the American Academy of Religion, vol. 45, no. 1 (March, 1977), pp. 73f.

611 Veatch, Henry, "Tillich's Distinction Between Metaphysics and Theology," Review of Metaphysics, vol. 10, no. 3 (March, 1957), pp. 529-533.

612 Vetter, Herbert F., Jr., "Paul Tillich: Existentialism and Neo-Naturalism," The Crane Review, vol. 2, no. 3 (1960), pp. 98-106.

613 Vilnite, O. T., "The Contemporary Development of Protestant Theology: Tillich and the Neo-Orthodoxy of Barth," Soviet Studies in Philosophy, vol. 7 (Spring, 1969), pp. 34-46.

614 Von Hase, Hans, "Paul Tillich in Marburg," Union Seminary Quarterly Review, vol. 4, no. 1 (1948), pp. 49-50.

615 Vulgamore, Melvin L., "Wesley and Tillich on the Legalistic

Influence in Justification," Rocky Mountain Review, vol. 2 (Winter, 1964-1965), pp. 35-47.

616 Vunderink, Ralph W., "The Significance of Existentialism for Christian Theology: An Examination of Paul Tillich's Philosophical Theology," American Catholic Philosophical Society Proceedings, vol. 44 (1970), pp. 241-248.

617 Wainwright, William J., "Paul Tillich and Arguments for the Existence of God," Journal of the American Academy of Religion, vol. 39 (June, 1971), pp. 171-185.

618 Wald, George, "Tribute," Prospect (Harvard Divinity School), vol. 5, no. 7 (November 4, 1965).

619 Walsh, Benedict, "Paul Tillich: An Existential View," At-One-Ment (Washington, D.C.), vol. 8 (1966), pp. 113-121.

620 Walsh, Benedict, "The Theology of Paul Tillich," At-One-Ment (Washington, D.C.), vol. 7 (1965), pp. 47-56.

621 Walters, O. S., "Psychodynamics in Tillich's Theology," Journal of Religion and Health, vol. 12 (October, 1973), pp. 342-353.

622 Warlick, H. C., "Tillich's Consciousness of Guilt and Autonomous Thinking," Foundations, vol. 16 (January-March, 1973), pp. 25-40.

623 Watson, Melvin, "The Social Thought of Paul Tillich," Journal of Religious Thought, vol. 10, no. 1 (1953), pp. 5-17.

624 Weigel, Gustave, "Contemporaneous Protestantism and Paul Tillich," Theological Studies, vol. 11, no. 2 (June, 1950), pp. 177-202.

625 Weigel, Gustave, "Myth, Symbol, and Analogy," Paul Tillich in Catholic Thought, Thomas F. O'Meara and Donald M. Weisser, eds. Garden City, New York: Doubleday & Company, Inc., 1969, pp. 241-255.

626 Weigel, Gustave, "Recent Protestant Theology," Theological Studies, vol. 14 (December, 1953), pp. 568-594.

627 Weigel, Gustave, "Reflections on 'On the Nature of Faith,'" Religious Experience and Truth, Sidney Hook, ed. New York: New York University Press, 1961, pp. 103-109.

628 Weigel, Gustave, "The Theological Significance of Paul Tillich," Cross Currents, vol. 6 (Spring, 1956), pp. 141-155. Included in Paul Tillich in Catholic Thought, edited by Thomas F. O'Meara and Donald M. Weisser (Doubleday and Company, 1969), pp. 32-55; in Theology Digest, vol. 6, Winter 1958,

pp. 45-50; and in Gregorianum, vol. 37, no. 1, 1956, pp. 34-54.

629 Weisbaker, Donald R., "Aesthetic Elements in Tillich's Theory of Symbol," Kairos and Logos: Studies in the Roots and Implications of Tillich's Theology, John J. Carey, ed. Cambridge, Massachusetts: North American Paul Tillich Society, 1978.

630 Weisbaker, Donald R., "Paul Tillich on the Experiential Ground of Religious Certainty," American Journal of Theology and Philosophy, vol. 1 (May, 1980), pp. 37-44.

631 Weisbaker, Donald R., "Process Thought in Tillich's Eschatology," International Journal for Philosophy of Religion, vol. 5 (Summer, 1974), pp. 91-107.

632 Weiss, Paul, "Thank God, God's Not Impossible," Religious Experience and Truth, Sidney Hook, ed. New York: New York University Press, 1961, pp. 83-93. A paper prompted by Tillich's essay, "The Religious Symbol."

633 Weisser, Donald M., "Paul Tillich, a Roman Catholic Appreciation," Paul Tillich in Catholic Thought, Thomas F. O'Meara and Donald M. Weisser, eds. Garden City, New York: Doubleday & Company, Inc., 1969, pp. 27-31. Appears also in Christian Advocate, February 10, 1966, p. 7ff.

634 Weldhen, Margaret, "The Existentialists and Problems of Moral and Religious Education: Tillich and Jaspers," Journal of Moral Education, vol. 1 (February, 1972), pp. 97-101.

635 West, Charles C., "Religious Socialism: Paul Tillich," Communism and the Theologians, Charles C. West. London: SCM Press, 1958, pp. 78-111.

636 Westphal, Merold, "Hegel, Tillich, and the Secular," Journal of Religion, vol. 52 (July, 1972), pp. 223-239.

637 Wheat, Leonard F., "Fifth Columnist Among the Theologians: Paul Tillich's Dialectical Humanism," Times Literary Supplement, March 19, 1971, p. 330.

638 Wick, Warner A., "The Pursuit of Wisdom: Reflections on Some Recent Pursuers," Ethics, vol. 59 (July, 1949), pp. 257-270.

639 Wiebe, Paul G., "From System to Systematics: The Origin of Tillich's Theology," Kairos and Logos: Studies in the Roots and Implications of Tillich's Theology, John J. Carey, ed. Cambridge, Massachusetts: North American Paul Tillich Society, 1978.

640 Wiebe, Paul G., "The Significance of 'The System of the Sciences' within Tillich's Thought," Tillich Studies: 1975, John J. Carey, ed. Tallahassee, Florida: (Florida State University), The Second North American Consultation on Paul Tillich Studies, 1975, pp. 76-87. A paper prepared for a consultation sponsored by the American Academy of Religion at its meeting in Chicago, October 30-November 2, 1975.

641 Wilhelmsen, F. D., "Paul Tillich: Being as the Power to Be," The Metaphysics of Love, F. D. Wilhelmsen. New York: Sheed & Ward, 1962, pp. 97-113.

642 Wilhelmsen, F. D., "Paul Tillich: The Primacy of Power Within Protestantism," The Metaphysics of Love, F. D. Wilhelmsen. New York: Sheed & Ward, 1962, pp. 113-124.

643 Williams, Daniel Day, "Paul Tillich's Doctrine of Forgiveness," Pastoral Psychology, vol. 19, no. 181 (February, 1968), p. 17.

644 Williams, Daniel Day, "St. Paul and Tillich," Union Seminary Quarterly Review, vol. 21, no. 1 (1965), pp. 27-34. A discussion between Daniel D. Williams, Tom F. Driver, and W. D. Davies.

645 Williams, Daniel Day, "Tillich, P. J.," Chicago: Encyclopaedia Britannica, vol. 21 (1967).

646 Williams, Daniel Day, "Tillich's Doctrine of God," The Philosophical Forum (Boston), vol. 18 (1960-1961), pp. 40-50.

647 Williams, George H., "Priest, Prophet, and Proletariat: A Study in the Theology of Paul Tillich," The Journal of Liberal Religion, vol. 1 (Winter, 1940), pp. 25-37.

648 Williams, John Norton, "The Christology of Paul Tillich: An Exposition and Evaluation," Encounter, vol. 21 (Autumn, 1960), pp. 423-438.

649 Williamson, Clark M., "Tillich's Two Types of Philosophy of Religion: A Reconsideration," Journal of Religion, vol. 52 (July, 1972), pp. 205-222.

650 Willimon, William H., "Tillich and Art: Pitfalls of a Theological Dialogue with Art," Religious Life, vol. 45 (Spring, 1976), pp. 72-81.

651 Wilson, Edwin H., "How Humanistic was Paul Tillich?" Religious Humanism (Yellow Springs, Ohio), vol. 1, no. 3 (1967), pp. 88-89.

652 Witmer, J. A., "Who was Paul Tillich?" Moody Monthly, vol. 66 (March, 1966), pp. 43-44.

653 Woocher, Jonathan S., "From Guilt to Reconciliation," Review of Existential Psychology and Psychiatry, vol. 15 (1977), pp. 186-209.

654 Woodhouse, H. F., "Some Pneumatological Issues in Tillich's 'Systematic Theology,'" Irish Theological Quarterly, vol. 41 (April, 1974), pp. 104-119.

655 Wright, C. J., "Courage and Systematic Theology: Paul Tillich's Existential Apologetic," Modern Churchman, vol. 43 (December, 1953), pp. 275-283.

656 Wright, E., "Paul Tillich as Hero: An Interview with Rollo May," Christian Century, vol. 91 (May 15, 1974), pp. 530-533. Replies to the above are found in the July 3, 1974 issue of Christian Century, pp. 753-754.

657 Wyschogrod, Michael, "Belief and Action," Religious Experience and Truth, Sidney Hook, ed. New York: New York University Press, 1961, pp. 180-187.

658 Young, N., "Some Implications in Tillich's Theology for Christian Education," Religious Education, vol. 60 (May, 1965), pp. 230-237.

659 Zietlow, Harold H., "Paul Tillich's Reformation Heritage," The Cresset (Valparaiso, Indiana), vol. 33, no. 10 (1970), pp. 12-13.

660 Ziff, Paul, "About God," Religious Experience and Truth, Sidney Hook, ed. New York: New York University Press, 1961, pp. 195-203.

661 Zimmerman, Marvin, "Faith, Hope, and Clarity," Religious Experience and Truth, Sidney Hook, ed. New York: New York University Press, 1961, pp. 187-195.

662 Zucker, Wolfgang, "The Demonic: From Aeschylus to Tillich," Theology Today, vol. 26 (April, 1969), pp. 34-50.

5. BOOKS OR PORTIONS OF BOOKS ABOUT OR RELATED TO PAUL TILLICH IN ENGLISH

1   Acheson, Russel R., ed. The New Theologians: Bultmann, Bonhoeffer, Tillich, Teilhard de Chardin. London: A. R. Mowbray, 1964.

2   Adams, James Luther. On Being Human Religiously. Boston: Beacon Press, 1976.

3   Adams, James Luther. Paul Tillich's Philosophy of Culture, Science, and Religion. New York: Harper & Row, 1965.

4   Aldwinkle, Russell. Death in the Secular City: A Study in the Notion of Life after Death in Contemporary Theology and Philosophy. London: Allen & Unwin, 1972.

5   Anderson, James F. Paul Tillich: Basics in His Thought. Albany: New York, Magi Books, 1972.

6   Anshen, Ruth Nanda, ed. Moral Principles of Action: Man's Ethical Imperative. New York: Harper and Row, 1952.

7   Armbruster, Carl J. The Vision of Paul Tillich. New York: Sheed and Ward, 1967.

8   Bader, Claudia. Oekumenische Arbeitstagung. Cambridge: Harvard Divinity School, July-August, 1936, pp. 7-11. A pamphlet which reports on the Oekumenisches Seminar, Geneva, July 28-August 15, 1936. Includes a summary of an address given by Tillich at the seminar.

9   Barnes, Hazel Estella. An Existential Ethic. New York: Knopf, 1967.

10 Barrett, William and Aiken, H. D., eds. Philosophy in the Twentieth Century: An Anthology. New York: Random House, 1962.

11 Bartley, William Warren. The Retreat to Commitment. New York: Knopf, 1962.

144

12 Binkley, Luther John. Conflict of Ideals: Changing Values in Western Society. New York: 1969.

13 Bloesch, Donald. The Christian Witness in a Secular Age: An Evaluation of Nine Contemporary Theologians. Minneapolis: Augsburg Publishing House, 1968, Chapter 7.

14 Borowitz, Eugene B. A Layman's Introduction to Religious Existentialism. Philadelphia: Westminster Press, 1965.

15 Braaten, Carl E., ed. Tillich's Perspectives on 19th and 20th Century Protestant Theology. New York: Harper & Row, 1967. An introduction to Tillich's thought is provided by Carl Braaten in his introduction, pp. xiii-xxxiv.

16 Brauer, Jerald C., ed. The Future of Religions. New York: Harper & Row, 1966. A book of essays by and about Tillich, collected in tribute to Tillich's impact on America.

17 Breisach, Ernst. Introduction to Modern Existentialism. New York: Grove Press, 1962.

18 Brown, Colin. Philosophy and the Christian Faith: A Historical Sketch from the Middle Ages to the Present Day. London: Tyndale Press, 1969.

19 Brown, D. Mackenzie. Ultimate Concern: Tillich in Dialogue. New York: Harper & Row, 1965.

20 Byran, Lawrence D. The Thought of Paul Tillich: A Select Bibliographical Companion to the Systematic Theology. Evanston, Illinois: Garrett Theological Seminary, 1973. Garrett Bibliographical Lectures, no. 9.

21 Cairns, David. God Up There: A Study in Divine Transcendence. Edinburgh: St. Andrew Press, 1976.

22 Carey, John J., ed. Kairos and Logos: Studies in the Roots and Implications of Tillich's Theology. Cambridge, Massachusetts: North American Paul Tillich Society, 1978. A book of essays which are listed separately in this volume.

23 Childs, James. Christian Anthropology and Ethics. Philadelphia: Fortress Press, 1978.

24 Clayton, John Powell. The Concept of Correlation: Paul Tillich and the Possibility of a Mediating Theology. Hawthorne, New York: Walter De Gruyter Inc., 1980.

25 Cobb, John B. Jr. Living Options in Protestant Theology. Philadelphia: Westminster Press, 1962.

26 Cochrane, Arthur C. The Existentialists and God: Being and

146 / Paul Tillich

the Being of God in the Thought of Kierkegaard, Jaspers, Heidegger, Sartre, Tillich, Gilson, Barth. Philadelphia: Westminster Press, 1956, pp. 77-99. Contains the chapter entitled "Being, Non-Being and Being Itself."

7 Cooper, John Charles. The Roots of Radical Theology. Philadelphia: Westminster Press, 1967, pp. 84-93.

28 Cushman, R. E. The Heritage of Christian Thought. New York: Harper & Row, 1965. Contains the section entitled "The Christology of Paul Tillich" by Robert E. Cushman.

29 Dewart, Leslie. The Future of Belief: Theism in a World Come of Age. New York: Herder & Herder, 1966, pp. 37-51. Contains the section entitled "Paul Tillich and Dietrich Bonhoeffer." The focus is on contemporary theology and the concept of God.

30 Diamond, Malcolm L. Contemporary Philosophy and Religious Thought. Ontario, Canada: McGraw-Hill Ryerson Ltd., 1974. Includes the section entitled "Tillich's Three Level Theory of Truth."

31 Dillistone, F. W., ed. Myth and Symbol. London: The Talbot Press (The Society for Promoting Christian Knowledge), 1966.

32 Dirks, Lee E. Religion in Action: How America's Faiths Are Meeting New Challenges. Silver Spring, Maryland: Newsbook, The National Observer, 1965.

33 Douglas, Paul F. God among the Germans. Philadelphia: University of Pennsylvania Press, 1935, pp. 304-305.

34 Dourley, John P. Paul Tillich and Bonaventure: An Evaluation of Tillich's Claim to Stand in the Augustinian-Franciscan Tradition. Leiden, Netherlands: E. J. Brill, 1975.

35 Duke, Robert W. The Sermon as God's Word: Theologies for Preaching. Nashville, Tennessee: Abingdon Press, 1980, pp. 30-48. Contains the chapter entitled "Existentialism: Paul Tillich."

36 Evans, Robert Allen. Intelligible and Responsible Talk About God: A Theory of the Dimensional Structure of Language and Its Bearing upon Theological Symbolism. Leiden: E. J. Brill, 1973.

37 Falk, Richard A. Martin Buber and Paul Tillich's Radical Politics and Religion. New York: National Council of Protestant Episcopal Churches, 1961.

38 Farley, Edward. The Transcendence of God: A Study in Contemporary Philosophical Theology. Philadelphia: Westminster

Press, 1960, pp. 75-102. Contains the section entitled "God as Transcendent Ground: Paul Tillich."

39   Ferre, Nels F. S. Searchlights on Contemporary Theology. New York: Harper & Brothers, 1961. Contains the chapter entitled "Three Critical Issues in Tillich's Philosophical Theology."

40   Ferre, Nels F. S. The Universal Word: A Theology for a Universal Faith. London: Collins Press, 1970.

41   Freeman, David Hugh. Recent Studies in Philosophy and Theology. Philadelphia: Presbyterian and Reformed Publishing Co., 1962.

42   Freeman, David H. Tillich. Philadelphia: Presbyterian and Reformed Publishing Co., 1962.

43   Gollwitzer, Helmut. The Existence of God as Confessed by Faith. London: SCM Press, 1965.

44   Hall, T. Paul Tillich's Appraisal of St. Thomas' Teaching on the Act of Faith. Rome: Catholic Book Agency, 1968.

45   Hamilton, Kenneth. The System and the Gospel: A Critique of Paul Tillich. New York: Macmillan, 1963.

46   Hammond, Guyton B. Man in Estrangement: A Comparison of the Thought of Paul Tillich and Erich Fromm. Nashville, Tennessee: Vanderbilt University Press, 1965.

47   Hammond, Guyton B. The Power of Self-Transcendence: An Introduction to the Philosophical Theology of Paul Tillich. St. Louis: Bethany Press, 1966.

48   Hanson, Anthony, ed. Teilhard Reassessed. London: Longman & Todd, 1970.

49   Haruna, Sumito. Tillich's Doctrine of God in Comparison to Kant's. Nishinomiya, Japan: Kwansei Gakuin University, 1967.

50   Harvey, Van Austin. The Historian and the Believer: The Morality of Historical Knowledge and Christian Belief. New York: Macmillan, 1966.

51   Henry, Stuart Clark, ed. A Miscellany of American Christianity: Essays in Honor of H. Shelton Smith. Durham, North Carolina: Duke University Press, 1963, pp. 268-291. Contains the essay entitled "Ontology and Christology: The Apologetic Theology of Paul Tillich" by John Pemberton.

52   Herberg, Will, ed. Four Existentialist Theologians: A Reader from the Works of Jacques Maritain, Nicholas Berdyaev,

Martin Buber and Paul Tillich. Garden City, New York: Doubleday Anchor Book, 1958.

53 Holmer, Paul F. Theology and the Scientific Study of Religion. Minneapolis: Denison, 1961.

54 Hook, Sidney. Pragmatism and the Tragic Sense of Life. New York: Basic Books, 1974.

55 Hook, Sidney, ed. Religious Experience and Truth. New York: New York University Press, 1961. Contains articles discussing or prompted by Tillich's essay, "The Religious Symbol" (pp. 301-321), together with Tillich's reply, "The Meaning and Justification of Religious Symbols" (pp. 3-11).

56 Hopper, David H. Tillich: A Theological Portrait. Philadelphia: J. B. Lippincott, 1968.

57 Hordern, William. A Layman's Guide to Protestant Theology. New York: Macmillan, 1955, pp. 165-183. Contains the section entitled "The Boundary Between Liberalism and Neo-Orthodoxy: Paul Tillich."

58 Hudson, William Donald. A Philosophical Approach to Religion. London: Macmillan, 1974.

59 Hutchison, John A. Faith, Reason and Existence: An Introduction to Contemporary Philosophy of Religion. New York: Oxford University Press, 1956.

60 Idinopoulos, Thomas A. The Erosion of Faith: An Inquiry into the Origins of the Contemporary Crisis in Religious Thought. New York: Quadrangle, 1971.

61 Jenkins, David E. Guide to the Debate about God. Philadelphia: Westminster Press, 1966.

62 Johnson, R. C. Authority in Protestant Theology. Philadelphia: Westminster Press, 1959, pp. 111-143. Contains the section entitled "The Contextual Approach."

63 Johnson, Wayne G. Theological Method in Luther and Tillich: Law-Gospel and Correlation. Washington, D.C.: University Press of America, 1981.

64 Kantonen, T. A., ed. Paul Tillich: Retrospect and Future. Nashville: Abingdon Press, 1967. A book of essays about Tillich by Nels F. S. Ferre, Charles Hartshorne, John Dillenberger, James Livingston, and Joseph Haroutunian.

65 Keefe, Donald J. Thomism and the Ontological Theology of Paul Tillich: A Comparison of Systems. Leiden, Netherlands: E. J. Brill, 1971.

66 Kegley, Charles W. et al. Politics, Religion, and Modern Man: Essays on Reinhold Niebuhr, Paul Tillich, and Rudolf Bultmann. Quezon City, Philippines: University of the Philippines Press, 1969.

67 Kegley, Charles W., and Bretall, Robert W., eds. The Theology of Paul Tillich. New York: Macmillan, 1952.

68 Kelsey, David H. The Fabric of Paul Tillich's Theology. New Haven: Yale University Press, 1967.

69 Kereszty, Roch A. God Seekers for a New Age: From Crisis Theology to 'Christian Atheism.' Dayton, Ohio: Pflaum Press, 1970, pp. 80-91. Contains the chapter entitled "Paul Tillich."

70 Killen, R. Allen. The Ontological Theology of Paul Tillich. Kampen, Netherlands: J. H. Kok, 1956.

71 Leibrecht, Walter, ed. Religion and Culture: Essays in Honour of Paul Tillich. New York: Harper & Row, 1959, pp. 3-31.

72 Leitch, Addison H. Winds of Doctrine: The Theology of Barth, Brunner, Bonhoeffer, Niebuhr, Tillich. Westwood, New Jersey: Fleming H. Revell Co., 1966.

73 Lo, Samuel E. Tillichian Theology and Educational Philosophy. New York: Philosophical Library, 1970.

74 Lowe, Adolf. The Price of Liberty. London: Hogarth Press, 1937. An open letter to Tillich on his 50th birthday.

75 Lyons, James R., ed. The Intellectual Legacy of Paul Tillich. Detroit: Wayne State University Press, 1969.

76 Macintosh, D. C. The Problem of Religious Knowledge. New York: Harper & Brothers, 1940, pp. 348-350.

77 Macleod, Alistair M. Paul Tillich: An Essay on the Role of Ontology in His Philosophical Theology. London: Allen & Unwin, 1973. Also published by Humanities Press, Atlantic Highlands, New Jersey, 1975.

78 Macquarrie, John. God-Talk: An Examination of the Language and Logic of Theology. London: SCM Press, 1967.

79 Mahan, Wayne W. Tillich's System. San Antonio, Texas: Trinity University Press, 1974.

80 Margolis, Joseph. Psychotherapy and Morality: A Study of Two Concepts. New York: Random House, 1966.

81 Martin, Bernard. The Existentialist Theology of Paul Tillich. New York: Bookman Associates, 1963.

82 Martin, Bernard. Paul Tillich's Doctrine of Man. Ullwyn, England: James Nisbet & Company Ltd., 1963.

83 Mascall, Eric Lionel. The Secularization of Christianity: An Analysis and a Critique. London: Longman & Todd, 1965.

84 May, Rollo. Paulus: A Personal Portrait of Paul Tillich. New York: Harper & Row, 1973. Appeared as Paulus: Reminiscences of a Friendship (London: Collins Press, 1974).

85 McKelway, Alexander J. The Systematic Theology of Paul Tillich: A Review and Analysis. Richmond, Virginia: John Knox Press, 1964.

86 McLean, George Francis. Man's Knowledge of God According to Paul Tillich: A Thomistic Critique. Washington: Catholic University of America Press, 1958.

87 Means, Paul B. The Things That Are Caesar's. New York: Round Table Press, 1935, pp. 135-139. The focus in these pages is on Tillich's concept of "Religious Socialism."

88 Mehta, Ved Parkash. The New Theologian. New York: Harper & Row, 1966. A joint treatment of Dietrich Bonhoeffer, Paul Tillich and John Arthur Thomas Robinson.

89 Meijering, E. Orthodoxy and Platonism in Athanasius: Synthesis or Antithesis? Leiden, Netherlands: E. J. Brill, 1968, pp. 160-172. Contains the section entitled "Paul Tillich."

90 Meynell, Hugo. The New Theology and Modern Theologians. London/Melbourne: Sheed and Ward, 1967, pp. 137-156. Contains the section entitled "Tillich's Theological Method" by Hugo Meynell.

91 Miceli, Vincent Peter. The Gods of Atheism. New Rochelle, New York: Arlington House, 1971.

92 Michalson, Carl, et al. Christianity and the Existentialists. New York: Charles Scribner's Sons, 1956.

93 Midgley, Louis C. Beyond Human Nature: The Contemporary Debate Over Moral Natural Law. Salt Lake City, Utah: Brigham Young University Press, 1968. A part of the Charles E. Mervill Monograph Series in the Humanities and Social Sciences.

94 Millard, David W., ed. Religion and Medicine: 3. London: SCM Press, 1976, pp. 91-200. Contains the essay entitled "Towards a Theology of Social Work" by David W. Millard.

95 Miller, Allen O. and Arther, Donald E. Paul Tillich's Systematic Theology. St. Louis, Missouri: Eden Publishing House, 1975.

96   Miller, Libuse Lukas. Knowing, Doing, and Surviving: Cognition and Evaluation. New York: Wiley, 1973.

97   Modras, Ronald E. Paul Tillich's Theology of the Church: A Catholic Appraisal. Detroit: Wayne State University Press, 1976.

98   Mondin, Battista. The Principles of Analogy in Protestant and Catholic Theology. The Hague: Martinus Nijhoff, 1968. Contains the section entitled "Tillich's Doctrine of Religious Symbolism."

99   Montgomery, John Warwick. Where Is History Going: Essays in Support of the Historical Truth of the Christian Revelation. Grand Rapids, Michigan: Zondervan, 1969.

100 Moreau, Jules Laurence. Language and Religious Language: A Study in the Dynamics of Translation. Philadelphia: Westminster, 1961, pp. 168-177.

101 Morrison, Roy D. Tillich's Telescoping of Ontology and Naturalism. Washington, D.C.: Wesley Theological Seminary, 1974. An unpublished manuscript.

102 Mullen, Ronald Eugene. Being Between. 2nd edition. Pasadena, California: JCK, 1976.

103 Murphy, Carol B. A Deeper Faith: The Theology of Paul Tillich. Wallingford, Pennsylvania: Pendle Hill, 1958.

104 Neville, Robert C. God the Creator: On the Transcendence and Presence of God. Chicago: University of Chicago Press, 1968.

105 Nicholls, William. Systematic and Philosophical Theology. Harmondsworth, England: Penguin Books, 1969.

106 Novak, Michael. A Time to Build. New York: Macmillan, 1967.

107 O'Connor, Edward Dennis. Paul Tillich: An Impression. New York: Fordham University Press, 1955.

108 Oden, Thomas C. Contemporary Theology and Psychotherapy. Philadelphia: Westminster Press, 1967.

109 O'Hanlon, Daniel J. The Influence of Schelling on the Thought of Paul Tillich. Rome: Pontifical Gregorian University, 1958.

110 O'Hanlon, Daniel J. The Influence of the Thought of Paul Tillich. Rome: Pontifical Gregorian University, 1957.

111 O'Meara, Thomas Franklin. Paul Tillich's Theology of God. Dubuque: Listening Press, 1970.

112 O'Meara, Thomas F., and Weisser, Donald M., eds. Paul Tillich in Catholic Thought. Garden City, New York: Doubleday & Company, Inc., 1969. A book of essays by various Catholic authors.

113 Orlebeke, Clifton, and Smedes, Lewis, eds. God and the Good: Essays in Honor of Henry Stob. Grand Rapids: Eerdmans, 1975. Contains the essays, "Tillich's Religious Epistemology" by Kenneth Hamilton, and "On Having Nothing to Worship: The Divine Abyss in Paul Tillich and Richard Rubenstein" by J. Daane.

114 Osborn, Robert T. Freedom in Modern Theology. Philadelphia: Westminster Press, 1967. Contains the section entitled "Paul Tillich: Freedom to Be."

115 Osborne, Kenen B. New Being: A Study of the Relationship Between Conditioned and Unconditioned Being According to Paul Tillich. The Hague: Martinus Nijhoff, 1969.

116 Owen, Huwe Parri. Concepts of Deity. London: Allen & Unwin, 1965.

117 Pauck, Wilhelm. Ecumenity in Tillich's Theology. Chicago: The Disciples Divinity House of the University of Chicago, 1974. From the William Henry Hoover Lectureship on Christian Unity.

118 Pauck, Wilhelm, and Pauck, Marion. Paul Tillich: His Life and Thought, Volume I. New York: Harper & Row, 1976.

110 Peerman, Dean G., ed. A Handbook of Christian Theologians. Cleveland: The World Publishing Co., 1965.

120 Pelikan, J., ed. Interpretation of Luther: Essays in Honor of Wilhelm Pauck. Philadelphia: Fortress Press, 1968, pp. 304-334. Contains the essay entitled "Paul Tillich on Luther" by James Luther Adams.

121 Piper, Otto. Recent Developments in German Protestantism. London: SCM Press, 1934, pp. 137-143.

122 Plaskow, Judith. Sex, Sin and Grace: Women's Experience and the Theologies of Reinhold Niebuhr and Paul Tillich. Washington, D.C.: University Press of America, 1980.

123 Porteous, Alvin C. Prophetic Voices in Contemporary Theology. New York: Abingdon Press, 1966.

124 Prinz, Joachim. The Dilemma of the Modern Jew. Boston and Toronto: Little, Brown, 1962.

125 Proudfoot, Wayne. God and the Self: Three Types of

Philosophy of Religion. London: Associated University Press, 1976.

126 Ramsey, Paul, ed. Nine Modern Moralists. Englewood Cliffs, New Jersey: Prentice-Hall Inc., 1962, pp. 181-208. Contains the section entitled "Paul Tillich and Emil Brunner: Christ Transforming Natural Justice" by Paul Ramsey.

127 Randall, John Herman, Jr. The Role of Knowledge in Western Religion. Boston: Starr King Press, 1958.

128 Ratschow, Carl Heinz. Paul Tillich. Iowa City, Iowa: University of Iowa--North American Paul Tillich Society, 1980.

129 Reinisch, Leonhard, ed. Theologians of Our Time. Notre Dame, Indiana: University of Notre Dame Press, 1964. Contains the essay entitled, "Paul Tillich" by Horst Buerckle.

130 Richardson, Alan. History Sacred and Profane. London: SCM Press, 1964, pp. 127-131. These pages contain a brief statement on how Tillich views the "Centre of History."

131 Robinson, James McConkey, ed. The Beginnings of Dialectic Theology. Richmond: John Knox Press, 1968.

132 Rome, Sydney Chester and Rome, B. K., eds. Philosophical Interrogations: Interrogations of M. Buber, J. Wild, J. Wahl, B. Blanshard, P. Weiss, C. Hartshorne, P. Tillich. New York: Holt, Rinehart and Winston, 1964.

133 Ross, Robert R. N. The Non-Existence of God: Linguistic Paradox in Tillich's Thought. Lewiston, New York: The Edwin Mellen Press, 1978. Volume One of the Toronto Studies in Theology.

134 Rottenberg, Isaac C. Redemption and Historical Reality. Philadelphia: Westminster Press, 1964.

135 Rowe, William L. Religious Symbols and God: A Philosophical Study of Tillich's Theology. Chicago: University of Chicago Press, 1968.

136 Rust, Eric Charles. Positive Religion in a Revolutionary Time. Philadelphia: Westminster Press, 1970.

137 Ryan, John Kenneth, ed. Twentieth-Century Thinkers: Studies in the Work of 17 Modern Philosophers. Staten Island, New York: Alba House, 1965.

138 Schacht, Richard. Alienation. Garden City, New York: Doubleday, 1971.

139 Scharlemann, Robert P. Reflection and Doubt in the Thought

of Paul Tillich. New Haven: Yale University Press, 1969.

140 Schrader, Robert W. The Nature of Theological Argument: A Study of Paul Tillich. Missoula, Montana: Scholars Press, 1975.

141 Slaatte, Howard A. The Paradox of Existentialist Theology. New York: Humanities Press, 1971.

142 Slaatte, Howard A. The Pertinence of the Paradox: A Study of the Dialectics of Reason-in-Existence. New York: Humanities Press, 1968.

143 Smith, H. S. Changing Conceptions of Original Sin. New York: Charles Scribner's Sons, 1955, pp. 219-227.

144 Smith, John Edwin. Reason and God: Encounters of Philosophy and Religion. New Haven: Yale University Press, 1961.

145 Soper, D. W. Major Voices in American Theology. Philadelphia: Westminster Press, 1953, pp. 107-152. Contains the section entitled "Beyond Religion and Irreligion."

146 Stone, R. Paul Tillich's Radical Social Thought. Atlanta: John Knox Press, 1980.

147 Stumme, John R. Socialism in Theological Perspective: A Study of Paul Tillich 1918-1933. Missoula, Montana: Scholars Press, 1978.

148 Sutphin, Stanley T. Options in Contemporary Theology. Washington, D.C.: University Press of America, 1979.

149 Tait, Leslie Gordon. The Promise of Tillich. Philadelphia: Lippincott, 1971.

150 Taubes, Jacob. Toward a New Christianity: Readings on the Death of God Theology. New York: Harcourt, Brace and World, 1967. Contains the section entitled "On the Nature of the Theological Method: Some Reflections on the Methodological Principles of Tillich's Theology."

151 Tavard, George Henri. Paul Tillich and the Christian Message. New York: Charles Scribner's Sons, 1962.

152 Tavard, George Henri. The Unconditional Concern: The Theology of Paul Tillich. New York: Fordham University, 1953.

153 Thatcher, Adrian. The Ontology of Paul Tillich. Missoula, Montana: Scholars Press, Oxford Theological Monographs, 1979.

154 Thomas, George F. Philosophy and Religious Belief. New York: Scribner, 1970.

155 Thomas, George F. Religious Philosophies of the West. New York: Charles Scribner's Sons, 1965, pp. 390-423. Contains the section entitled "Philosophical Theology: Tillich."

156 Thomas, John Heywood. Paul Tillich. London: The Carey Kingsgate Press Ltd., 1965.

157 Thomas, John Heywood. Paul Tillich: An Appraisal. Philadelphia: Westminster Press, 1963.

158 Tillich, Hannah. From Place to Place: Travels with Paul Tillich, Travels Without Paul Tillich. New York: Stein and Day, 1976.

159 Tillich, Hannah. From Time to Time. New York: Stein and Day, 1973.

160 Tinsley, E. J., ed. Paul Tillich: 1886-1965. London: Epworth Press, 1973.

161 Trigg, Roger. Reason and Commitment. London: Cambridge University Press, 1973.

162 Unhjem, Arne. Dynamics of Doubt: A Preface to Tillich. Philadelphia: Fortress Press, 1963.

163 Van Dusen, Henry Pitney, ed. Christian Answer. New York: Charles Scribner's Sons, 1945.

164 Vogel, Arthur Anton. Reality, Reason, and Religion. New York: Morehouse-Gorham, 1957.

165 Vunderink, Ralph W. The Significance of Existentialism for Christian Theology. Washington, D.C.: Catholic Philosophical Association Proceedings (1970), pp. 241-248. no. 44.

166 Wand, J. W. C. The Minds Behind the New Theology. London: A. B. Mowbray & Co., 1963. Chapter 4 is entitled "Paul Tillich."

167 West, Charles C. Communism and the Theologians: Study of an Encounter. London: SCM Press, 1958, pp. 78-111. Contains the section entitled "Religious Socialism: Paul Tillich."

168 Wheat, Leonard F. Paul Tillich's Dialectical Humanism: Unmasking the God above God. Baltimore: The Johns Hopkins Press, 1970.

169 Wieman, Henry Nelson. Intellectual Foundation of Faith.

New York: Philosophical Library, 1961, pp. 81-106. Chapter 4 is entitled "Paul Tillich Answers."

170   Wieman, Henry Nelson, and Meland, Bernard E. American Philosophies of Religion. Chicago: Willett, Clark, & Co., 1936.

171   Wilhelmsen, Frederick D. The Metaphysics of Love. New York: Sheed & Ward, 1962.

172   Williams, John Rodman. Contemporary Existentialism and Christian Faith. Englewood Cliffs, New Jersey: Prentice-Hall, 1965.

173   Williamson, Rene de Visme. Politics and Protestant Theology: An Interpretation of Tillich, Barth, Bonhoeffer and Brunner. Baton Rouge: Louisiana State University Press, 1976.

174   Zahrnt, Heinz. The Question of God: Protestant Theology in the Twentieth Century. New York: Harcourt, Brace and World, 1966. Contains the chapter entitled "The End of the Protestant Era?"

KEYWORD INDEX: SUBJECTS

The underscored numerals (1, 2, 3, 4, and 5) refer to the five bibliographies; following the colon are the entry numbers.

Absolute 4: 267T, 289T
Absolutes 1: 282T; 3: 20T, 41T, 73T, 143T, 166T, 265T, 267T
Abysmal 2: 239T
Abyss 4: 237T; 5: 113A
Academic 4: 66T
Accepted 1: 483T, 484T
Act 4: 517T; 5: 44T
Action 1: 44R, 331R; 4: 462T, 657T; 5: 6T, 32T
Acts 4: 104T
Actuality 1: 12T
Adam 4: 268T
Adolescence 2: 217T
Advaita Vedanta 2: 107T
Aesthetic 2: 15T, 188T; 4: 213T, 629T
Aesthetics 2: 90T, 248T; 4: 152T, 594T
Aesthetischen 1: 71T
Afrikanerdom 4: 177T
Afterword 1: 19T
Aim 1: 223T
Aims 1:462TA; 4: 138T
Alienation 2: 66T; 4: 61T; 210T, 274T; 5: 138T
Ambiguities 4: 174T, 467T
Ambiguity 1: 18T; 4: 328T
America 1: 108T, 110R, 177R, 180A, 208R, 389T, 419T; 2: 46T; 4: 77T, 445T, 537R; 5: 16A, 32T
American 1: 27A, 86A, 158T, 212T, 249A, 304A, 458A, 468R; 2: 7T, 184T, 225T, 229T, 257T; 4: 91T, 244T, 358T, 383T, 440R, 550R;

5: 51T, 145T, 170T
Americans 2: 104T
Analogia 2: 28T, 110T; 4: 428T
Analogical 2: 230T
Analogy 2: 152T; 4: 81T, 202T, 376T, 393R, 465T, 625T; 5: 98T
Analysis 1: 30T; 2: 5T, 16T, 27T, 33T, 58T, 60T, 73T, 85T, 89T, 123T, 146T, 152T, 166T, 182T, 192T, 208T, 234T, 238T, 267T; 4: 104T, 159T, 162T, 177T, 301T, 325T, 389T, 465T, 470T, 506T, 579T; 5: 83T, 85T
Anglicanism 4: 464T
Anguish 4: 573T
Answer 1: 24T, 25T, 87R, 362T, 376R, 479AR; 3: 9T; 4: 573T; 5: 163T
Answers 4: 222T, 389T; 5: 169A
Anthropocentric 4: 55T
Anthropologies 2: 40T
Anthropology 2: 113T, 138T, 143T, 204T, 258T; 4: 334T, 395T; 5: 23T
Anthropomorphic 4: 169T
Anti-Semitism 1: 182A
Anticipation 4: 112T
Antinomy 4: 116T
Anxiety 1: 23T, 26T, 27RT; 2: 65T, 77T, 89T, 246T; 4: 59T, 260T, 413T
Apologetic 2: 128T, 157T; 4: 88T, 214T, 389T, 397T, 440T, 543T, 655T; 5: 51A

157

KEYWORD INDEX: PERSONS

The underscored numerals (1, 2, 3, 4, and 5) refer to the five
bibliographies; following the colon are the entry numbers.

Aeschylus 4: 662T
Allers, Rudolph 1: 128T
Altizer, Thomas J. 2: 47T
Aquinas, Thomas 2: 148T,
  152T; 4: 202T, 207T,
  208T, 357T, 376T, 487T;
  5: 44T, 86T
Augustine, St. 4: 361T
Barth, Karl 1: 25T, 125T;
  2: 2T, 12T, 19T, 26T, 75T,
  79T, 114T, 141T, 152T,
  164T, 215T, 230T, 262T,
  264T; 4: 16TA, 158T, 238R,
  480T, 593T, 613T; 5: 26T,
  72T, 173T
Baum, Gregory 2: 208T
Bennett, John C. 1: 54T, 369A,
  418A
Berdyaev, Nicholas 1: 55T,
  298T; 2: 117T, 158T, 203T,
  239T, 256T; 5: 52T
Blakeney, Raymond B. 1: 56T
Blanshard, B. 5: 132A
Boehme, Jacob 1: 342R; 2:
  194T; 4: 399T
Bohr, Niels 2: 132T
Bonaventure, St. 2: 52T;
  4: 154T; 5: 34T
Bonhoeffer, Dietrich 2: 78T;
  4: 604T; 5: 1T, 29A, 72T,
  88A, 173T
Boss, Medard 2: 189T
Brameld, Theodore 2: 100T
Bridgeman, Percy 2: 266T
Brightman, Edgar 2: 14T, 239T
Brunner, Emil 1: 57T, 58T,
  363TR; 2: 128T, 179T,
  237T, 262T; 4: 458T;

  5: 72T, 126A, 173T
Buber, Martin 1: 21T, 259T,
  260T, 261T; 4: 137T,
  382T, 449T; 5: 37T, 52T,
  132T
Bulman, R. F. 4: 563T
Bultmann, Rudolph 2: 26T,
  73T; 4: 48T, 129T, 276T,
  431T; 5: 1T, 66T
Bushnell, Horace 2: 53T
Buttrick, George A. 2: 66T
Calvin, John 2: 212T
Cantor, Nathanael 2: 102T
Cassirer, Ernst 2: 4T, 81T
Cobb, John 2: 47T
Collingwood, R. G. 2: 109T
Cone, James 4: 301T
Croce, Benedetto 2: 251T
Davies, W. D. 4: 268A, 644A
Dawson, Christopher 2: 251T,
  255T
Demos, Raphael 1: 458A; 5:
  143T, 596T
Dewey, John 2: 124T, 263T
DeWolf, L. Harold 2: 245T
Dilthey, Wilhelm 2: 109T
Dobzhansky, Theodosius 2:
  263T
Dodd, C. H. 2: 154T
Driver, Tom F. 4: 268A, 644A
Dunn, Angus 1: 424A
Ebeling, Gerhard 2: 197T
Eckhart, Meister 1: 56T
Edwards, Jonathan 2: 30T,
  84T
Einstein, Albert 1: 215A, 408T
Emerson, Ralph Waldo 2: 108T
Emmet, Dorothy 2: 132T